MAKING A DIFFERENCE

Also by Sheila L. Murray

HOW TO ORGANIZE AND MANAGE A SEMINAR
What To Do and When To Do It

MAKING
A
DIFFERENCE

*Twelve Qualities That
Make You a Leader*

SHEILA MURRAY BETHEL

G.P. PUTNAM'S SONS   NEW YORK

G. P. Putnam's Sons
Publishers Since 1838
200 Madison Avenue
New York, NY 10016

Library of Congress Cataloging-in-Publication Data

Bethel, Sheila Murray.
Making a difference: Twelve qualities that make
you a leader / by Sheila Murray Bethel.
p.   cm.
ISBN 0-399-13467-0
1. Leadership. I. Title.
HM141.B47   1990   303.3'4—dc20

Illustrations by Matt Spergel

Grateful acknowledgment is made for permission to reprint excerpts from the following copyrighted material:

Gray Matter by Harry J. Gray, (c) United Technologies Corporation (1986); *The
Changemasters* by Rosabeth Moss Kanter, (c) copyright 1983. Reprinted by permission of Simon & Schuster, Inc.; *Chapterhouse: Dune* by Frank Herbert, (c) copyright
1985. Reprinted by permission of The Putnam Publishing Group; *The Tao of Power*
by R.L. Wing, (c) copyright 1986 by Immedia. Copyright by permission of Doubleday, a division of Bantam Doubleday Dell Publishing Group, Inc.; *The Art of Living
Treasure Chest* by Wilferd A. Peterson, (c) copyright 1977. Reprinted by permission
of Simon & Schuster, Inc.; *The Art of Supportive Leadership* by J. Donald Walters,
reprinted by permission of Crystal Clarity Publishers, Nevada City, CA 95959 916-
292-3482 $7.95; *The Great Decision* by Allan A. Michie (Reader's Digest, August
1944). Excerpted with permission from: "The Great Invasion" by Allen A. Michie,
Reader's Digest, August 1944. Copyright (c) 1944 by The Reader's Digest Assn., Inc.;
Whatever It Takes, by McCall and Kaplan. Morgan W. McCall, Jr./Robert E. Kaplan,
Whatever It Takes: Decision Makers at Work, (c) 1985, p. 94. Prentice-Hall, Inc.
Englewood Cliffs, New Jersey; *Power and Influence* by John P. Kotter. Copyright (c)
1985 by John P. Kotter, Inc. Reprinted with permission of The Free Press, a Division
of Macmillan, Inc.; *The Leader* by Michael Maccoby, copyright (c) 1981 by The
Project of Technology, Work and Character. Reprinted by permission of Simon and
Schuster, Inc.; *Impossible Dream*, 1965 Helena Music Company and Andrew Scott,
Inc. Words, Joe Darion, Music, Mitch Leigh; *Mastering Change* by Leon Martel,
copyright (c) 1986. Reprinted by permission of Simon and Schuster, Inc.; *The Lessons
of History* by Will & Ariel Durant, copyright (c) 1986. Reprinted by permission of
Simon and Schuster, Inc.

ACKNOWLEDGMENTS

In the five years it has taken me to write this book, there have been many wonderful people who have been supportive, especially my dear friend John Hammond and his late wife, Avy. There have been people whose professionalism and concern have made a major difference in the completion and success of this book: Ken Braly, my friend and computer whiz, who kept bailing me out of my computer problems; Joan Minninger, who dissolved my writer's block; Eleanor Dugan for her expertise and deep concern in editing the first draft; my assistants, Linda Eskew and Zan Sloan, for their patience, caring, and attention to detail; Mike Murray and Rick Enright for critiquing the manuscript; Duane Newcomb for his friendship and resources; Howard Morhaim, my literary agent, for his expertise and encouragement; Lindley Boegehold, my Putnam editor, for her confidence and enthusiasm; Trish Todd, my Berkley editor, for her sensitivity, skill, and friendship. This book would not have been started, let alone completed, without my husband Bill's encouragement and assistance. His criticism, editing, and research have played a major role. Last but not least, I would like to thank all of my leadership clients. I have learned much from them.

DEDICATION

This book is dedicated with love and appreciation to
Dean and Julia Stribley, my father and mother;
my sons, Mike and Shannon, and my husband,
Bill, who is the finest man I've ever known.

CONTENTS

present in all of us to some degree. To develop and use them, you don't have to study complex psychological theories. They are basic, common sense ideas and attitudes that individually and collectively can make you a more dynamic leader. Some of these qualities are "how-to" *skills* and *aptitudes*. Others involve *philosophies* and *attitudes*.

THE TWELVE QUALITIES OF LEADERSHIP

A leader:

1. Has a mission that matters
2. Is a big thinker
3. Has high ethics.
4. Masters change
5. Is sensitive
6. Is a risk taker
7. Is a decision maker
8. Uses power wisely
9. Communicates effectively
10. Is a team builder
11. Is courageous
12. Is committed

WHAT THIS BOOK WILL DO FOR YOU

In defining and explaining the twelve qualities, this book will:

- Equip you with skills, tools, and techniques to maximize your natural leadership talents.
- Expose you to disciplines, concepts, and theories that will build the confidence you need to make leadership decisions.
- Sharpen your curiosity, fire your idealism, and reinforce your commitment to making a difference.
- Challenge you with questions about yourself that will help you discover the best way you can make a difference.

Leadership is not something that you learn once and for all. It is an ever-evolving pattern of skills, talents, and ideas that grow and change as you do. To become a leader you must first have clear definitions of these leadership qualities, a mission, and an honest desire to better yourself by making a difference to others.

MAKING A DIFFERENCE
Where To Begin

If you thought you could make a difference, would you be willing to try? If you discovered that you possessed leadership qualities and skills, would you use them? If you knew that you could motivate others to make a difference, would you be inspired to do so?

I'm sure the answer to these questions is yes! And I'm going to show you how you *can* make a difference—in your home, your job, and your community.

Whether you choose to serve in scouting, in business, or in your community, you can become an effective and more powerful leader. You can build your leadership skills and use them to motivate and influence others.

Right now there are men and women just like you, from every walk of life and every social and economic level, making a difference because they, like you, care deeply about something. They're using their leadership skills to make that difference. They are different.

What sets them apart from other people? It's not how much education they have, how much money they make, where they come from, or who they know. It's not their age, sex, or occupation. It's their awareness of the needs of others, their awareness of the challenges they face. It's their enthusiasm for improving things and creating new opportunities. They have a passion for a cause, or they want to give something back to society. They've reaped the rewards of serving others. In looking for ways to make a difference, they have tapped their personal power and leadership potential.

There are twelve common denominators—twelve *qualities*—that all effective leaders possess. These qualities are characteristics

LEADING BY EXAMPLE

We lead first by example! Everything we say or
do sends a message, sets a tone, or teaches
people what to do or what not to do.

As leaders, we live under a microscope. Nothing we say or do
escapes the scrutiny and examination of our followers. This is one
of the most important secrets of leadership: Followers mirror the
example set for them.

As we employ the twelve qualities of leadership, we need to ask
ourselves repeatedly, "What message am I sending?" "What environment am I creating?" "What example am I setting?" When
you set out to make a difference, your actions inspire others to
follow. You lead first by example. You are accountable.

—————The Shock of a Lifetime————

Paul Jeffers is an insurance salesman from Sacramento, California. I shared the speaking platform with him at a gathering of
insurance people, and, as I listened to him speak, I watched the
powerful impact his story had on the audience.

Paul was a very successful insurance salesman, respected by his
peers and his community. He had a happy family and would have
been considered successful by anyone's standards. One night he
and his wife went to bed, chatted, kissed, and went to sleep. When
he awoke the next morning he first thought he was still asleep.
Then he realized he was living a nightmare. Paul woke up permanently and profoundly deaf.

As he described the trauma that instant tragedy can inflict on
your life, you could see the audience's astonishment: Most of them
had not realized that he was deaf! He brought tears to our eyes as
he talked of never again hearing his wife's voice or the sound of
his children at play. He had to learn to deal with the equilibrium
problems of the inner ear. He knew he had to earn a living, but
how could he function in a job that depended so much on telephone
contact and personal interviews? The enormity of the problem was
nearly overwhelming.

Paul could give up or he could fight back. Although it would be tremendously difficult, he decided to try and continue life as he had been living it. Paul picked up the pieces of his life and learned to compensate for his deafness. His would be an inspiring story for any of us. But what makes Paul even more special is his commitment to using his disability to set an example. He continues a successful insurance career and a happy family life. But now through his speeches he also inspires people, helping them understand that they, too, can overcome adversity. His courageous example motivates and influences people all across the country.

─────────A Woman Who Got Mad─────────

There probably isn't a parent in the United States who is not familiar with the story of Candy Lightner. On May 3, 1980, Candy Lightner's daughter, Cari, was killed by a drunk driver. Psychologists tell us that the loss of a child is the most stressful and tragic event that can happen to a parent.

But Candy's anger over the waste of her daughter's life caused her to take action. On May 7, Candy Lightner met with four friends to decide what they could do to help prevent such tragedies in the future. That meeting was the beginning of MADD—Mothers Against Drunk Driving.

One of the first things they did was to gather twenty or so people together for a demonstration in Sacramento, the capital of California. Then the power of their desire to change the drunk-driving problem took them to Washington, D.C., where they marched with 100 people in front of the White House. Today, there are 360 chapters in forty-seven states, with affiliates in Canada, Great Britain, New Zealand, and Germany. Through MADD's lobbying and initiative, we now have a National Commission Against Drunk Driving and more than 400 new laws against drunk driving in fifty states.

Candy's leadership example also inspired the founding of SADD—Students Against Drunk Driving. Now there are numerous chapters of SADD across the nation involving thousands of young people who want to prevent the deaths of their friends.

Candy says that MADD's first job was to convince people that drunk driving was actually a crime. But obviously, Candy's job has become more than that. Her commitment is an inspiring example to the thousands of people who have joined her effort to make a difference.

About her personal loss, Candy Lightner says that MADD "gave positive meaning to [my daughter] Cari's death." And when asked about the success of MADD, she says, "If you care enough, you can accomplish anything."

GRASS ROOTS LEADERSHIP—WHAT CAN YOU DO?

You don't have to go through a trauma like Paul Jeffers and Candy Lightner did to make a difference. You don't have to speak in front of large audiences or form a worldwide organization either. You can find something close to home that matters to you and go to work on it at your own pace. You can join thousands of men and women making a difference on a daily basis, leading by example.

* Join the man in Kentucky who told me he gives one hour every Saturday afternoon to teach someone to read. He was so encouraged by the results that he was able to get three of his friends to do the same thing.
* Join the woman in Washington who has organized a group to read to nursing-home patients.
* Join the elderly man in California who saves all year so he can cook and serve free Christmas dinners to hundreds of his poor neighbors.

One of the best things about grass-roots leadership is that it belies our feelings of powerlessness in the face of the overwhelming problems the world faces today. Anyone of us facing any of these problems alone could say, "What difference could I possibly make?" When you feel that way, remember, you are *not* alone. We all feel that way at times. Remember also, there are other people all across this country who feel the same and, like you, have resolved to try to make a difference. Our combined efforts do matter. This is the power of grass-roots leadership. Together we can go a long way in solving our most pressing problems, we can create great opportunity, we can literally change the world.

Our country has always grown best through grass-roots leadership. Throughout our more than 200-year history, we have depended on grass-roots leadership to move us forward. Our destiny has found expression in "we the people"—the people of the small towns and big cities taking up a cause, speaking out, serving others, giving their personal effort. Our representatives legislate, create laws, and administer what the *people* have decided must be done.

MANAGE THINGS—LEAD PEOPLE

For the past few decades, we have been overmanaged and underled. At the end of World War II, the world turned to rebuilding its war-torn countries. We learned to manage objects and procedures, money and time, equipment and machinery. But somewhere along the way we lost the emphasis on leadership. We forgot that while management is important, leadership is what builds and maintains great nations and great peoples.

We all want to be inspired, motivated, and encouraged to do our best. We feel this way when we are being led, not just managed. That's why it's so important to distinguish between management and leadership. Doctors Hersey and Blanchard gave us an excellent definition in their 1969 book, *Management of Organizational Behavior:*

Management: Working with and through people and groups to accomplish organizational goals.

Leadership: Influencing human behavior, regardless of the goal.

That's what leadership is: *influencing others.* To make a difference and to be effective leaders, we have to influence others to think and to act, as well as to follow. We must set an example that others *choose* to follow. And the secret to eliciting that choice is the very essence of leadership.

SERVING MAKES THE DIFFERENCE

Lao-tse, the sixth-century Chinese philosopher, said: "A leader is one who serves."

To make a difference we must be willing to serve. Real service has a high value. If we contribute our time, emotions, energy, and effort, we can have real impact on people and problems. When we contribute to the well-being of others, our joy and fulfillment are immeasurable. As President George Bush said when he addressed a group of college students in St. Louis, "From now on, any definition of a successful life must include serving others."

Service has two main ingredients. They are:

1. The willingness and ability to serve others. How deep does your personal service ethic go? Service is a two-way street. Do you acknowledge and appreciate the services that others give you? Or do you treat those who serve you with indifference, arrogance, even contempt? What does this tell others about your dedication to service?

2. The type, kind, and quality of service given. Regardless of the type, size, or kind of organization you work with, it is important to emphasize that:

• Service is an attitude, not a department.
• Everyone in an organization is responsible for the service ethic.

Some people think that "service" requires only lip service—a written policy statement or an occasional commendation to an employee. True leaders know that service starts at the top. It starts with one person. Imagine your desk with two signs. One says, "The Buck Stops Here." The other says, "Service Starts Here." Wouldn't that send a powerful message to others?

There is a direct correlation between how a leader serves his or her followers and how the followers serve others. If we want to make a difference in our organization, we have to ask ourselves, "How do I serve my people?" "How do I treat them?" Because that's exactly how they will turn around and serve others.

These aren't easy questions. Anyone who wants to make a difference has to recognize that everything we do is an example to our followers and to our co workers. Service is a most appealing example. It is one others will *want* to follow.

The philosophy of history's leaders who have had a positive effect on our world has been one of service. It is invariably the servant-leaders who have advanced mankind.

Freeway Service

My husband, Bill, and I were driving home from a meeting with one of our clients. We had agreed to prepare a proposal for a training program in sales and leadership, and to get it to our client in time for their weekend executive retreat. It was Wednesday afternoon and our working schedule on the complex proposal was very tight.

We were driving along at 55 mph, discussing how to juggle our schedules, when a white van pulled up beside us. On its side in big red letters were the words EXPRESS IT. Underneath, it said "Courier Service 24 hours a day, 7 days a week," and gave a telephone number and an address. "Wow," I said to Bill, "that's the answer to our delivery problem." I grabbed a piece of paper and started to write down the telephone number.

Just then the driver saw me, tooted his horn, and waved. I waved back. In sign language he asked, "Do you want our services?" I nodded and showed him the piece of paper on which I was writing the phone number. He rolled down his window, and, at 55 mph, held out a brochure. I was so excited that I started to roll down my window to take it. Bill said, "For heaven's sakes, we don't want to get in a wreck. Wait!" So I signaled to the young man, making a dialing gesture to indicate that I would call the company. He smiled, tooted the horn, and off he went!

When it comes to service, that's what I call going the extra mile. We did indeed call his company and have used its services many times. When their employees pick up packages at our office, I hear the same story over and over. They talk about how the owner, Sal Grassia, sets the example of serving. He cares about his people, and does his best to serve them. His attitude is reflected in how they serve us and their other customers.

Sal worked for Federal Express for eight years and saw how they became successful by giving excellent service. He says, "I'm out to beat their service record." Apparently, he learned his lessons well, because he has three offices (as of this writing) in the San Francisco Bay area and is opening another in Sacramento soon.

Once you get Sal started talking about leading by example and his service philosophy, you can't stop him. He is passionate about what he calls "our service philosophy. It's the only thing we have to offer." He says, "I keep telling my team that we are all in this together. The managers, supervisors, telephone people, delivery people—we are all here to help our customers." With pride Sal says, "We have a ninety-six percent-efficient service level, and we're still improving." When I asked him what he thinks makes the difference, he was quick to say, "People make the difference, it's a team effort. My philosophy is first, image—how you look.

Then professionalism—do it right the first time, and third, service—get it there on time." I told him that I'd noticed that even his newest people seem to emulate his service philosophy. I wondered how he trained them so fast. He said, "It's not hard. I just explain that increased service = increased volume = increased profits = increased benefits to all employees. It doesn't take them long to catch on to why Express It is making a difference."

THE SERVICE BOOMERANG

Why should you want to be a servant? Because, as the old saying goes, everything that goes around comes around. What you sow, you reap. These are not empty platitudes. If you want to influence others to serve and help you make a difference, you will get back what you give out. The service ethic always boomerangs. Remember: People don't care how much you know until they know how much you care. They are not interested in your title, your college degrees, or how much money you have. First, they want to know if you care about *them* as a person, if you care about helping them solve their problem. Then your knowledge and experience becomes important.

When serving, ask yourself two questions. First, "What would I want if I were dealing with *me?*" That brings the idea of service to a very personal level. And second, "Who am I really serving?" If leadership serves only the leader, it will fail. Ego satisfaction, financial gain, and status can all be valuable tools for a leader, but if they become the only motivations, they will eventually destroy a leader. Only when service for a common good is the primary purpose are you truly leading.

We have intelligence quotients and personality quotients. If there was a service quotient, an *SQ*, how would you score? How would your organization score? We all have the responsibility to ask for, expect, and give good service. But serving must be a part of our personal leadership philosophy if we are to succeed and prosper. There has never been a better time for leaders who can motivate the service ethic in their followers.

WHERE TO BEGIN

When you have the courage to say, "I will try to make a difference. I'll take up the challenge of becoming a leader," you become part of the grass-roots leadership so badly needed today. If you lead by example and use the power of a service ethic, people will be motivated to follow. When you manage things but lead people, you will influence their behavior and productivity.

Where should you start? There are more opportunities for making a difference than we would ever have room to mention in this book. In chapter 1, "A Leader Has a *Mission That Matters*," we will talk more about deciding where and how you can make a difference.

A LEADER HAS A MISSION THAT MATTERS

The Secret of Building Charisma

> "Make no small plans for they have
> no power to stir your soul."
> —ANONYMOUS

How do you begin to make a difference? What do you want to make a difference *about?*

You'll find the answers to these questions when you define your mission that matters. A mission is not just a duty or task. Your mission that matters will be a dream, vision, or purpose that drives you. It can be small and personal or large and world-shaking, but your mission will have some positive effect on people around you.

The important thing to know about missions that make a difference is that they usually start out as something you do naturally just because you want to help a little. We don't usually say, "Well, now I'm going to be a leader with a mission that matters." What often happens is that your mission grows out of your activities at home, at work, or during volunteer work. Then your commitment becomes an example of leadership that inspires and motivates others to join you or to have their own version of a mission.

Your mission can take a few hours a week or your whole life. Whatever the scale, it is a powerful and magnetic leadership quality. Missions make leaders different from other people. Missions are at the very heart of the leadership/service ethic.

On June 22, 1989, President George Bush stood on the White House lawn and told 3,000 students, "Make it your mission to make a difference." When you start to look for ways to make a difference, there are no restrictions. Nothing is off-limits or out of reach. When you begin to look for your mission, do not feel restricted by your age, health, ethnic background, or social, economic, or educational status. You might begin by looking at your personal life. Is there a way you can help those closest to you?

A Personal Awareness Mission

Ten years ago, Meg Franklin's husband was killed in a plane crash, and Meg was left a widow with a fifteen-month-old daughter, named Montine. As a single parent with increased responsibility, she became acutely concerned about the quality of daycare Montine was receiving. She began to talk to other women who were faced with the dilemma of finding safe, affordable, quality childcare.

Meg is the manager of Benefit Services at Levi Strauss & Co. in San Francisco. Because of her involvement with Levi Strauss's community projects, she volunteered for several committees that were surveying and advocating improved child-care facilities. She knew that good child-care facilities would help children, parents, and, ultimately, the businesses that supported them. She has become very involved in the Bay Area Employer Childcare Coalition.

Meg's personal concerns for others grew into a mission that is making an important difference. Your mission can also develop from your work. Is there a way you can help others by using your professional expertise?

A Work Mission

Dr. Dick Henning makes enormous contributions to his community as the dean of Community Services for Foothill College in Los Altos, California. In this job he serves the community on behalf of the school. But Dick also found a way to serve the community on behalf of his own concerns. He founded the "Celebrity Forum," one of the most prestigious lecture forums in the United States. Six to eight times a year 2,400 people from all around the San Francisco Bay area fill a local performing-arts auditorium to hear outstanding leaders present their views at the forum. Presidents Ford and Carter have appeared, as have Henry Kissinger, Jeane Kirkpatrick, Jane Goodall, Nobel Peace Laureate Elie Wiesel,

Helmut Schmidt, Jehad Sedat, Mario Cuomo, Sam Donaldson, and George Will, just to name a few.

I asked Dick what motivated him to dedicate so much time and energy to the Celebrity Forum. He answered, "I was deeply concerned about the fact that people get their view of the world from the brief, tidy, safe quotes that we are fed on the television news. I wanted to get people away from their television sets and in touch with the real newsmakers, people with divergent views that can stimulate our thinking. We get to ask these people questions, challenge them, and have a meaningful exchange that sends the audience away with a broader view of the issues and an increased appetite for this sort of exchange."

Dick's forum is certainly a worthy mission that matters. He is making a difference in people's lives. There are dozens of ways you could help make a difference if you are willing to volunteer. Is there a worthy cause that you could help?

Volunteering

Peter Cousin is very passionate about his mission. Pete is corporate-sales coordinator for Cenit Bank in Norfolk, Virginia. He has volunteered for many projects and joined several organizations over the years. But he never felt like he was really making a difference until he decided to use his sales and marketing talents and skills to serve his community. Pete knew about SMEI (Sales and Marketing Executives International), an international organization with a chapter in every major city in America, but he had never joined. When he inquired he found that their aims and his matched. He immediately joined the Tidewater chapter. Within two weeks he was asked to be on a committee and he accepted. Since then he has been on many other committees and has served on their boards of directors. Pete says, "Volunteering is fulfilling and adds to all the parts of my life." His pet program is a scholarship fund for students studying marketing. He and other SMEI members have raised several thousand dollars for deserving scholars.

Pete will sometimes telephone 50 to 100 members a week to get their views on issues or to ask them to volunteer for an activity. He says, "Having a mission and commitment are key." One of his favorite sayings is, "Don't be a watcher, be a doer." Pete started with a small idea and it has grown to be a worthy mission that is making a difference.

START SMALL—START NOW

There are three major roadblocks to building a mission that matters.

* The first is thinking you are too old or too young or too *anything* to have a mission.
* The second block is to put off beginning.
* The third is even worse—it is to do nothing because you feel you can do so little!

All missions have modest beginnings. Don't hesitate to start small. As your mission grows, you'll grow with it. To become a leader with a mission that matters, you don't have to be a statesman, celebrity, or business giant, or have a lofty position, numerous degrees, or huge bank accounts. Your desire to make a difference is what matters. Even your smallest effort counts.

A LEADERSHIP TEST

You need drive and ambition to accomplish your mission, but drive and ambition shouldn't be confused with the energy some people use to pursue what they want. Successful people can influence others without necessarily meaning to, but that does not automatically make them leaders, nor does it mean that they have a mission.

There is a good way to find out if a person is truly a leader. Ask them what their mission is. You won't have to explain the term "mission"; they will understand. After you ask the question, just keep quiet because they will immediately give you an answer.

When I spoke with Tom Landry, former head coach of the Dallas Cowboys, I asked him which of the twelve qualities he thought were most important. He said: missions that matter, decision making and communications. He quickly said missions were first, "because in my business we all know what our goal is—to win football games. Missions are tremendously important. I translate that, in our terms, as having a philosophy about what we want to be as a football team. This is what I try to stress with the Cowboys that we must all believe in the philosophy that we have to be successful.

Once you get your staff, your players, and organization in tune with that, everything else falls into place as far as the leadership is concerned.''

─────────── *A Mission for Michigan* ───────────

Joan Hutchinson is director of Education and Information for the Michigan Municipal League. When I asked her what her leadership mission was she quickly answered: "My mission is to improve the leaders of our [Michigan's] cities so we can make government better for everyone. I want to do our share here in Michigan, to educate people and to improve the quality of life for our citizens." That's a pretty clear mission!

Joan has been with the Michigan Municipal League for eleven years. When she came on board as a trainer there were ten educational programs a year. With her leadership, by the end of 1988, there were 134. These programs benefit everyone in the state. They range from programs on basic government for the elected officials, to public relations programs for the park and Recreation departments, and special programs for the police include command-officer training. For the first time in 1989 she is organizing a four-state regional meeting to train municipal attorneys who all appear before the Sixth District Federal Court.

Joan produces results. She says that "training is contagious. People get caught up in it." About her mission she said: "It is about serving. It gives me a real sense of accomplishment and contribution to see what we achieved."

CLARIFYING YOUR MISSION

To help you clarify your mission and to focus on how you can make a difference, you need to ask yourself some questions:

1. *What is the most important thing in the world to me?* Your mission grows out of your own unique view of what is important in your life and the world.

Alfred Tutela, Cleveland superintendent of schools, found a very creative mission. It began with his belief that education is the best way to give young people a fair chance in the world. Cleveland's forty-nine percent drop-out rate indicated to Tutela that far too many young people were throwing away their most valuable asset. He decided to try appealing to kids in two areas they understood—money and having a future.

He devised a plan to pay kids in grade seven through twelve $40 for every A grade they received in an academic course, $20 for Bs and $10 for Cs. The money would be escrowed for them in an account bearing their name. At the end of each year they would receive an accounting of how much they had earned. Then they could take up to eight years, after graduation, to use the money for college or job training. Sounds like a crazy idea, doesn't it?

Tutela hit the nail right on the head. The kids got excited about earning the money and having the chance to receive the kind of education that was otherwise unavailable to them. Tutela took his plan to the Greater Cleveland Roundtable, a group of influential business, community, and religious leaders. They too saw the enormous problem and felt the plan had merit. They got together and raised $5 million to fund the program. During the program's first week, Cleveland received requests for information from Washington, Baltimore, and Toronto.

2. *Where do I start and how?* Taking the first step is often the hardest part of any endeavor. Look around for inspiration and directions.

- Meg Franklin's mission began because of her awareness of the need for childcare. If you are concerned about child-related issues, perhaps you, too, could get involved with childcare. You might make an important difference in your community.
- Do you work in a manufacturing industry? Your company may be able to use your input to build a better, safer, more efficient product. Your commitment could inspire other employees who are working on these products to get involved.
- If, like me, you have an aged parent and are worried about the quality of care available for older people, you could become active in senior programs. Or as a smaller mission, you could help one elderly person by making his or her life safer and more comfortable. You'll be surprised at how your personal leadership example can motivate others.
- If you are fortunate enough to be financially successful, you

could share that success with groups that need individual funding.

Eugene M. Lang of New York City has spent $125,000 on his "I Have A Dream" program for the sixth-grade students of P.S. 121, in East Harlem. Lang attended P.S. 121, and as a successful business man and a role model for the students, he was asked to speak at their commencement exercises. In his speech he encouraged them to stay in school, not to let their ghetto life engulf them. But he got carried away with his enthusiasm and told them that if they stayed in school and graduated from high school he would pay for their college tuition. To his delight thirty-four of those youngsters have been accepted at colleges or have applications pending. He says, "We're trying to give these ghetto kids the kind of support they would get if they had been born into a relatively affluent family."

3. *How much time can I devote to my mission?* You need to decide what part it plays in your life. Will it be all-consuming? Or will it be something for which you carefully allocate the needed hours? Even the busiest person can schedule time for something that matters.

John P. Polychron, President and CEO of Planters LifeSavers Company, is willing to put in the time and effort to attack what he sees as an enormous problem in America's business. "Illiteracy is a huge debit hiding above the bottom line. Corporate America must make fighting it a priority." Polychron also knows the emotional cost of illiteracy. He knows his employees can not be fulfilled people without being able to read. "It takes guts to admit that you can't read," he says.

In 1978 he created the PET (Planters Employee Training Program) in his Suffolk, Virginia, plant. He worked with the city school system and the state department of education to set up the system. PET offers basic education in reading, writing, grammar, math, and other studies. Since its beginning, over 150 employees have improved their basics skills. Some have earned their General Education certificates; others have learned to read, and many have increased their skills to help them on the job. John Polychron's mission is worth the time and effort he gives to the program.

4. *Do I have the skills and knowledge I need?* Do you need further education or training to have an impact, to make a difference? When and where can you get this education? How much would it cost? Are you willing to put in the effort to acquire this new knowledge? Does your employer provide training programs you could take advantage of? Have you looked into programs at state or local colleges? There are many ways you could avail yourself of the knowledge you need to clarify your mission.

5. *Am I staying open to all the possibilities?* Openness and flexibility is important. One of the most exciting elements of having a mission is growing beyond your original vision because you stayed flexible.

Several years ago I had the privilege of meeting and becoming friends with Bob and Dorothy DeBolt. When Dorothy Atwood and Bob DeBolt were married in 1970, their combined children numbered ten. He had one and she had nine, four of whom were adopted children from Korea and Vietnam who had been emotionally or physically handicapped by the ravages of war. To their brood of ten, Dorothy and Bob added nine more children, some from Vietnam, Korea, and Mexico.

Eventually the DeBolts had nineteen children, many of them considered "unadoptable." There was Karen, the spunky black child born without arms and legs. In several of Dorothy's speeches she tells the story of Karen sitting on the toilet and accidentally slipping in and calling out, "Don't flush—don't flush!!" Dorothy says a good sense of humor was often their saving grace.

There was Tich and Ahn, two teenage paraplegics who took a paper route that no non-handicapped youngster would accept—it included a delivery up five flights of stairs. There was Sunee, who had lost her first two foster homes and had given up hope of having a family. Bob and Dorothy DeBolt had a joint mission: to help these special children and others with similar problems.

As the DeBolts' mission grew, they found there was great need for an adoption agency to find homes for such children. So the DeBolts founded AASK (Aid to the Adoption of Special Kids), an organization to find and help families willing to permanently adopt physically and mentally handicapped children of all races. It was the first agency of its kind, and now it has several branches in the United States.

When Bob and Dorothy began their mission, they didn't care whether anybody knew about it. They were adopting these children because of their deep desire to help and to try to make a difference. But mission building is like climbing a mountain whose top is covered in fog. When you reach what you think is the summit, you discover even higher mountains and bigger challenges you could not see from the ground.

The DeBolt children are all grown now and have left home. Bob and Dorothy are enjoying their grandchildren. The last time I saw them, I was again struck by how "normal" they are. You would never imagine that they have affected thousands and thousands of lives around the world. If you sat down to have a cup of coffee with them, they would be as easy to talk to as your best friend. I guess that's one of the things that makes them so unusual. While they are ordinary people they are quite extraordinary leaders.

POLITICAL LEADERS CAN INSPIRE US, TOO

Political leaders walk a difficult line, having to be simultaneously skillful politicians—with all the necessary compromises that are traditionally involved—and skilled leaders, able to persuade and overcome opposition. They need the power of a vision—a mission that matters.

Political leaders usually have an easily recognizable mission. Lech Walesa of Poland, Pakistani Prime Minister Benazir Bhutto, Bishop Desmond Tutu of South Africa, and President Corazon Aquino of the Philippines have missions of such scope and magnitude that, successful or not, will affect our world. If television had existed in the days of George Washington or Abraham Lincoln, we might have a more intimate knowledge of how they implemented their missions. Yet the words of Lincoln and Washington still ring out with clarity and power. Their missions are perhaps more inspiring today than they were in their own lifetimes.

————————*One Nation Indivisible*————————

I work in Washington, D.C., often and every time I'm there, I visit the Lincoln Memorial. My favorite time is late at night when I can be alone to think. As I stand at the bottom of the steps and look up at the floodlit memorial, I think about the men and women who trekked across the continent to start a new life in the frontier.

I think about all the small and large missions that mattered, that gave us the states whose names are carved around the top of the building.

As I walk up the steps in the silence, I am overwhelmed by Lincoln himself, looking down with those benevolent eyes that seem so real. I often think that I wouldn't be surprised if he stood up and said "hello" and asked about America today. When I stand and read the words of his Gettysburg Address inscribed in the marble, I am always deeply moved and feel the power of his mission that mattered. It is an incredible experience. It makes me want to "do" something—something meaningful.

It's rumored that since the memorial was built, every sitting President has visited Mr. Lincoln in the wee hours of the morning, seeking inspiration or solutions to critical problems.

Lincoln was a shy man, often beset by bouts of depression. He lacked the formal education of a Jefferson or a Hancock, but he led a country to survival of a terrible Civil War.

Lincoln's mission was to maintain "one nation, indivisible, with liberty and justice for all." The Emancipation Proclamation was framed by a statesman, not just a politician. After Lincoln's untimely death, it took a full hundred years before other leaders stepped forward to complete Lincoln's mission of racial equality under the law. Lincoln gave us a powerful example to live by and to lead by. Even though it was far too slow in coming, the fight for racial equality was fired and driven by the brilliance, clarity, and power of Lincoln's mission.

If you have never been in Washington, D.C., I hope you will take the opportunity to visit this incredible monument. Be sure to have a tissue with you. You'll need it.

BUSINESS LEADERS CAN SET POWERFUL EXAMPLES

The corporate mission statements of the world's best-run companies often reflect the personal missions of their leaders. These missions are the driving force behind their profits and success.

Profits and missions that matter are not exclusive of each other. In fact, successful organizations with clear-cut, clearly defined mission statements usually benefit both employees and customers, while adhering to a high sense of ethics and social responsibility. These companies and organizations seem to have a spirit and staying power that others do not.

—————————*A Different Method*—————————

In 1979 Harry J. Gray, chairman of United Technologies Corporation, decided to use an unconventional method to convey the company mission to the business world. He did this with a series of "Messages" about the kind of company United Technologies was trying to be. These messages were short poems printed in *The Wall Street Journal* in place of traditional advertising. Here is Gray's foreword to the book compiling the messages:

Seven years ago, when some of us at United Technologies decided we needed to let the business world know more about our corporation through advertising, we had a choice to make: We could launch the traditional sort of ad series to explain our product lines, our research investments, our operating philosophy, our financial results. Or we could take a flier on a strikingly *un*traditional series of messages which would discuss life in general instead of life at the corporation.

The conventional approach probably would have worked as a way of telling what the corporation does. But the messages we decided to go with . . . have let the world know about the *kind* of company this is. It has done that job with extraordinary effect.

We have received requests for more than 3,600,000 reprints. We have opened over 691,000 letters—many of them long and thoughtful. I have been sent candy, flowers, product samples of various kinds, offers for investment, civic awards.

Johnny Carson read one of our messages on his show. Ann Landers has reprinted many of them. School boards in several big cities have made copies by the thousands for distribution to students. Military leaders have told me our ads are used by the services as motivational messages. Five of these messages were among the ten best-read ads to appear in *The Wall Street Journal* in the past decade. None of us at United Technologies knows for sure why this series has been so astonishingly effective. But we have some theories.

For one thing, we believe we were right to invite readers to think— instead of telling them how to think. We believe we did well to discuss everyday subjects that affect everyone in some way, instead of talking about ourselves.

We think we were wise to stay with problems that can be solved rather than tackling complex, abstract problems that elude solution.

Most basically, we believe we struck a responsive chord with the underlying theme for this campaign: *How we perform as individuals will determine how we perform as a nation.*

In a democracy, this has to be so. In a corporation, too, individual behavior is the key to organizational performance. Our readers evidently find the theme sensible and inspiring at the same time.

So do we, and we have been proud to put it forth as the premise for this unique communications effort.*

Harry J. Gary
Chairman
United Technologies Corporation

*A message as published in *The Wall Street Journal* by United Technologies Corporation, Hartford, CN 06101.

Gray's mission that matters is stated very clearly in the crux of his letter: *"How we perform as individuals will determine how we perform as a nation."*

Each of our missions is like a pebble thrown into a still pond, causing concentric circles to expand in ever-widening circles of influence. The combined effect of our missions that matter has a positive and powerful cumulative effect.

EVERYDAY LEADERS AS ROLE MODELS

Everyday leaders are everywhere. They are you and others like you who want to make a contribution. They are in your town and mine. They are factory workers, company managers, corporate executives, homemakers, clergy, scout leaders, salespeople, small business owners, and city council persons. They are young and old, rich and poor, every color, size, and shape.

Their missions may be on a more modest scale than those of world leaders, but they are equally important. Everyday leaders influence us as much as world leaders because they act as role models and set examples for us on a much more personal level. They offer us easily accessible motivations, hope and inspiration for daily living.

────────────A Personal Example────────────

In the late 1960s I was deeply impressed by a couple in our town who had a brain-damaged child. They asked for volunteers to help with a rehabilitation program for their daughter. I volunteered. Five days a week I would go to their home and, with other volunteers, would do what was called "patterning." It was a system of physical rehabilitation designed to stimulate learning and train the muscles to bypass the damaged portion of the brain, training the unused portion to perform normal body functions such as walking, standing, speech, and large and small muscle movements.

As I became involved with the family of this child, I met many other families who were also using this same program. They had to travel to Philadelphia, where the program was initiated, every few months for re-evaluation and updating of their training. If you have ever worked with a brain-damaged or retarded child, you know that traveling is not an easy matter. It is also very expensive, and most of the families were of modest incomes.

So we volunteers got together as a group and formed a nonprofit corporation. We sponsored fund-raising events and with the proceeds we formed the Institute for the Achievement of Human Potential in the San Francisco Bay area. We hired staff trained at the institute in Philadelphia. I ended up as coordinator of the institute and had the privilege for several years of working with the neurologists, psychologists, surgeons, therapists, ophthalmologists, and other professionals who were committed to helping these children.

While working at the institute, I met hundreds of teenagers, men, and women, people of all ages who were making a difference by volunteering to help these children reach their maximum capacity. The couple in our town were fine role models for me and many others. We worked together to make a difference. And our combined efforts achieved much more than any of us could have alone.

BUILDING YOUR MISSION

When you have begun clarifying those areas in which you'd like to make a difference, you can begin to build your mission. By the end of this section you will have an idea of where to begin to put your time, effort, and energy. Here are four categories to spark your imagination.

1. *Analyze your skills, talents, and abilities.* This can be a pleasant and self-motivating task. Take three pieces of paper and label them as follows:

(1) My Physical Skills
(2) My Intellectual Abilities
(3) My Special Talents

Under physical skills, list everything you can think of that describes your physical skills. List large and small skills. For example, I value physical fitness and like to snow ski. With this skill, I could help small children learn the basics. I value fitness, so I could be helping children begin a life of exercise and fitness. I also have very strong hands and arms, and I used this strength when I volunteered for the physical rehabilitation program.

You may have many physical talents when you stop to think about it. Can you play an instrument or paint? That might inspire you to donate some time to teach others and build their interest in the arts. Can you repair cars or other machinery? If so, perhaps you could help a young person looking for work or someone who is out of work to build similar skills and find employment. Use your imagination and don't take anything for granted. We will come back to this list.

Under intellectual abilities, list things that represent your mental capacities. Did you have special training of some kind? Do you have degrees of higher education? Can you speak other languages? Are you an especially logical thinker? Are you one of the lucky people who understands and can work well with computers? Do you have an affinity for numbers? Don't be shy. We'll come back to this list also.

Under special talents, list the things that are unique to you. How about writing skills? Are you one of those rare people who can weave words and sentences together to inspire and motivate others? Perhaps you have an excellent voice and could use it to record books for the blind. Are you good with animals? How about raising guide dogs for the blind? Don't forget that special talent called "people skills." Think about any special talent that you have.

Even if you don't realize how you might use it to make a difference, put it on the list.

2. *Recall your childhood and youth.* When you were a child what did you dream of doing? What excited you? What took your imagination off to far places or to great deeds? Think about where you came from. If your childhood was poor, your mission might be directed at one of the many issues related to poverty. If you had a wonderful education, you might choose to organize groups to tutor poor readers or help immigrants learn the English language and American customs. Was a parent an alcoholic? Perhaps fighting addiction is your mission.

What influenced you as a child or teenager? Did you discover the beauty of dance or music or art? Did you have a deaf, blind, or handicapped friend? Were your family migrant farm workers? Did you lose a father or brother in the Korean or Vietnam wars? Did someone close to you die of cancer? Good, bad, easy, hard, rich, or poor—we were all influenced and affected by our childhood environment and could build a mission on our experiences.

3. *Open your eyes and ears.* Most of us tend to see and hear the same things every day. We have set patterns and avoid or block out anything unfamiliar. This is a natural thing to do, and it creates a sense of calmness and security in our lives. However, when we are considering how we can make a difference and trying to find our mission that matters, we have to really see and feel the world around us.

Here are some ways to start expanding your view of the world around you.

- Buy your local newspaper and read the fine print on the third or fourth or fifth page. See what the articles are about. Look at the want ads and the personal columns to see what is being sold and what people's concerns are.
- Go to a museum and watch a group of children on a field trip discovering the world of great paintings.
- Go to a depressed area—a destitute rural area or inner-city ghetto—and feel the weight of poverty and hopelessness. It will move you beyond what you think you would feel.
- Visit the cancer or AIDS ward of a hospital and listen to people talking about life, living, and death.
- Talk to a group of senior citizens. They could give you enough

missions to last a lifetime. With luck, we will all be old some day and we can ask ourselves, "How do I want to live then?"
• Go to your local police department and find out about the drug problem in your town and schools. Could you help educate children about the dangers of alcohol and substance abuse?

Don't be afraid to open your emotions and intellect and observe what is really going on around you. It can be painful sometimes. But when we deal with these kind of emotional issues we often find our deepest passions. And passion is a vital ingredient of missions and leadership.

———————————*A Way of Life*———————————

"Project Self-Help and Awareness (PSA) isn't a program, it's a way of life," says passionate Director John Kinsman of La Valle, Wisconsin. Supported solely on donations, PSA funds and organizes exchange programs between families in Mississippi and Wisconsin. PSA volunteers have taught courses on nutrition, sewing, farming, and Black history; worked on voter registration and canvassing; served as poll watchers; started self-help pig, calf, and garden projects; and worked building, repairing, and painting homes in countries of Mississippi that are the poorest in the nation.

John Kinsman is a leader that most people have never heard of, but his mission and that of PSA is explained very clearly in one sentence: "We believe that through awareness of racism and prejudice, we begin to eradicate the ignorance that causes it." The passion of John Kinsman's mission that matters is making a difference.

4. *Sit Quietly.* There is more that needs to be done than you could ever do. But don't let the need overwhelm you. You CAN make a difference.

Our lives get so cluttered that it is easy to be trapped in the here and now. We forget to look at the horizon. The best way to build your mission is to expand your experience and thinking. For this kind of introspection, you need to get away from our noisy world. Create a time to let your mind wander, a time to give your imagination room to soar, to dream great dreams.

Now you have a list of your skills, talents, and abilities. You've thought about your youth and childhood, observed your daily world, and have begun to develop a philosophy about missions, making a difference, and leaders. Let's see how you can use all this information. As you are sitting in your quiet place, go back and review the lists of your skills and talents and abilities and decide which one of them is the most fulfilling to you.

If you start to build your mission around something you are truly excited about, you will be much better at it. You will have much more stamina and passion.

Go on to look at your youth and childhood. See if some of the things that you listed might be interesting to you as an adult. If you combine these interests with your skills and talents, this may be the beginning of a way to make a difference.

After you've looked at those two sections, think about the things that you observed. How might they be combined with the other two sections? The best way to build your mission is to expand your experience and thinking. The more you can do to stimulate your emotional, intellectual, physical, and spiritual capacities, the more sensitive you become to potential missions.

Once you have an idea about your mission, there is one important thing left to do: Have the courage to question your preconceived ideas, prejudices, and conditioned responses. When you examine these roadblocks, you can open a floodgate of possibilities. For example: If you decide to make a difference by helping someone learn to read, you might have some preconceived ideas about the simplicity of the task because it is not a problem for you. One way to test that preconception is to spend a day or two trying to learn a foreign language. This can be a very humbling experience and might give you an idea of what it is like for someone else to learn to read. Building a mission can be as rewarding as implementing one. You can make a difference on the road to a clear mission and then expand it when you arrive.

DON'T WORRY—BE PATIENT!

At this point I want to warn you about becoming discouraged because you may not know exactly what your mission is or what kind of difference you are going to make. Don't worry about it. Going through this process of mission building will get your personal mental computer on the right track.

If you relax and let your mind take over, you will have a delightful surprise in a very short time. Something will come up that can inspire and motivate you. In the computer industry, they have the expression GIGO—garbage in, garbage out. It means that if you start with garbage, you can't get anything better back.

The same principle works in your mental computer, and obviously the reverse is also true. If you insert good thoughts about building a mission, and you go through these mental exercises, you will get back some good information from your mental computer. Don't be impatient. It can take time. Meanwhile, congratulate yourself for having gone through the process. That alone will make you a better leader and help you make a difference.

MAGNETISM AND CHARISMA

We may not always be able to define a particular leader's mission, but we recognize leaders who have missions. We are drawn to them and their energy, we solicit their options, and we follow their lead. They help us redefine our lives, our purpose, and perhaps our own missions.

Often, acquiring a mission that matters catapults a person into a leadership role. That is what happened to Martin Luther King, Jr., when, as a young minister, he organized a local boycott of segregated buses in Selma, Alabama. He attracted followers of all races. His personal magnetism as a leader grew as the scope of his mission became clear to him and to others.

A mission that matters is part practical and part magical. The practical part is the result. The magical part is what the mission does to your mind and heart. These two parts are interrelated.

• The more clearly defined the mission, the more effective you become and the more you can make a difference.
• The deeper the passion for your mission, the more it acts as a magnet for others and creates what is called *charisma*.

If you think you lack brilliant speaking skills or personal magnetism, don't worry. Your mission doesn't depend on it. But it is interesting to see how some people's missions have transformed them into charismatic leaders because of the depth and passion of their desire to make a difference. Your enthusiasm can make you eloquent. The example that you set can speak more forcefully than words.

In biblical and historical time there are many examples of missions that produced charismatic, magnetic leaders. When Moses saw the Burning Bush and heard the angel of Jehovah, he was transformed into the leader that led his people out of bondage. The tentmaker, Saul of Tarsus, was on the road to Damascus when lightning flashed around him. He was converted to Christianity and became Paul the Apostle whose writings were the charismatic, dynamic force of Christianity. Joan of Arc's heavenly voices created such passion in her that men followed her into battle.

Mahatma Gandhi organized nonviolent protests against British rule that hastened the independence of India. The force of his example lessened violent retaliation by the Indian population in a turbulent time. Gandhi demonstrated to all future generations that peaceful change is both possible and more effective than blood-soaked revolutions.

Eleanor Roosevelt was another person whose belief in peace and the basic goodness of all people formed a lifelong mission. Homely, shy, and modest, she had an intense personal interest in others that gave her powerful personal magnetism. She drafted no laws, was never elected to public office, and made no political appointments, yet her vision is woven throughout our nation's recovery from the Great Depression, our survival during World War II, and our search for world peace through the creation of the United Nations and its charter.

KEEP ON KEEPING ON

When I become discouraged about my mission I read the biographies of people like these and I am encouraged to go on.

This is a good place to say that it is very human to get discouraged at times. Sometimes your mission may be criticized by others. Sometimes your mission may seem harder than you thought it would be. There is always an element of personal sacrifice in making a difference. At some point you will need to put others first—this is a test of your commitment. There are times when you will wonder if you are making even a dent in what you want to accomplish. I feel the same way at times. But when I read about people who persist, who keep on keeping on, it buoys me up and gives me courage to continue.

Being famous or having world recognition for your mission is not what matters. What matters is that you are trying to make a difference. When it is the last day of your life and your spiritual bags are packed and you've *tried* to make a difference, then you can go peacefully off to our Maker, knowing that the world is a little bit better because you have been here.

LEADERS WITHOUT MISSIONS

Can someone be a leader without having a mission? Can you make a difference without a mission? Possibly, but true leadership qualities are developed and sustained by having a mission. Some leaders identify a lifetime mission. Others have different missions at different stages of their lives. It isn't "wrong" not to have a mission that matters, but without one you can't reach your full potential as a leader. Your mission is your driving force.

Big things come from small beginnings. The mighty oak tree comes from the tiny acorn, and a tiny seed of wanting to serve others can help you make a difference. Your mission that matters can be the driving force that inspires others to follow. Your example of service will be your legacy of leadership.

A LEADER IS A BIG THINKER
The Magnet That Attracts Others

"Some men see things as they are and say why?
I dream of things that never were and say why not?"
—ROBERT FROST

Leaders that make a difference are "big thinkers." They know that seeing things others can't see is not only a quality of leadership; it is a responsibility. Being a big thinker means being part pragmatist and part mystic. This talent is not as rare as you might think; it's as much an attitude as it is an aptitude. Big thinkers use their visionary capabilities to expand their missions and make a difference.

Certainly the first people who predicted that man would walk on the moon or send pictures through the air were greeted with knowing smiles and the spiraling of index fingers around ears. When President John F. Kennedy proposed putting a man on the moon, others before him had already ventured into space. But Kennedy's vision pushed their exploration to its then-conceivable limit. Now space stations and colonies on other planets are on the drawing boards. Someday we may extend our vision to other solar systems, maybe other universes.

For every great idea that works, there are hundreds that don't. Both heart transplants and turning lead into gold sound like good ideas. But experimentation shows that one works and the other is impossible. Both ideas were valuable because we learned from both. Without big thinking we'd make very little progress.

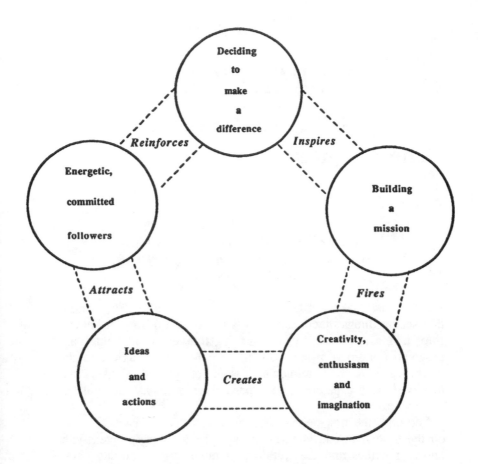

TRANSFORMING BIG THINKING INTO BIG RESULTS

The path from big thinking to big results has five parts. Once you decide to make a difference, you set off a chain reaction of inspiration, creativity, and action.

Your big thinking is an attitude that sees people, places, and things bigger and better than they see themselves. As a visionary leader you'll find beauty where others do not, you'll seek opportunity where others find only problems, and you'll see answers where others haven't yet recognized the questions.

──────────*Father Joe Carroll, Visionary*──────────

When Joe Carroll left the Bronx for San Diego in 1962, he was going to become either a priest or an administrator for the Boy Scouts. He chose the priesthood. His first assignment as a priest was in a wealthy neighborhood in El Cajon, California, where he quickly learned to solicit money for worthy causes. With his Irish wit and Bronx savvy, he persuaded parishioners to give money freely and with good humor. People often joked, "Quick, grab your wallet, here comes Father Carroll."

By 1983 he had served in several parishes and his reputation as a fund-raiser had spread. By that time he also had severe arthritis and an artificial knee. Father Carroll could have rested. But when Bishop Leo Maher asked him to take over the St. Vincent De Paul Center in San Diego, Father Carroll could not say no. There were 4,000 homeless people in San Diego sleeping on beaches, in parks, in abandoned buildings and automobiles. The center would be a shelter for them. The diocese had already purchased an old building downtown. They estimated it would cost one million dollars to convert the building to a shelter. Father Joe rolled up his sleeves and went to work.

Six months into the job Father Carroll had a big idea. He went to Bishop Maher and convinced him to buy a full city block and construct a building fashioned after the old California missions. It would be a place of beauty and utility. It would house a clinic, school, play area, children's library, 350 residents' rooms, and a kitchen that could feed 2,000 people daily. The cost would be $7 million!

Father Joe went to work collecting money once more. He solicited the majority of the contributions from individuals and institutions. He went on television to ask for money; he worked with a car dealer who donated $100 for every car he sold. San Diego Charger Eric Sievers gave twenty-five dollars for each pass he caught and fifty dollars for every touchdown he scored against the Miami Dolphins. Father Carroll used all his creativity and influence to raise the money needed for his vision. But he was still short of his goal.

At this point Joan Kroc, widow of Ray Kroc, of McDonald's fame, had already donated $500,000 dollars. She called to see how the fund-raising was progressing. Father Carroll told her he was still $3 million short. "O.K," said Joan, "I'll send you a check for the $3 million tomorrow." Father Joe Carroll's vision was a reality.

The St. Vincent De Paul Joan Kroc Center has received much national attention for its programs and architectural design. Father Joe's vision has spread, and the center is now a model for other programs across the nation.

He's been called the "Hustler For the Homeless," a title he doesn't mind at all. Father Joe Carroll says, "I've had jobs since I was eight years old. No matter who you are you can always hustle and earn a few bucks." He runs the center as a business and says, "My product is dignity."

INNOVATION, IMAGINATION, AND VISION

> Managers have "to do" lists.
> Leaders have "to create" lists.

Creativity and imagination are abilities, distinct from the capacity to acquire knowledge. "It is better to create than to be learned. Creating is the true essence of life," said Reinhold Niebuhr. Albert Einstein said that imagination is "something more important than knowledge."

To enhance big thinking and productive innovation, give yourself permission to let your imagination flow. Children and creative adults allow their minds to give all possibilities an equal chance. They don't reject any idea immediately or automatically. Einstein said, "I think and think for months, for years. Ninety-nine times the conclusion is false. The hundredth time I am right."

Vision, in its most exalted form, reaches even beyond the limits of imagination. Vision is "a waking dream" (Longfellow), "the art of seeing things invisible" (Jonathan Swift). Making a difference often means seeing invisible challenges. It's having faith that you can accomplish the mission you've chosen, and imparting that faith to others.

The architects of the Constitution clearly saw Swift's "things invisible." Our Constitution has held up under the enormous social and economic change that has occurred since its inception. During the past two hundred years we have grown from thirteen colonies to fifty states, and the population has increased thousands of times.

The delicate balance of political power, the separation of church and state, and control of the military are constantly being tested, yet our nation survives under this same constitution. Since the original ten amendments—the Bill of Rights—were approved in 1789, only fifteen have been added. The inspiration and vision of our founding fathers has attracted millions of people from around the world and that vision continues to be our "waking dream."

THE HIGH-FAITH FACTOR

There is the story of the kindergarten teacher who asks a child what she is drawing. "I'm drawing a picture of God," the child replies. "But, sweetheart," says the teacher, "no one knows what God looks like." "They will in a minute!" says the child. That is thinking big.

True leaders possess a similar childlike faith. Not a *childish* faith that lacks maturity and understanding, but an attitude of deep faith in themselves and others. They have a high-faith factor.

If you are a big thinker you have faith in your own God-given skills, talents, and abilities. More importantly, you have faith in the desire of other people to do well, to make a contribution, to have a meaningful life. You know that most people don't want to feel like losers. Your faith in them can make a world of difference in how they perform because your faith acts as a catalyst to their courage.

INSPIRING OTHERS

As Dr. Kenneth Blanchard wrote in *The One Minute Manager,* some people "may be *disguised* as losers." However, as a visionary leader, you won't be fooled. You know that they may never have been shown how to tap their hidden skills and potential, or never had enough positive feedback to build self-confidence or ever learned to take risks. Your challenge is to identify and inspire these people, turning them into productive contributors.

Big thinkers can transform the world. They believe that people want to be the best they can be. When circumstances keep people from developing and achieving, they welcome a leader who points out a new direction.

History tragically demonstrates that in desperate times, despairing humans will follow almost anyone. As a positive visionary you have two tasks: To point your followers in a positive, productive direction, and to provide an outlet for energy that might otherwise be destructive. As a big thinker your power to make a difference is incalculable.

ACTORS AND RE-ACTORS

There are two kinds of people in this world: actors and re-actors. Most people are *re-actors*, waiting for events to affect them. They lack the ability to anticipate events. They don't know if something is good or bad until its effects are obvious. When re-actors try to use their imaginations, they are often overwhelmed by options and potential problems. In contrast, a leader is an *actor* in life, a person who uses imagination and analysis to direct and control events in a positive, powerful way.

People will follow you when your vision inspires them and adds meaning to their lives. The leader who has a goal and a way to achieve that goal helps people see past today. This vision of the future greatly influences human behavior because it means anticipating needs, expressing common concerns, and identifying common goals. You can motivate people and give them something to aim for beyond their own interests. When you are a big thinker, you can help *them* make a difference.

A group of young volunteers working on a local election were discussing why they were involved. One young man said: "I was very excited when I met him [the candidate], because he actually asked me to help him reach his goal. No one has ever asked me to get involved before. I felt like he was sharing his vision with me." A young woman who had been standing toward the back of the group said, "I'm tired of feeling like I don't matter. I think if he wins he will do some things about the problems we have, and I will have been a part of the solution for a change."

STRATEGIES OF BIG THINKERS

How do you take your vision and turn it into reality? As a big thinker there are specific strategies you can use.

- Check your assumptions and expectations periodically.
- Develop and define your personal philosophy.
- Challenge tradition and the prevailing wisdom.

- Nurture curiosity, both in yourself and others.
- Look for simplicity, wherever possible.

Let's look at how each of these strategies work.

CHECK YOUR ASSUMPTIONS

Attacking your assumptions is crucial to making a difference. It helps you avoid getting trapped in a bog of false concepts that stagnate your creativity. You need to let your imagination flow.

The dictionary defines imagination as "recombining former experiences in the creation of new images different from any known or experienced." When facing a challenge, start by listing your assumptions about the situation. Then ask, "What if this happened?"—"What if I did this instead?"—"How would it work if I did this first and then this?" Don't be afraid that your assumptions won't stand up to scrutiny. If they don't, you're strong enough to reframe them or replace them with better ones.

Here are the four steps for a "reality check" about your assumptions.

1. State your assumptions
2. Decide on their validity
3. Outline the actions (if any) you need to take
4. State your expectations for the future

You can begin right now by checking your assumptions—about yourself, your relationships, your career.

Assumptions Check

Make a statement you believe to be true about each of the following areas of your life.

About Yourself
  —your health and fitness
  —your spiritual development
  —your educational improvement

About Your Relationships
  —with your spouse
  —with your children
  —with your parents
  —with your siblings

   —with your closest friend
   —with your boss
   —with your coworkers

About Your Work/career
   —your promotions
   —your income
   —your career direction
   —your fulfillment from your work
   —your responsibilities
   —your challenges

About Your Company/group
   —your job description
   —your areas of responsibility
   —your decision-making skills
   —your ability to communicate
   —your time management
   —your people skills

Check validity and expectations. Now test the validity of the above statements, your "assumptions," by playing devil's advocate. Look at each statement/assumption and ask yourself:

1. Is my statement really true?
2. To what degree is it true or not true?
3. Is there something I am overlooking?
4. What am I taking for granted?

Now go back and evaluate your expectations.

5. What actions do I need to take?
6. What are my expectations for the future?

Some of your answers to these questions will identify areas in which you need to re-evaluate your assumptions. Assumption-validity checks are an extremely valuable way to stay on top of situations. Too many people spend their time fire fighting because they don't take the time to clarify the present and prepare for the future.

An example of an assumption-validity check might look like this:

Example of a Leadership Assumption

Statement: My people are doing well at their jobs.

Validity check: Have they been upgrading their education so that they can change with the times and continue to do well?
Are there people who are resting in a comfort zone, when they should be striving or challenging themselves? If so, who?

Action plan: What can I do to move them along?
Should I review job descriptions to check their validity against the actual job and the performance criteria required to do the job well?

Expectations: My people will constantly improve under my leadership.

Example of a Personal Assumption

Statement: I feel well and seem to be fit.

Validity check: When is the last time I have had a complete checkup? Would such a checkup reveal some deficiencies in my diet or exercise level, cholesterol level, resting heart rate, etc.

Action Plan: Schedule a checkup immediately and follow through with regular checkups. Determine an improved health routine with my doctor and other experts, and then follow it.

Expectation: I will always be aware of my physical self and do everything necessary to maintain and improve my health.

Erroneous assumptions and *invalid* expectations are at the bottom of most bad decisions, difficult relationships, or poorly functioning groups. Checking assumptions tells you where you are and where you should be going. It's not always easy. Assumptions are familiar and comfortable. However, if you are going to tap your creativity and be a big thinker who makes a difference, you need to be willing to let go of some outdated assumptions.

DEVELOP YOUR PERSONAL PHILOSOPHY

Business and organizations have long known that they need a clear philosophy, a mission statement, to be effective. In Chapter 1 you saw that if you are to be a productive leader, you need a mission statement. Your philosophy of life is larger than your mission statement. It will strengthen your resolve and help you recognize outside pressures that may be harmful to your mission. A statement of your personal philosophy should express the meaning of your life and what you want to make a difference about.

Have you ever tried to define your life philosophy? It is a little like writing your own epitaph. Your mission is an important part of your definition, but you should also include statements about how you will lead your life and why the things you are doing are important to you. This statement will change and expand as you become a better leader. It will grow as you do.

—A Man With A "Think Big" Life Philosophy—

When Leon Peters died, California Governor George Deukmejian said, "Leon Peters was a man with bold visions and dreams." For over fifty years Leon Peters had been deeply involved in hundreds of causes and projects in Fresno, California. He stood just over five feet tall, yet he was a man everyone looked up to.

Peters had the ability to inspire others to look beyond the common and ordinary. He was the classic big-thinker leader, seeing people, places, and things as bigger and better than others saw them. When you spoke with him about his causes, it was obvious that he had a clear philosophy about his life.

Even without a college education, Leon Peters achieved what few people ever achieve. He said that he compensated for his lack of university training by working harder. Peters was of Armenian descent. In the earlier part of this century, Armenians were discriminated against in Fresno. Despite ethnic discrimination and the difficulties of the Great Depression, Peters became an example of the free-enterprise system that he valued so much.

Peters's energy and commitment to his country were remarkable. He worked to protect the national parks and forests of the Sierra Nevada, was involved with the Boy Scouts for fifty years, served as chairman of the California State University, Fresno, Board of Governors, and worked to create Fresno Community Hospital. More than anyone, Peters was responsible for establishing the hospital and making it one of the leading medical centers in the central San Joaquin Valley. In 1971, the Leon S. Peters Rehabilitation Center of the Fresno Community Hospital was named in his honor. And because of his hard work at California State University, Fresno, the university now has a $12.4 million business building and service center named for Leon Peters.

Peters always saw beyond the immediate. His vision showed him opportunities that others didn't see. "It is a privilege," he insisted, "to serve the community." He often said that "only in America could my dream come true."

Once, when Peters was given an award, he said, "How can I think I'm an outstanding citizen? I don't think I've done as much as I could have. When I look back and see what I've received from this community and compare it to what I've done, I realize I've received a lot more than I've given. It's important to be able to do something for the community and for future generations." With those words Peters defined his personal philosophy, the foundation of his leadership skills. Today the Fresno Chamber of Commerce presents an annual Leon S. Peters Award for outstanding leadership to people who have devoted their time and talents to the community.

When he died in 1983, he left what the Indians call a "long shadow." He was described as "a towering figure in the business, cultural, and civic life of Fresno," who had "intense community loyalty—he believed that he had a responsibility to be involved in civic projects," and "he always looked beyond the roles people played and saw the individual that was each of us."

In his quiet way, Peters demonstrated great leadership by turning his vision into reality. His philosophy and example of community service has made a difference to thousands of people in many cities. His "long shadow" will not soon fade. He is missed greatly!

A personal philosophy, like that of Leon Peters, is built over a lifetime. It is always changing and expanding. Don't be afraid to express yours with whatever words you can at first. You'll polish and refine it soon enough. The very act of beginning to cultivate your life philosophy will add depth to your mission. This philosophy is the springboard of your power as a big thinker.

CHALLENGE TRADITION

"This is how we have always done it." That's one statement you can't afford to make if you are to make a difference. The world is changing too fast. But challenging tradition and the prevailing wisdom takes courage because people have a lot invested in the way things are currently done.

Challenging tradition does not necessarily mean making radical changes. It may not mean making any changes at all. But when you examine tradition, you will discover ways to improve the way you do things. You will gain a better or broader perspective of people, places, events, and situations.

—————A Big-Thinker Sales Manager—————

I was working with a sales organization whose goal was to increase sales. We started by examining their traditional ways of doing things, including the weekly Monday morning sales meeting. "Why Monday morning?" I asked. The new sales manager grinned. "Well, that's when the previous manager held the meeting."

We asked some of the other executives if they knew any special reason why the sales meeting was held on Monday. "It's always been on Mondays," they replied.

It quickly became obvious that they were living with a tradition that had no real bearing on their needs. After some discussion, the sales manager said, "Actually, in our current situation, Monday is not really the best day for the meeting. I would rather have my sales staff come in on Monday morning, touch base, and then get out in the field. Monday through Wednesday are our best selling days. Thursday is less good and by Friday our clients are too busy to see my sales people." So he decided to break tradition and hold his weekly sales meeting on Friday afternoon.

It worked out very well. He found that Friday was a good time to discuss the week's problems and to work with his staff to find solutions.

This sales manager was an excellent human motivator. He used his new Friday afternoon meetings as a time to give recognition for the week's successes. Together he and his sales staff set plans for the next week, and his people went home for the weekend on a positive note.

The sales staff liked the new schedule better, too. On Monday mornings they were fresh and anxious to be out in the field, not sitting around a conference table. Some said that the traditional Monday meetings had slowed down their initial enthusiasm for the week. The sales manager was a big thinker and was smart enough not to get caught in a tradition that needed updating. He instituted several other policy changes, discarding outdated traditions, and his sales increased.

What traditions can you challenge? If you made some changes, could you achieve better results as this sales manager did?

Examining traditions doesn't mean that you automatically discard them. Most traditions have grown from sound, even profound reasons. When you examine the traditional, you end up strengthening the traditions that deserve preservation. Knowing what to change and knowing what *not* to change are equally valuable.

This same sales manager started questioning the traditional monthly sales awards breakfast. He soon found that all the sales people and his bosses enjoyed the opportunity to get together and share "war stories" and successes. He kept the monthly sales award breakfast exactly as it was.

——*Big Achievement through Big Thinking*——

Big thinkers are not awed by "the way it's always been done." When you have the courage to challenge tradition, some very exciting things can happen. Big thinking always precedes big achievement.

In 1959 Pope John XXIII convened Vatican II, the first ecumenical council in ninety years. In 1962, 2,860 Catholic leaders met at the Vatican to discuss major, difficult, and sensitive changes in the Catholic church. They came from nearly every nation in the world (excepting the communist-bloc countries who denied exit visas to their priests and bishops). Because these men had the courage to challenge tradition, they opened wide the windows of the Catholic church as had never been done in modern times.

Traditions die hard and many of their decisions are still controversial today, more than twenty-five years later. In an effort to make the Holy Mass more accessible and meaningful, priests are now allowed to conduct services in their native languages rather than traditional Latin. The position of the altar has been moved so that priests now face their congregations during Mass. The Folk Mass has become popular, attracting and meeting the needs of millions of young people.

Could you make a difference by looking beyond the obvious? Has everyone else written off an idea that you think still has merit? Perhaps they are stuck in an outmoded tradition? Maybe you should take another look. You may very well be the Pope John XXIII of your organization.

NURTURE CURIOSITY

Curiosity is one of the key ingredients for being a big thinker. Not ordinary inquisitiveness but real curiosity, what Cavett Robert calls "divine discontent." He is describing the internal voice that prompts us to do better or nags us that something is not right. This discontent can motivate you to seek new answers, new approaches—sometimes with sublime results.

Leaders nurture this kind of curiosity in themselves and others, welcoming the mental gymnastics of looking at things backwards, upside down and inside out. They enjoy being curious.

Here are some ways to help arouse your curiosity, innovation and creativity:

Look up: Most people walk down the street with their minds intent on their destination. They don't really "see" where they are. The next time you are walking on a downtown street, open your awareness to what is going on around you. Look up at the second- and third-story windows. It is amazing what kind of businesses and shops you will find. Take a few minutes to visit one of them. Who works there? What kind of work are they doing?

Do you remember the book *The Maltese Falcon* or the movie starring Humphrey Bogart? Sam Spade (Bogart) is partners in a detective agency with Miles Archer. In the beginning of the story Miles Archer is shot. Sam gets involved in finding the killer and recovering a statue of a Maltese falcon. The adventure twists and turns amid the dark, foggy, back streets of San Francisco.

Today if you walk down Bush Street where it roofs Stockton Street and look up at the corner you will see a sign that notes the untimely death of Miles Archer at the hand of Brigit O'Shaughnessy. It reads: "On approximately this spot Miles Archer, partner of Sam Spade, was done in by Brigit O'Shaughnessy." As you can tell, San Francisco takes its landmarks very seriously.

Reroute yourself: Do you drive to work every day? Try taking a bus, cab, or train and really *look* at the passing scenery. Or try driving to work on a different route. Or leave an hour or two earlier. You will see different people than you usually do. Where do they work? What do they do? Can you guess their occupation by the way they are dressed?

Running on half a staff: What if you had to do without half the people in your department, work group, or committee? What would you do to get the same amount of work done? What would you have to eliminate for lack of personnel? Could you still function? If so, could any of these ideas be implemented to increase productivity with your current level of staff?

Alternately, imagine that your staff has just doubled. How would you use the new people? What new projects or responsibilities could you take on? How would these affect the efficiency, productivity, and power of your unit? Can any of these ideas be implemented using your current staff?

Learn from the young: As children we had Erector sets, Tinker Toys, Lincoln Logs, and Logo blocks. We were allowed and encouraged to "build something." Our curiosity was one of the most important factors in our development, and we drove our parents crazy with repeated *whys* and *hows*.

To rekindle your innate childhood curiosity, watch a group of kindergarten children playing. Stop at a nearby playground or visit a nursery school if necessary. Notice their enthusiasm for creating new things. Join the children in their play if possible. Make up a game with them and see if you can be as creative as they are. We have much to relearn from children.

Play "That's impossible!": Get a group of friends or coworkers together and have an anything-goes session on a current problem. Tell them that all possible solutions, no matter how crazy or remote, will be welcome. People will usually balk at first, so you will need to offer a couple of outrageous suggestions yourself to get them started. Tell everyone to turn off their judgmental-parent mindset and look for possibilities. Use "What if" statements. Pretend there are no boundaries. Playing and having fun with these ideas is a catalyst to innovation. The first session may be a little stiff or slow to start. But if you plan creativity sessions often, people will soon learn to break the old "that's impossible" thinking habit.

Ask why? Not how?: To really make a difference, you need to start asking "why?" first instead of "how?" In our society we are so busy figuring out how to do things that we forget to ask why we are doing them. We get into trouble with our bias for action.

Many times you will clarify and totally reframe a situation by asking, "Why do you want to do it that way?" or "Why is it done that way?" "Why?" will get you much more interesting and imaginative responses than "How?"

Ask the person cooking dinner, *"Why* are you doing it that way?" You'll probably get a standard answer: "Oh, because I've always done it that way," or "Because that's what the recipe says," or "That's the way my mother did it." Keep asking "Why?" and if you don't get the dish thrown at you, you might end up with a creative cooking idea.

Ignore the "right" answers: Roger von Oech, author of *A Whack on the Side of the Head,* an insightful book on innovation and creativity, says we often disregard the "second-best idea" in our search for the "right idea." Von Oech says we need to *unlearn* some of our thinking in order to get to the new ideas. We get stuck on what we know, instead of looking for what we don't know. What one thing are you absolutely sure you know the answer to?

Learn when to take a break: Don't let deadlines intimidate you. Time frames and urgency can jam your mental computer. When you are under pressure, be sure to get away from the problem occasionally. Changing what you are doing will allow your mental computer to do the processing you need.

We've all had the experience of trying and trying to solve a problem with no success. Then when we finally give up and go on to something else, the answer pops into our minds. Taking a break is essential for free-flow thinking. Free-flow thinking unlocks the imagination. Relax and take your imagination for a walk—literally. Creativity rarely comes when you are stagnating behind a desk or locked into a structure. Even if you are under time pressures or deadlines, stop what you are doing and change your environment to let the mind relax.

————A Woman Who Thought Big————

Frances Perkins was an extraordinary woman. She was the first woman to hold a cabinet post in the federal government of the United States. She was secretary of labor under President Franklin D. Roosevelt from March 1933 to July 1945. Above all, she was a big thinker.

Labor was one of the most sensitive issues during the first years of Roosevelt's presidency. The world was in the midst of the Great Depression and millions were jobless. With masses of unemployed people willing to take any job at any wage, there seemed little chance of shortening the work week and guaranteeing a minimum wage.

As secretary of labor, Perkins was the instigator of the revolutionary and bitterly contested Social Security Act. Because she was a big thinker, she could envision its enormous value to future generations. In 1935, both the Social Security Act and the Fair Labor Standards Act (establishing minimum wages, overtime pay, and child-labor laws for employers engaged in interstate commerce) became law. Perkins was the framer, the driving force, and the negotiator between the opposing factions. She challenged tradition and the prevailing wisdom of the time in which she lived. She had the courage to be a big thinker. Frances Perkins used her ability to be innovative and creative in ways that have profoundly benefited your life and mine. She unquestionably made a difference.

LOOK FOR SIMPLICITY

As leaders we must be careful that, in our enthusiasm for the new, we don't complicate it. Productivity and progress depends on leaders who simplify, not complicate.

We humans have made the world much too complicated. Our language is one of the worst examples of needless complication. People and groups have created language and buzzwords to justify their existence and enhance their exclusivity and importance. To get things done, to make a difference, we need to simplify language so we can get to the heart of matters. As leaders, we need to make language more precise, not less, and to build communication bonds, not erect walls.

Leaders in science create exciting new ideas and processes every day. But we must remember not to complicate these ideas. The computer is an example of a technology that simultaneously simplifies and complicates our existence. As society becomes more dependent on "high-tech," leaders must become more "high-human" oriented. It is up to us. Technology can make life easier, or it can rob us of warmth, compassion and feelings.

The problems of the 4 billion (and climbing) people on the earth are staggering. We must learn to break complex issues into simpler parts. "Simplifying" does not mean that issues suddenly become simple. It means that they are easier to handle in smaller, more manageable pieces. People can see how to complete a larger task if you explain and define it in workable segments.

VISION BEYOND THE CONCEIVABLE

Vision starts with imagination. The next time you go to the beach, play the childhood game of writing your name in the sand. Then watch it wash out to sea and imagine it washing up on some faraway land. The imagination of leaders can cross oceans to affect people they have never seen. There are millions of ideas waiting to be discovered and acted on by big thinkers. Eden Phillpotts said, "The universe is full of magical things patiently waiting for our wits to grow sharper." Just one new idea could change the world.

The world needs your ideals and your idealism. We have negative, narrow thinking in abundance, and more than enough cynics. Now we need people who can look for the brave and the beautiful where others see nothing. We need big thinkers to nourish the imaginations of others and help them expand their own creative powers.

──────────An Example of Big Thinking──────────

When Ralph Montelius graduated from Pepperdine University's PKE (President Key Executive) Masters Program in 1987, it was both the end and the beginning of his lifetime commitment to education. Ralph was twice the age of the average master's recipient. He had already completed one twenty-year career in the Air Force and was well established in a second career as vice president of Customer Services with Triad Systems. He had also wrestled with cancer twice. Clearly, Ralph was no narrow thinker.

Ralph's company surprised him with a special graduation present. They instituted an award for the people at Triad who continue their education, and they called it the Ralph Montelius Award for Special Achievement and Personal Development.

In 1988 I was keynote speaker at a Triad award banquet, one of the most exciting and motivating meetings I have ever attended. When Ralph Montelius stepped forward to present his namesake awards, a roar came from the audience. Over fifty young people, selected from 700 candidates, received the award. Some were in master's and bachelor's programs, others in continuing development programs. The recipients were pursuing this education on their own time, carrying full work loads, caring for families, and maintaining many outside interests. Because of Ralph Montelius's example of big thinking, they are stretching to emulate him because they believe their education will make a difference.

You might be thinking, "What's the big deal about someone graduating from the Pepperdine program? Many other people have. And millions of people have master's degrees." But Ralph Montelius did not arrive at Pepperdine in any ordinary way.

Ralph never graduated from high school, but, he says, he learned good habits young. At the age of ten he went to work in his stepfather's meat market where he developed a strong work ethic.

As soon as he turned seventeen, Ralph joined the Air Force where he spent twenty-one years as an enlisted man. He talks about those days with great pride. The work ethic he learned as a child enabled him to take advantage of special training and opportunities. He went to the Air Force Non-commissioned Officer Academy and excelled once again.

1971 was a tough year for Ralph. Doctors discovered he had cancer, but Ralph's positive attitude and determination got him through major surgery and radiation therapy. By the time he was in remission, he had been to the private hell that only other cancer victims can understand, but he was alive and well and eager to get on with his life. He was a senior master sergeant in charge of three launch complexes at Vandenberg Air Force Base when he left the Air Force that year.

Unfortunately there was not much call for launch experts in the business world. Ralph went to work for a finance company and in a short time was a branch manager. He says, "I had learned people skills in the Air Force, and in the finance company I acquired business experience and knowledge."

In 1974, Ralph joined the newly formed Triad Systems customer service department. Ralph smiles when he recalls that, "In those days we had thirty-five customers and three field engineers. We still have twenty-five of those customers today!" By 1985 Triad had more than a thousand employees, and Ralph was vice president in charge of field service personnel across the nation. He had reached what most people would consider the peak of his career. Yet when the two-year Pepperdine program was offered, he jumped at the chance to complete his formal education. Ralph says, "No matter how old you are, you're able to learn new things."

Ralph plunged into the program with his usual zeal. He was excited about graduating and managed to juggle his time between family, work, and studying. But fate was to deal him another tough hand. Halfway through the program, Ralph began having problems with the old radiation and cancer operation. He was forced to spend a month at the Stanford Medical Center, having major surgery to remove old scar tissue from the cancerous area. Despite this serious setback Ralph's determination never wavered. With pride and gratitude Ralph completed his thesis and graduated in December 1987.

Everyone at Triad, young and old, has a courageous big-thinker role model in Ralph. Ralph's big thinking is affecting people in 3,200 communities that Triad services across this country. His young staff is highly motivated and educated. They believe in his philosophy of service and reflect his example of personal growth. Ralph Montelius is a perfect example of how a big thinker can make a difference.

The world is changing so fast and the amount of information we must assimilate daily has increased so tremendously that leaders *must* see beyond the present and the obvious. Reinhold Niebuhr said, "Nothing worth doing is completed in our lifetime." But a leader knows it must begin in our lifetime. We must have high expectations for what is ahead, projecting ourselves and others into a positive future scenario.

Thinking big and having vision is more than a major responsibility of today's leaders; it is a biblical injunction: "Where there is no vision, the people perish" (Proverbs 29:18).

A LEADER HAS HIGH ETHICS
Building Trust With Your Followers

> "Ethics is the maintaining of life
> at the highest point of development."
> —ALBERT SCHWEITZER

Legend says that when young George Washington was asked who cut down the cherry tree, he replied, "I cannot tell a lie." Our first president has become a folk hero reflecting many of our shared values, especially high ethics. I believe people still want to identify with Washington's philosophy of honesty and his strong sense of right and wrong, his personal integrity, and his rejection of deception, artificiality, and shallowness. High ethics are still valued by people across all of our social, economic, and political spectrums. People still look for high ethical standards in their leaders. And leaders need strong ethics to guide them in their actions and decisions.

WHAT ARE ETHICS?

If you make a list of words related to ethics, it would include morals, integrity, honesty, values, trust, duty, virtue, truth, decency, courage, prudence, loyalty, honor, goodness, fidelity, and conscience. Most of us would agree that these words are descriptive and appropriate, but they do not comprise a definition. We need a working definition of ethics to guide us and help us in making a difference.

First, ethics are not morals. They are an *outgrowth* of morality. Ethics represent *actions* based on a concept of right and wrong. If this seems too fine a distinction, let's look to some definitions that may help.

Morals: A personal philosophy based on the ability to know right from wrong. What we believe about right and wrong affects our thinking and shapes our character traits. Morals are a *philosophy.*

Ethics: High standards of honest and honorable dealings based on our morals. Ethics are a set of basic working tenets for life and business. How we act and what we do, our methods of functioning, and how we apply our morals is our ethical behavior. Ethics are *application.*

The stronger our ethical behavior, the better leaders we become. As Harry J. Gray, chairman of United Technologies said in chapter 2, *"How we perform as individuals determines how we perform as a nation."*

There are unethical people in business. But we can't condemn all businesses for those whose unethical behavior makes headlines. We have many outstanding leaders in businesses large and small. H. J. Gray is one. John Ackers, chairman of IBM, is another highly ethical leader. He spoke to the Bay Area Council in San Francisco and included some powerful comments on ethics. He said:

> Like you, I've been reading a lot about ethics in the news recently. Though ethics is forever its own reward for each individual, ethics is a crucial force in our strength as a nation. And I especially include our economic and competitive strength.
>
> We compete as a society. And you can't have a good society with everyone stabbing everyone else in the back, with everyone trying to steal from everyone else, with everything requiring notarized confirmation in writing because you can't trust the other fellow, with every little squabble ending in litigation, and with Congress writing more and more pages of regulatory legislation to tie American business hand and foot to keep it honest. That's a recipe not only for headaches in running one's company; it is a recipe for a wasteful, inefficient, noncompetitive society.
>
> I don't think the sky is falling. I don't think we had a great ethical

height in the good old days from which we've been tumbling downhill. But when all is said and done, I agree with Thomas Jefferson who said, "All human beings are endowed with a moral sense." The average farmer behind a plow can decide a moral question as well as a university professor. I have confidence in the person on the street. But that common moral sense doesn't come out of nowhere. We must consciously and vigorously work at fortifying our ethical buttresses.

Each of us has a personal responsibility for ethical behavior. As Mr. Ackers says, we must consciously work at it. When we do, we set an influential example for others. One person's high ethics do make a difference.

THE ETHICS SCALE

Ethics are generally measured by setting up two extremes at opposite ends of a scale. One end of the scale is the concept of absolute right, whether it be defined by religion or law. The other end of the scale rejects the idea that anything is inherently right or wrong. The philosophy is, "If it works, it's okay," "If it feels good, do it.' Because of the distance between these two extremes, ethics can never be reduced to an indisputable formula. Ethics remain emotional and spiritual as well as intellectual. We are forced to live with this irritating and intriguing paradox because to live otherwise would be chaos.

Nevertheless, societies create general rules of conduct to guarantee their own survival. The rules established by our forefathers and still agreed upon by most of us are what protect us from anarchy, leaving us free to advance without having to decide the same issues over and over again. Somerset Maugham said, "The great truths are too important to be new." In our Judeo-Christian society we have many truths that have served us well for generations. Even though we may have lost sight of some of them, they are still there, waiting to be rekindled by people like you who want to make a difference.

SETTING AN EXAMPLE

If we are going to lead, we need strong ethics for two reasons: to guide ourselves and to set examples for others. When we have strong ethical values, we raise the level of conduct and aspiration for both ourselves and our followers. As leaders we perform three important functions:

1. We constantly define and communicate ethical behavior in our words and actions.
2. We translate that definition into a working premise that everyone understands. When we do that effectively, we build trust and cohesiveness in our organization.
3. We resolve ethical conflicts that arise. When we do, we strengthen the foundation of our organization.

The leader with consistently high ethics fulfills these functions and becomes an inspiration for everyone. Problems occur when ethical behavior is *not* clearly defined, understood, or demonstrated.

SITUATIONAL ETHICS

Each of us makes daily decisions about our ethical behavior in various situations. This is *situational ethics*. Since we are not perfect, we rarely operate consistently at the highest ethical level. Instead, the best we can do is to try to develop the wisdom and judgment to get as close to perfection as possible. For example, absolute honesty means never lying. That sounds like a good idea. But all of us have told "white lies" to keep from hurting someone's feelings.

Remember the last time a friend asked if you liked a new outfit? If you didn't, there was little point in saying so. If you found a neutral comment that was appropriate but did not tell the absolute truth, were you unethical? Most of us would answer "no." So we use our experience (wisdom and judgment) and our conscience (moral character and integrity) to tell us how far we can stray from absolute honesty without compromising our ethics and our integrity.

If something is ethically or morally repugnant on a personal scale, it is equally repugnant in our jobs and professions. In both areas a leader sets the standards, tries to live by them, and communicates the same expectations to others.

THE POWER OF TRUST

Management expert Peter Drucker said, "The leader's first task is to be the trumpet that sounds a clear sound." With every example of high ethics and integrity, we send a "clear sound" to others. It builds trust and loyalty which are at the base of all effective relationships.

When standards and performance do not match, when they do not send a clear sound, we lack authenticity, confuse our followers, and set bad examples. Our people must be able to trust us or the consequences can be detrimental, not only to profits or success, but to attitudes and actions. If you are a leader who combines high ethics with a genuine concern for others, personal competence, and fairness in the exercise of power, you will inspire trust. Without trust, the contract between you and your followers collapses. Your ability to make a difference will be greatly diminished.

————*A Leader Builds Trust and Loyalty*————

Barbara Smith Nivala lives and works in Phoenix, Arizona. She is executive vice president of the National Speakers Association and has a staff of nine. Barbara is a fine example of a leader who produces excellent results through high ethics and service to her people. Her understanding of the importance of trust and loyalty is at the heart of her effectiveness. She delegates effectively by letting people know that they are accountable and that she trusts them to do their best. They know that she will support them with the members of the association and the board of directors, when they need it. She praises freely and never criticizes someone in public. Directing an association of over 3,000 very independent members can be stressful at times. But Barbara knows that she must keep the stress to a workable level. Her staff know they can trust her not to let things get out of hand. She plans well and asks others to do the same in order to avoid fire-fighting situations. She is a leader who makes a difference by quietly and patiently building trust and loyalty in her people by being trustworthy and loyal to them.

WHO CAN WE LOOK UP TO?
In this age of ethical controversy, it would be easy for us to become cynical, to lose our faith in each other. We all need heroes and people with high ideals to inspire us. If we were sitting together now, I'm sure you could tell me some inspiring stories of people you know whom I could look up to. I have one to tell you about.

We've all read about medical scams and the unethical behavior of a few doctors. It is unfair to judge the many fine and dedicated men and women in the medical profession by the few who are unethical. Here is an example of one of their finest.

―――――*C. Everett Koop―Surgeon General*―――――

One doctor who has been called many things, but never unethical, is Dr. C. Everett Koop who served as surgeon general during the Reagan administration. Despite the unpopularity of some of his directives, he has become a folk hero and an example of someone who does not abandon beliefs to political expediency. Indeed, many of his health directives were in direct opposition to government policies: He declared nicotine an addictive drug and spoke out against tobacco subsidies and administration-backed tobacco exports to Third-World countries; he suggested exploring free-needle programs for drug addicts to prevent the spread of AIDS. When Koop was appointed in 1981, over liberal objections to his personal views on abortion (he was against it) and conservative objections to his personal views on sex education (he was for it), the office of surgeon general was a position with little power, no budget, and no staff. Through strong personal leadership, Koop turned the office from a rubber stamp of administration positions to a powerful advocate for the health of a nation that shaped public health policy on issues from organ transplants to child abuse.

A deeply religious man, Koop's personal views on homosexuality (''antifamily'') did not keep him from seeing the AIDS virus as a health issue, not a moral one. *U.S.News & World Report* told the story of Koop's sitting by the bedside of a young man dying of AIDS. A compassionate man, Koop decided that when someone is dying, life-styles are irrelevant: ''I am surgeon general of all the people.'' Despite vigorous opposition, he printed 107 million AIDS information booklets and sent them to every home in America, so that people would know how to protect themselves from the deadly epidemic.

Koop's invested his job with a moral mission, "to espouse the cause of those who lack justice." During his twelve-hour days and seven-day work weeks, septuagenarian Koop advocated the medical rights of handicapped babies, bans on smoking in public places, the reduction of violence on TV (network executives, he says, are "caught between their conscience and their pocketbooks"), organ-donor programs, condoms, and sex education about AIDS, "starting at the lowest grade possible." He has opposed mandatory AIDS testing and euthanasia. Of his ability to survive in Washington, D.C., without resorting to political solutions for medical and social problems, he said: "I have a sense of right and wrong. A lot of other people in this town don't have that."

You don't have to agree with Surgeon General Koop's views to appreciate his legacy of high ethics and his example of sensitive, powerful leadership.

RESPONSIBILITY

There was a time when our ethical standards were formed at home. But with so much of our population in the work force, leaders in all occupations and professions have more moral and ethical responsibility than ever before. Our occupational leaders must have the courage to speak out for ethical behavior and justice. "Justice is truth in action," said Benjamin Disraeli. Indifference or silence to unethical behavior demoralizes people, destroys organizations, and strangles our nation.

In these days of mergers, acquisitions, and corporate takeovers, we read and hear so much about unethical behavior. It exists on an alarming scale. It makes headlines that sell newspapers and boost newscast ratings. But this sensational unethical behavior is *not* the norm. There are hundreds and thousands of ethical business transactions conducted every day by ethical men and women. We must be sure that we do not become desensitized to unethical behavior because we see and hear so much about it. If we become indifferent or remain silent, we will destroy our freedoms.

"Freedom comes from human beings, rather than from laws and institutions," said Clarence Darrow. We cannot legislate or litigate ethics. We must *live* them. If we are going to make a difference, it is critical that we set the example of high ethics for others to follow.

THE RIGHT MOTIVES OR THE RIGHT MOVES?

A young executive recently said to me, 'How can I worry about ethics when we are involved in a hostile takeover and we're fighting for our existence?''

My answer was, "You don't have to put ethics on the shelf while doing corporate battle. Without ethics, even if you win, you lose." Every time we say or do something unethical we chip away at the foundation of our moral character. The more we are unethical, the easier it becomes. We diminish ourselves and our ability to make a difference.

The vast majority of successful businesses are based on ethical behavior and standards. When I discussed ethics with Bill Weisz, vice chairman of Motorola, Bill said, "Ethics is the most important leadership quality because you have to have that to play in the game at all. Honesty and integrity are required of everyone in a business or a company, but most especially the leaders. After that, the other [leadership qualities] become critical. But first everyone in the system must have high standards.''

All organizations have rules and regulations by which they operate, but our policy manuals alone are insufficient and imperfect decision-making tools. They're effective only when we use them in combination with ethical judgment.

—————— An Ethical Business Judgment ——————

You have just finished a lovely cruise. You have disembarked in Miami and are ready to fly home. Unfortunately, the airline you planned to fly home on has gone on strike and your cruise line leaves you to solve the problem. You're pretty upset. You have the right to expect the cruise line to help.

That's exactly what happened when Eastern Airlines went on strike, stranding hundreds of cruise line passengers returning from cruises originating in Miami.

If you had cruised on Royal Viking Line or Norwegian Cruise Line, your expectations of assistance would not have been disappointed (as they were for hundreds of passengers on other lines).

Kloster Cruise Line, the travel arm for Royal Viking and Norwegian, jumped in and in one day rebooked 350 outbound (disembarking) and 350 inbound (arriving) passengers. Those disembarking in Miami were put on a bus and taken to a nearby hotel ballroom where each person was reissued an airline ticket to their home. The team spirit of the Kloster staff infected the passengers. They were patient and cooperative and very appreciative of the service they were receiving. Kloster said "it was our job to take away the fear of our passengers."

While this is certainly a story of excellent customer service, good public relations, team work, sensitivity, and many other qualities you'd expect in a leading cruise line, it is also an excellent example of high-ethical business practice. Whatever it cost Kloster, Royal Viking, and Norwegian, they will receive much more in return from the goodwill generated.

High ethics can be demonstrated in many ways and the R.O.I. (return on investment) is not always measured in terms of money. The long-term investment in high ethics builds and reinforces the foundation on which an organization is built.

An Entrepreneur with Ethics

The first time I met Sybil Ferguson, the founder of Diet Center, Inc., I was prepared to meet a guru. The heads of organizations that deal with personal betterment often are gurus. I was invited to give the keynote speech at the Diet Center's national convention. There were nearly 1,000 Diet Center staff in attendance, and many were having their picture taken with Sybil. It was obvious they all admired her tremendously.

When I had a chance to sit and talk with her, I was delightfully surprised to meet a very warm, humble, and down-to-earth lady. Sybil and I talked about her business and personal philosophies. I asked her how she would rank the twelve qualities of leadership. "Ethics," she told me, "is number one, because to be honest, ethical, and true to your word is essential. Your business is no stronger than the leadership at the top. Ethics exemplify what you stand for and what you are. Without that, you have no leadership qualities. You can't bluff people for long. If you want to go for the long term, you must be ethical."

PROFIT MOTIVE AND SOCIAL RESPONSIBILITY

I'm sure you'd agree that the prime purpose of business is to make a profit. But when profits become the *only* measure of success, we have lost sight of our shared values. When unethical business practices create unfair situations that go beyond a healthy competitive environment, we are in deep trouble. We have very serious economic monsters looming in our future. National debt and trade deficits top the list. When we read about these huge economic problems our eyes tend to glaze over. We lose sight of what they really mean. It is hard to imagine a billion or trillion dollars. We cannot lose sight of the fact that *people* are involved in these economics. Economic problems are human problems, and so human values must be applied to their solutions. These human values and solutions come from you and me. Our economic problems will affect your son or daughter's hopes of going to college and someday buying a home. They affect your right to equal opportunity in the market place. They affect my eighty-one-year-old mother's right to health care. Numbers are not just figures on a page; they are people!

The good news is that profit motive and social responsibility can coexist and prosper when we operate with high-ethical standards and compassion.

No one ever said that being ethical is easy. Living a life of high ethics is hard. Circumstances pull at us every day, urging us to take the easy way out, to twist something just a little or close our eyes for just a second. Unethical actions are committed all around us every day. We can see them, identify them, and make decisions and judgments about them. Saying and doing nothing—acts of omission—can be just as unethical as the committed act, and often much more destructive. The distinction between what is illegal and what is unethical has become blurred.

Mervin Morris founded the national chain of department stores, MERVYN'S. He is a highly ethical man and is a distinguished leader in the retail industry. When I asked him what he thought were the most important qualities of a leader, he said, "I don't think that one can truthfully say there is a single most important quality, but I will refer to two that are so often lacking." (His second reference was a lack of listening, which we'll cover in a later chapter.)

Mr. Morris referred to the surprising lack of ethics and what greed can do to a person.

> We all know some very prominent and successful leaders who are not too meticulous when it comes to ethics. It is amazing how bright they are in some areas, how they can motivate people, but are still motivated by greed themselves. Greed does have a way of blurring and making fuzzy one's ethics.

We live in a world with more and more gray areas. Abortion and euthanasia are perfect examples of the blurring of what's legal and what's ethical. Abortion and euthanasia are legal in many parts of the world. But it's not that simple. Both issues involve ethics, too. There are strong arguments on both sides. How do you feel about them? Are you sure you are right in your opinions? Can anyone be completely sure that their stand is correct? Correct for whom? According to what standards?

To make a difference we must take a stand on difficult, complex issues. We can't lead if we are wishy-washy and indecisive. That doesn't mean we should never change our minds or that we shouldn't be open to new arguments (if for no other reason than to test our principles). You and I may have completely different views, but we can't let that stand in the way of respecting each other's differences. We can't be judgmental or we cease to lead, and without followers we are alone in our effort to make a difference.

DEFINING PERSONAL ETHICS

Most of us would say that we are ethical. If I questioned your ethics, you might take offense and you would certainly be willing to defend your position or actions. But both of us can benefit from examining our personal standards of conduct—our ethics. We must have the courage to turn the spotlight on our actions, habits, and examples if we are to be leaders who can make a difference.

————————————*Spotlight*————————————

What is your opinion of the following scenario?

You become sexually involved with someone other than your marriage partner. It happened only once and you deeply regret your actions. You vow never to be unfaithful again. You decide not to tell your partner because you are positive it would damage or destroy the relationship. Since you will never again be unfaithful, you decide silence is best. You regard your actions as a sin and plan to atone.

Is your silence right or wrong? If you confessed and the marriage broke up, would your honesty have served any purpose?

When a serious mistake such as infidelity has occurred and is not admitted, does this make it easier to repeat the activity? Can a long-term relationship survive the strain of such a secret?

Ethical dilemmas like this one can produce as many opinions as there are respondents. As leaders, we know that personal ethics are the foundation of our relationship to the rest of society. That's why we begin by being honest with ourselves, by asking uncomfortable questions, and then by examining our answers closely.

Here are some other ethical problems to consider:

- After a delay of many months, you are finally reimbursed for some medical expenses by an insurance company. A few days later you get another check for the same amount from a different insurance company. You really need the money and are furious over the red tape that led to the delay. What do you do?
- You are sitting at the dinner table with your children. You and your spouse are exchanging lively stories about a friend or coworker. The children hear the discussion, the exciting half-truths, exaggerations, and humorous comments. You regard this as sophisticated, socially acceptable banter. Do you then tell your children never to gossip or lie about others? How do you explain the difference to them?
- You get an extra ten dollars in change at a checkout stand. You notice it and your friend who is with you notices, too. Do you return the money or keep it? Would your actions be different if your friend was not there? If the amount was just a dollar? What about $100? Would it make a difference if the clerk had been insulting? If the items you bought were highly overpriced? Or if you had torn your jacket on a nail sticking out from the counter? What justifications would you use if you kept the money?
- One of your employees comes to you and confesses stealing

money from the company. He has a moving story of personal problems and offers to repay the money. He begs for another chance. Other employees know about the situation. Do you turn him over to the police so that he can be punished? Or simply fire him? Or allow him to stay on in another department where he won't handle money? Or let him keep his job where he still has access to company funds? If you don't take legal action, what message does this give to your other employees? Will it strengthen or weaken office morale and discipline? What will your future relationship with the culprit be? (Reread the above story, substituting "she" for "he" and see if your response would be any different.)

- A real story from the front page of the *San Francisco Chronicle:* The back door of an armored truck comes open, dumping bundles of cash all over a busy street. The truck drives off, the driver is unaware of what had happened, and dozens of citizens stop their cars or run from the sidewalk to chase the wind-blown money. Some stuff their pockets and flee. Others round up the money and guard it until the police come. What would you have done? Would you have to think about it very long?

- The culmination of a cherished project has been reached. You have just been introduced to a very important person who has generously offered to help you achieve your goal. During the next hour he makes numerous obscene jokes about various religions and races. You find these crude jokes extremely offensive and would never tolerate them in a different situation. Do you remain silent, thankful for the help you are receiving? Is your discomfort balanced by the future success of your project and what it will mean to others? Or do you become outraged and leave? Or try to remain calm while you tell him that you find the jokes offensive? What if he laughs at you and increases his diatribe to needle you? What if he throws you out and refuses to work with you?

Many of our ethical decisions are easy and automatic. Others are intensely complex and painful. As leaders, we face both kinds every day, and how we deal with them reveals the quality of our leadership.

When expediency, comfort, social customs, or everyday practicality seem to confuse the issue of integrity, ask yourself: Am I proud of this action? Would I want my children, parents, or friends to see this written on the front page of the paper? Is this the kind of example I want my followers to live by?

Defining personal ethics can be difficult. But we can make a bigger contribution and be a better leader when we have the courage to tackle this issue.

BUSINESS ETHICS

How can a nation that prides itself on free enterprise, creativity, and business savvy survive when business ethics are inconsistent with right and wrong? The answer is, it can't. Businesses and nations are both made up of individuals who must share rules about living and doing business.

Peter Drucker, the father of modern management, warns, "Executives cannot use 'business ethics' as a defense for acts that would be condemned if committed by anyone else."

"Just because it's legal doesn't mean it's ethical" has become a common expression today. There shouldn't be a difference between what is legal and what is ethical. But there is.

In a competitive market, doing business often involves beating out the other guy, getting the best of a deal, turning $1 million into $5 million. In this adversarial climate, clear definitions of ethics can be difficult. How do you know whether an action is brilliant tactics or unscrupulous double-dealing?

One way is to ask yourself if this action might harm an individual or business. If a group of your peers got together, would what you are doing be viewed as ethical? Would your *opposition* view it as ethical? Would your action reflect a good competitive spirit? How would you feel if someone was doing to you what you have done to them?

————————Questionable Ethics————————

Today, in the face of massive medical evidence, tobacco and chemical companies still vigorously deny that their products can cause illness. Manufacturers decide that it is cheaper to pay fines for polluting our air and water than to invest in non-polluting equipment. Tobacco companies and advertising companies seduce young people and unsophisticated or uneducated people by creating ads depicting smokers as sexy, sophisticated, and successful. Where do ethics and social responsibility come in? Are the ads just good business, or is the advertising dangerous mental and emotional manipulation for profit?

Recently I found a magazine advertisement aimed at the upwardly mobile career professional. The ad, for a well-known hotel, read:

One way to get away from the office during the week:
Lie.
Sure, honesty is the best policy, but there is an
exception: a midweek getaway to . . .

How would you feel, as an employer, if your people lied to you so they could spend time at this hotel? How would you feel about a hotel that urged your employees to lie? Does such an ad contribute to unethical behavior? When is it ethical to lie, cheat, or steal? And what responsibility do the hotel and advertising agency that created the ad have to our national ethical climate?

When I first saw this ad, I got angry. I gave myself a few days to cool off and think it over, but my reaction didn't change. That week I was conducting a leadership seminar for a group of middle and upper management. It included a section on ethics. I handed out copies of the ad without comment, then opened the floor for discussion.

At first there was silence while everyone read the ad. Then there was a different kind of silence, filled with understanding nods. The majority of the people saw what I saw and expressed their concern for the reaction that the public might have to the ad. A few felt the readers were responsible for making their own decisions, and that the hotel and advertising agency had no ethical responsibility. A few were torn between the two opposing views. How do you feel?

After the seminar I contacted the hotel's general manager and the owner of the advertising agency, passing on my impressions and those of the people in the seminar—who were the kind of people at whom the ad was aimed. We discussed ethical responsibility and the implications of the ad.

The hotel manager said he couldn't believe anyone would take the ad literally. The president of the advertising agency said he thought the ad was clever and he saw no harm in it. Each promised to consider my input. I asked them to let me know what conclusion they came to. While both were willing to listen to me, neither called me back. What's your opinion?

Here are some other examples to consider:

- A major U.S. baby food company admits that its "100% pure apple juice" is just colored sugar water with a small quantity of apple flavoring.
- Substandard "counterfeits" are sold as high-test metal bolts and used to build aircraft, creating the potential for massive loss of life.
- Discount stores offer inferior merchandise stamped with the brand names of quality products.
- A new tranquilizer is implicated in the deaths of over a hundred hospital patients; a representative of the drug company jokes that they had expected to make $40 million with the new product, "but if we had known how potent it was, we would have projected $80 million."

Where do you stand on ethics in examples like these? A tougher question is, can you and I do anything to affect these situations? I believe we do make a difference when we speak up or take a stand. Here's how:

First: by making sure that *our* ethics are not in question.
Second: by involving our followers in discussions to increase their awareness of incidents like these so that we can raise their standards and expectations.
Third: by setting the example of taking the small but powerful step of writing a letter to the offending company and sending a copy to the editorial section of your local paper.

John Ackers concluded his comments to the Bay Area Council by saying,

> Among the ethical buttresses, there are business codes of conduct like those many of us have long had in our companies, which spell out strict policies on such things as insider trading, gifts and entertainment, kickbacks, and conflicts of interest.
> Last is to keep our sense of order straight—put first things first. We've

all heard short-sighted business people attribute a quote to Vince Lombardi: "Winning is not the most important thing; it's the *only* thing." Well, that's a good quote for firing up a team, but as an overreaching philosophy it's just baloney. I much prefer another Lombardi quote. He expected his players, he said, "to have three kinds of loyalty: to God, to their families, and to the Green Bay Packers. In that order."

Lombardi knew—and you and I know—that some things count more than others. All of us are proud of our companies, but the good of our entire society here in the U.S. transcends that of any single corporation. The moral order of the world transcends any single nation-state. And you can't be a good business person—or good doctor or lawyer or engineer—without a just understanding of the place of business in the greater scheme of things.

If we concentrate on these ethical issues, I believe we'll contribute to our country's strength, heighten its capacity for leadership in an increasingly competitive world, and keep it on the right track as it closes out this century and enters the twenty-first century.

Can you imagine the impact we could have if each person who reads this book would do two things:
1. Write a letter on behalf of high ethics.
2. Ask one other person to do the same thing.
That's grass-roots leadership. That's how we make a difference.

TEACHING OUR YOUTH

My heart jumps with pride as I watch our young Olympic athletes competing. I get a lump in my throat and a tear sneaks down my cheek when they stand on the platform to accept their medals. With hand over heart, they stand so proud and tall, singing our national anthem. Did the same people who taught them to compete also teach them that they don't need drugs, TV contracts, and kickbacks from equipment manufacturers to succeed? I hope so!

What are our young people to believe when they are exposed to events that highlight an alarming lack of ethics in every sector of our society? We have created educational curricula that are ethically deficient, and we are seeing the harmful results. Students in business schools and law schools are being taught that "situational ethics" means solving problems on a pragmatic instead of an ethical basis. They are learning to be financial and business survivalists, to be shrewd and manipulative in-fighters. If "thou shalt not kill" does not apply in the heat of battle, why should "thou shalt not steal" apply in the heat of business competition? "Careerism" now dominates the balance between personal success, financial success, and social responsibility.

IBM's Chairman, John Ackers, also had some powerful comments about this issue.

> We learn first from our parents and others who, by precept and example, set us straight on good and evil, right and wrong. Role models are a major force in our concept of ethics.
>
> We must reinvigorate our children's study of the past. We must take a hard look at ethical teaching in our schools. And it begins at the lowest level, not graduate school, because it's too late then. The place to start is kindergarten. Start with a clear-cut study of the past, because our ethical standards come out of our past, out of our cultural inheritance as a people—religious, philosophical, historical. The more we know of the past, the more surefootedly we can inculcate ethical conduct in the future.
>
> There is the honor system we live with every day. It is college students policing themselves—no plagiarism, no cheating on examinations. It's downright ludicrous that divinity schools, law schools, and departments of philosophy—plus all the other parts of the university—have to pay proctors to pad up and down the aisles at exam time to make sure nobody is looking at crib notes or copying from a neighbor. We can do better than that.

Mr. Ackers is right! We *can* do better than that. When I work with educators and school administrators, I am always impressed by the power they have over our lives. If we make quality education a national priority and give educators our commitment, our expectations, and our resources, we will be living in a wonderful world in the twenty-first century. If not, our standard of living will drop, our productivity will plummet, and we will pay a heavy price. Ethics is at the heart of this issue. If we wait until graduate school to teach ethics, it's too late. First-graders can learn about ethics. If you have ever had a child in first grade, you know that seven-year-olds can understand the difference between right and wrong. And they look to role models to reinforce that understanding.

A few years ago, sports figures ranked with movie stars as national heroes. Babe Ruth and Babe Didrikson, Joe DiMaggio and

Joe Louis, Ty Cobb and Wilma Rudolph were names that made us all stand a little taller, feel a little better about being Americans and members of the human race. Their victories became our own. Unfortunately, today's children have some new role models, sports figures with the maturity of sulky three-year-olds, the manners of alley cats, and the greed of Midas. Giving one's opponent a concussion rates cheers from the crowd and a few minutes in the penalty box or a slap-on-the-wrist fine. The term "good sportsmanship" has nearly disappeared from our vocabulary. We are making it impossible for the next generation to tell the difference between leaders and self-indulgent prima donnas.

How can we counteract these bad examples? I think we have to become activists. When we work with children, we can discuss good and bad behavior. We can give them some guidelines for an ethical life, not just for winning. America is so consumed with winning and success that each of us can make a difference just by reinforcing the value of balance in our children's lives. Of course that assumes that *we* have balance in our views of success and winning. We can also let the owners, coaches, and athletes know what we think of their bad behavior and the effect it has on our young people. This may sound like a lot of work, and it is. Fighting for your beliefs and values is never easy, but I've learned one thing in my fifty years and that is *it is always worth the effort,* and it does make a difference.

In the past we have permitted this insidious moral climate to go unchallenged. Now we must take responsibility for ending it. Education, advertising, corporate policy, civil law, and religious tenets all need to be re-examined and updated by courageous leaders who are willing to tackle tough or unpopular issues. You and I can make a difference by questioning those things that do not seem ethical, by speaking up and letting our views be known.

I am happy to report that when I work with youth groups and we discuss ethics, they ask excellent questions that really keep me on my toes. For example, I was working with a group of high school seniors and we were discussing the topic of ethics and business. I gave them several scenarios, such as the recent insider-trading scandals. While they all admitted that they couldn't completely understand the technicalities and the complications of business, it was refreshing to hear them talk about the importance of ethical behavior even in the face of major temptations like profits. These bright young people have yet to be tested, but it was reassuring to see their level of awareness.

POLITICAL ETHICS

We've been calling ourselves Americans for over two hundred years. We've been rightfully proud of our republic. But if America is to survive the next two hundred years, we must maintain strong political and social ethics.

We can refuse to tolerate officials at any level who believe they are above the law. We are a nation of laws that govern every citizen, including the men and women who serve us politically. Unless we insist on high ethics from our officials, we are not living up to our own ethical responsibilities.

We Americans have always had a soft spot for the "clever scoundrels" of our past. But confusing the mythical past and reality is dangerous. Richard Nixon might have gone down in history as one of our great presidents because of his important foreign policy. Re-establishing relations and trade with China was one of his most brilliant accomplishments. But Nixon overstepped his power. His arrogance, his belief that he was above the law, led him to lie. He would probably have survived the Watergate scandal if he had admitted his guilt and asked for forgiveness. We are a magnanimous people and like to forgive repentant people. But he did more than lie. He scoffed at us. That arrogance, what the Greeks called *hubris,* was his downfall. He stepped way over the ethical line. His conspiracy theory of government, so prevalent elsewhere in the world, appealed to few Americans.

COURAGE TO PUT ETHICS FIRST

Not making waves, doing the easiest thing, is often the safest activity. It has at various times led to feeding traitorous Christians to the lions, burning heretical astronomers at the stake, and lynching integrationist civil-rights workers. In each example, the political, religious, or social order was seriously threatened.

While the need for order, consistency, and continuity is important, we need the courage to put ethics first. Albert Einstein said, "Never do anything against conscience even if the state demands it." The excuse that "it was orders" or "that everyone else was doing it" can no longer be accepted.

Great leaders have often been extremists in some sense, and their vision makes them disruptive to the established order of things. The men and women who put their lives on the line to bring about social change—the end of slavery, the recognition of unions, women's right to vote, the end of segregation, and nuclear disarmament—are good examples of people who put ethics first. You and I can make a difference by *not* allowing our minds to be closed or to fall victim to the status quo. We can keep an open mind to changes and issues that may at first appear extreme. We must be courageous in our ethics regarding political and social concerns.

ETHICAL DECISIONS OF THE FUTURE

The best way to have an ethical future is to prepare for it now. Dr. Gregory Stock wrote a little book called *The Book of Questions*. Each page asks two or three questions to stimulate your thinking, many of them about ethics. The next time you have a group of followers or friends together, try using this book to stimulate ethical thinking. I guarantee you'll have some interesting discussions.

Here are some other dilemmas about ethics that would also be challenging to consider. We will be facing them in our society in the next few years. Today's leaders will be key forces in forging the ethics of the next century.

- Scientific advances are raising new questions. For instance, a few years ago a person was considered dead when they were no longer breathing. Then the definition of death changed to the absence of a heartbeat. Currently brain waves are the definitive sign of life. Since it is now technically possible to keep a body alive long after brain activity has ceased, we have had to redefine what life is.
- New biotechnology and gene splicing will make it possible to create more food than the world's current population needs. When this happens, what ethical measures can the world use to prevent a population explosion?
- What is our ethical responsibility to starving people in countries where governments are seeking control by starving opposition groups to death? Do we interfere with the internal policies of other nations? Is it ethical to use force?

- Should surrogate mothers be banned? (They are, after all, prominent in the Bible.) If not, what should be done when the child is defective? When the pregnancy produces twins? When one party to the contract wants to break the contract?
- Consciousness-altering drugs have been around as long as alcoholic beverages, but have only recently been introduced to Western culture—with devastating effect. Cultures in which drugs are traditional have strict standards and rituals for their use, just as Western culture has ancient customs and proscriptions for the use of alcohol. How should the United States cope with the so-called recreational drugs? Given that both drugs and alcohol harm the unborn fetus and alter the brain in permanent and destructive ways, is it logical to ban one and not the other? Some countries have tried to contain drug use by legalizing drugs. They have not succeeded. Others have tried to end drug use by strict death penalties. They also have not succeeded. What answers can today's leaders offer?
- We like to think our justice system has come a long way since seven-year-old children were hanged for stealing bread two hundred years ago. But has it? If a society is judged by its prisons, how do we rate? Does anyone believe that people come out of prison any better than they went in? Yet, for the daily cost of incarcerating someone in a dangerous, overcrowded prison, one could stay in a luxury hotel with room service. Jessica Mitford wrote in *Kind and Unusual Punishment*, "Those of us on the outside [of prisons] do not like to think of wardens and guards as our servants. Yet they are, and they are intimately locked in a deadly embrace with their human captives behind the prison walls. By extension, so are we. A terrible double meaning is thus imparted to the original question of human ethics: Am I my brother's keeper?"
- Since the invention of the long bow, each new weapon has been heralded as so horrible that it will put an end to war. Yet no weapon made has ever gone unused. Our country now possesses the bombs and poisons to kill every living thing on this planet ten times over. Can the inevitable be postponed or prevented? What role will today's leaders play in the outcome?

THE RESPONSIBILITY OF MATURITY

Our nation is maturing and with that maturity comes responsibility. With 250 million (and rising) people in this country we cannot afford to be careless about ethics. We preach human rights around the world. We criticize nations who enslave. Now we must seek our own counsel. We must look candidly at our nation's actions, policies and standards, and examine our ethical values. The world is watching. Do we practice what we preach? Having high ethics does not mean reciting a list of pious platitudes. It means defining our beliefs and then living by them.

In his book *Winning Through Integrity,* Cliff C. Jones says, "It takes maturity to walk the fine line between avarice and ambition." If we are collectively committed to making a value system work, it will. If not, no policy can enforce high ethics. We owe it to our nation and ourselves to meet the highest ethical standards and then to expect others to do likewise.

Words like "virtue," "honor," and "duty" have fallen out of fashion. We need to return them to our vocabulary as power words, not terms of derision. Virtue is not virginity. Honor is not a plaque or trophy. Duty is not a punishment. Let's recognize virtue as a restless quest for justice, honor as rejecting shoddiness, duty as a moral obligation.

Our pledge of allegiance says "with liberty and justice for all." If our nation is to remain great we must re-establish what our forefathers created for us: *E pluribus unum,* one composed of many. That means working together for our common interests, hopes, and values. Our differences are part of our great strength. We are a melting pot of peoples, religions, and ideas. Out of this wonderfully diverse mixture has come our shared system of ethical values.

America's uniqueness lies in its ability to draw strength from new insights and ideas, to use change as a positive force. We cannot succumb to elitism and special interests that use differences to tear us apart. Our shared ethical values keep us free. And our ability to change and grow keeps us strong. We make a difference when we set an example of high ethics.

ANCIENT WISDOM

The Greeks and Eastern philosophers have much wisdom to offer us as we change and grow. Confucius predated Plato by only a few decades and both wrote extensively about ethics. Confucius's ideas are still revered and provide rules of conduct for millions of people.

Here are a few of his thoughts on ethics:

- The essentials of good government are: a sufficiency of food, a sufficiency of arms, and the confidence of the people. If forced to give up one of these, give up arms. If forced to give up two, give up food. Death has been the portion of all men from of old, but without the people's trust, nothing can endure.
- Hold fast to what is good and the people will be good. The virtue of the good man is as the wind and that of the bad man as the grass. When the wind blows, the grass will bend.
- Let the leader show rectitude in his personal character and things will go well, even without directions from him.

Twenty-five hundred years later, these words are just as meaningful as the day he wrote them.

Our short history is an exciting one. We will continue to have a bright future if we can encourage and produce leaders who put ethics at the top of the list of leadership qualities. If you are an ethical person you will attract others to you. If making a difference means having great concern for ethics, you will be one of those who leads us into the next century.

A LEADER IS A CHANGE MASTER
Creating The Future

"God grant me the serenity to accept the things
I cannot change, the courage to change the things I can,
and the wisdom to know the difference."
—THE SERENITY PRAYER

THIS IS THE AGE OF CHANGE

We are living in an exciting age of unprecedented change. The futurists report that in the fifty years between 1970 and 2020 we will experience change equivalent to that of the last 500 years! The "winds of change" have given way to an "earthquake of change." In an earthquake the topography of the land changes. Life today is undergoing the same intensity of change.

Change is not new. It is the *rate* of change that is affecting us so dramatically. This acceleration has presented us with unique challenges. As the rate of change increases, we will have to increase our willingness and our ability to adapt. Rosabeth Moss Kanter coined the term "Change Masters" and defines these people and organizations as "adept at the art of anticipating the need for and of leading productive change." The future is in your hands if you are a change-master leader.

————An American Seeking Change————

Can a young Mexican-American migrant farm worker change his family history of illiteracy and hard manual labor? Can he overcome the barriers and become a community leader?

Does that sound like the plot of a soap opera? It should, because this story has all the ingredients from which TV plots are woven.

Esau Ruiz Herrera was born in Del Rio, Texas, fifty yards from the Mexican border. His parents were migrant farm workers and there was not much in the family history to indicate that young Esau would be different from them. In 1951 the Herrera family heard that wages were high in the Santa Clara Valley, so they packed their meager belongings and went to San Jose, California. They lived in a tent in the fields where they worked. They followed the crops from city to city. Sometimes they lived in garages of other farm workers' homes. Yet Esau says he was lucky, because his parents insisted that he go to school.

Esau spent as much time as possible in the library. At home he pored over the worn religious books and Bible his father was able to provide. Esau realized that if he was going to change the pattern of his family's history he must learn to speak English fluently. By the time he was ready for high school his father managed to buy a small house using his G.I. Bill, and Esau stayed in the same school for the entire four years. While at Overfeldt High School he got his first job out of the fields. He cleaned the bathrooms. "It was great," says Esau. "No hot sun, no bending over all day, and I even got a twenty-minute rest break. My father never had a twenty-minute break in the fields."

Life was changing for Esau. The family had a small home. He had completed high school with high grades. He looked around and saw all the great things you could do in life if you went to college. He started to inquire and found out that Santa Clara University was recruiting minorities.

This was the turning point in his life. His excellent grades in high school won him a scholarship to Santa Clara. By this time Esau had become an activist in the Hispanic community. He says, "One of the first things I did in college was organize all *six* minority students and hold a demonstration."

Esau was getting smarter by the day! He discovered that if you want to change the system, you can do it one of two ways: Fight it from the outside or get into the system and work for change from within. A friend told him that if he went to law school he could "change the world." Those were the kind of words that stirred Esau's soul. He deeply wanted to make a difference. He wanted to help other Hispanics improve their lives, and he knew the key was to influence the youth. "They have so few role models," says Esau. "They just don't see themselves as being able to make it."

After law school he established himself as a successful trial attorney and began his activist role. He is director and past president of the school board. He speaks to East San Jose High School classes and says, "Look. If I could do it, so can you."

Esau is president of the Pathway Society, the premier organization in Santa Clara County for fighting drug abuse. He is president of the Hispanic Caucus, a group of all-Hispanic school board members in California. He is on the board of directors of Santa Clara University's East Side project. This is a project that directs college students to work with the poor. He is legal council for the American G.I. Forum, a group of Hispanic veterans who focus on education needs. He has done their legal work for ten years, at no charge. Esau also coaches girl's and boy's basketball and plays music for senior citizens at rest homes and retirement communities.

Esau Herrera is a passionate man. He believes he makes a difference in the community because he has the ability to help others change, to help them see beyond where they are. He says, "People want to do and to be better. They need inspiration to change and to try to make a difference. They need a catalyst to inspire faith and to encourage them to take a risk. That's my job.

"My theme is to make a difference right here in my own neighborhood. I don't have to fight the whole world. If I do well where I am, it will make a difference in the rest of the world." Esau Herrera is making a difference.

AMAZING AND WONDROUS CHANGE

The last half of the twentieth century has become a landmark of creative, innovative change in world history. We are experiencing some amazing and wondrous technological changes:

- We can now fly halfway around the world, nonstop from Sydney, Australia, to Los Angeles in under fifteen hours.
- Organ transplants are common occurrences and eye-cataract surgery is an out-patient procedure, with restored sight in a matter of days.
- A television program can be viewed simultaneously by millions of people around the world. It is common to see satellite dishes in backyards. Even nomad tribes living in tents have their own satellite dishes and television sets.
- The microchip has revolutionized every aspect of our lives. Briefcase-size computers have the same capacity as their predecessors that filled entire rooms a few years ago. We can program our homes' lighting, heating, and security systems from a panel on the wall the size of a hand calculator.

There have also been some complex social changes:

- Working for a corporation no longer means security. We used to make long-term plans for life and business built around the company we worked for. With mergers, acquisitions, and buyouts, this has all changed.
- Deciding which company to use for telephone service has become a major decision.
- The modern woman must make much more complex life and business choices than her sisters of past generations.

Positive changes, negative changes, amazing changes, complex changes. Letting go of the old and taking hold of the new. Just when we are sure we have seen it all, we again face adaptation and change.

JAPANESE CHANGE DOMINATES
Question: #1—What do the Japanese know about management that we don't?
#2—Where did they learn their successful management principles?
Answer: #1—Nothing, it's just that we've forgotten what we once knew.
#2—From us.

In 1946 General Douglas MacArthur was commander of the U.S. Occupation Forces in Japan. Among his many goals for rebuilding the nation was to have the Japanese produce radios for mass distribution so that he could broadcast important messages to every corner of the country.

He had heard of young Homer Sarasohn, an engineer at MIT and Raytheon. MacArthur called Sarasohn and enlisted his help. Sarasohn was to teach management philosophies and skills to the Japanese. Sarasohn and his associate Charles Protzman began what was to be the most pervasive change ever experienced in Japanese management history. While they were teaching the theories that have helped build the Japanese into a world power, Americans have been forgetting these same lessons.

The theories Sarasohn and Protzman taught were basic. They espoused respecting each individual employee, delegating and giving responsibility and accountability. Sarasohn and Protzman had a message that the Japanese took to heart. An important part of that message was capsulized in these words: "Every business enterprise should have as its very basic policy something of this nature, [to aim] the entire resources and efforts of the company toward a well-defined target, a target that would benefit society." The Japanese people feel they make a difference because they are involved not only in producing quality products, but in bettering their society. Can Americans change and once again embrace that philosophy? Or are we so caught up in immediate gratification and me-ism that we care little about society as a whole?

A Change Master Corporation

Bill Weisz, vice chairman of the Motorola Corporation, was outlining the leadership qualities he felt were important. He described how a company, as well as an individual, can take on the responsibility of being a change master. Bill said:

Motorola has taken on being an agent of change.

For example as a company, we have always believed that it is important to participate in those things that affect our business activities, our community efforts, our employees, and our country. We have a written objective to be a good citizen in every country in which we operate. That includes standing up for issues that involve employees.

Here in the U.S. we have a group in Washington to deal with regulatory organizations, such as the FCC. We've spent much effort and time working with government, sometimes working hard to change things, with reasonable success. I think we've a reasonably high image for credibility in the Washington environment because many times we've taken positions that we believe are best for the country, even when they are in opposition to those of some key customers.

As another example, we can talk about how difficult it is to get into the Japanese domestic marketplace. How regulations and attitudes had to change, both here and there, how Motorola took on being an agent of change. We worked very hard with the U.S. and Japanese governments and Japanese industrial organizations over many years, particularly in the past ten years. We worked hard to enforce existing trade laws in the U.S. while trying hard to be successful as a good supplier in the Japanese domestic market. That's what you have to do to be successful.

YOUR ABILITY TO HANDLE CHANGE

You don't have to be a major corporation or a world-famous figure to make a difference. If you are willing and able to change, you can affect people, situations, and systems.

Some self-evaluation will begin the process of determining your effectiveness as a change master-leader. Once again questions play an important role in shaping your potential for leadership. These questions will help you see where you've been and where you want to go. They help you shape your mission and open the door for big thinking. Begin with these questions; you can add your own as you go along:

—What changes have I experienced in the last two years?
—What have I learned from these changes?
—Have they improved my ability to lead? If so, how and why?
—How comfortable am I with change?
—How skillful am I in anticipating future change and its effects on my mission?
—How eager am I to face change?
—Do I accept change willingly?
—Can I examine my perception of change candidly?
—Can I maintain my creativity while working through the change?
—Can I find innovative ways to affect the outcome of change?
—Do I have a flexible leadership style in response to change?

—Do I keep my perspective during change?

The answers to these questions will help you determine your willingness and ability to accept and handle change. They will also help you set proper examples so that others may also change.

THE KEYS TO ENHANCING YOUR ABILITY TO CHANGE

To be a change master you must first learn to handle change yourself. Then you can take your skills, talents, and abilities and help others change. Let's look at some specific ways to enhance your mastery of change.

KEY #1—"DON'T FIGHT IT!"

That is easier said than done. The natural tendency is to protect what you know and value, what has become familiar or comfortable. Psychologist Perry Buffington says: "When one is young with pristine goals upon which to focus, the effects of change are more easily minimized. As one ages, with more and more accumulated failures and less time to achieve, change takes its toll."

It seems that just as you adjust to one change, anticipating a chance to relax and adjust, here comes another change. It's easy to say, "Wait a minute, I don't need any more change." Unfortunately the world will change with or without you. So you adapt once again.

Fighting and refusing to recognize change are natural, human reactions. "Our dilemma," says columnist Sydney Harris, "is that we hate change and love it at the same time; what we want is for things to remain the same but get better."

All of us resist change at some level and on some issues. And there are some things we *should* resist changing, because change does not always translate into "better." Change does not automatically mean progress. Change for the sake of change alone can destroy valuable situations, assets, and relationships. Many values deserve to be defended: values like ethics and morals.

I speak in Washington D.C., several times each year. Every time I am there I get up very early in the morning when it's quiet and there are few people on the streets. I go out to the Vietnam Memorial and walk to panel 23 East. I reach up to line 67 and run my fingers over his name. Each time I do, I'm reminded that there

are people in this world who feel strongly enough about their beliefs and values to defend them against change, to the death if
necessary.

Have you ever asked yourself, "What would I defend to the
death, if necessary?" When you have the answer to that question
it affects how you think, act, and feel. It puts passion in your
leadership. As a leader in today's fast-changing world, you must
ask yourself, "What will I change and what will I defend?"

THE THREE TRAPS OF RESISTING CHANGE

Leon Martel, in *Mastering Change, The Key To Business Success,* describes three common traps that keep us from recognizing
and using change:

1. Believing that yesterday's solutions will solve today's problems.
2. Assuming present trends will continue.
3. Neglecting the opportunities offered by future change.

As leader you can't afford this kind of comfort-zone thinking.
You have to develop a constant flow of new solutions. Two important questions for you to ask yourself are:

• At what level do I resist change?
• About what issues do I resist change?

To accept change is commonsense, but as Will Rogers, the great
American humorist, said, "Just because it's commonsense doesn't
mean it's common practice." Key #1 in becoming a successful
change master is not fighting change.

KEY #2—"YOU DON'T HAVE TO LIKE THE CHANGE"

You don't have to like change or agree with it. But as a leader
you need to take an intellectual approach to understanding change
so you can adjust to and progress with a situation or experience.

You must study, explore, and read everything you can about the
change in which you are involved. You have to commit time each
day to reading about current matters that affect your perception
and handling of change. It is said that "The person who won't
read is no better off than the person who can't read." People who
can but won't read run the risk of becoming a literate illiterate—

that's a person who leaves school and never reads another meaningful book.

The old saying, "What you don't know won't hurt you," doesn't work when it comes to change. What you don't know could paralyze you as the rest of the world goes rolling by. So you need to be prepared and knowledgeable about the change in which you are involved.

Leaders stay on top of the information about the changes in business, industry, and their personal lives. Our future is directly linked to our ability to respond quickly and with flexibility. We are more effective when we are informed.

Life is not always about "liking." It's about getting on with it! It's about doing the best you can at the time, with whatever resources you have available! You don't have to *like* the change, but you must anticipate it, recognize it, and understand it.

KEY #3—"BE WILLING TO LET GO OF THE PAST"
Handling change and getting control of our life comes about
when we are willing to let go. Let go of
old ideas, concepts, resentments, and
attitudes. Only then is there room for new
successful ideas.

With the rate of change accelerating every day, being able to let go of the past is vital to your ability to lead. When you make a conscious effort to turn off the old tapes that are constantly playing in your mind, when you release yourself from the burden of other people's "oughts and shoulds," when you resist peer pressure to stay with what is comfortable, and when you break the chains of the pressures of society, you make giant strides toward becoming a change master.

————————*A Man and An Idea*————————

Henry Ford changed more than how we get from one place to another. He was a key figure in changing the United States from an agricultural economy to an industrial one.

Ford was born on a Michigan farm during the Civil War. His childhood was spent tinkering with threshers, reapers, and other horse-drawn farm equipment. When he was twelve Ford saw a steam-driven traction engine. From then on engines were his passion; he was ready to let go of the past.

When he was sixteen, Ford went to Detroit as an apprentice machinist. Eventually he became chief engineer for the Edison Illuminating Company. Ford, however, was intrigued by a recent invention, an internal combustion engine powered by gasoline. His wife shared his enthusiasm, and his earliest models were tested on their kitchen table.

All of America was automobile-mad, Ford along with them. When he was an apprentice machinist he had an idea for mass producing inexpensive pocket watches. He adapted this concept and it became the basis of the automobile assembly line.

Ford founded the Ford Motor Company with several partners in 1903. Using efficient production methods he was able to produce more and more cars each year at lower and lower prices. Soon an automobile was within reach of nearly every American family. Over 15 million Model T Fords were sold. If general literacy revolutionized the way Americans thought, general mobility revolutionized the way Americans lived.

Henry Ford developed a manufacturing system that changed the world by giving us freedom of movement. He truly made a difference.

KEY #4—"HAVE A SENSE OF HUMOR"

When things are changing all around us a sense of humor keeps us sane and allows our followers to develop their own sense of balance. Humor can counteract the pain of change. A good sense of humor sustains people when life becomes difficult. It can give everyone a momentary "emotional vacation" so they can recharge and get on with the job at hand. Kahlil Gibran wrote that humor "gives us a sense of proportion."

The leader who can use humor to relieve the stress of change is a powerful and sensitive leader. Using humor doesn't trivialize serious situations. It puts overwhelming circumstance in perspective.

President Ronald Reagan gave us a perfect example of how a leader can use humor. After he was shot by a would-be assassin and rushed to a hospital, the medical staff was astonished to find the president of the United States as their patient. Soon his wife arrived to find him being worked over by a corps of doctors and nurses. In the midst of fear and uncertainty, the president's sense of humor relieved everyone's stress. Despite his pain, he grinned and said to his wife, Nancy, "I forgot to duck."

A sense of humor can conquer pretense and subdue inflated egos. It can diffuse anger and hostility. It can take an impossible situation and change it to an acceptable one. Victor Borge said, "Laughter is the shortest distance between two people." A sense of humor helps others in times of change by acting as an emotional safety valve. Research has shown that people and organizations rarely succeed unless some fun or humor is involved.

The old axiom, "If you take yourself too seriously, no one else will," is key. The most effective leaders are self-accepting, spontaneous, and can laugh at themselves when they make mistakes. They can see the lighter side of a situation. They can use humor as a vehicle to express their feelings, and to renew and encourage others. They know how to have fun and can turn routine tasks into enjoyable experiences.

A well-developed sense of humor is one of the most charismatic qualities of leadership. In times of change, humor can make a difference.

KEY #5—"EXPECT TO SUCCEED"

When unexpected events occur, the value of a leader with a high-faith factor cannot be underestimated. Expecting success to follow a period of change affects your attitude and that of your followers. It is a powerful motivator. A high-faith factor is faith in your own God-given skills, talents, and abilities. It is your faith in other people's desire to do well. When you have faith that you and others in your organization will handle change well, you'll be a strong leader.

It's that childlike (not childish) faith that we talked about in chapter 2 that can make you strong in times of change. It is the magnet that draws followers to the leader. Childlike faith is imagination, seeing the light at the end of the tunnel, believing in the higher qualities of self and others. In times of change, what better quality could you have as a leader than that of expecting to succeed and motivating others to succeed also?

But don't mistake what I mean by "succeed." There are times in life when the change is negative. Then success means getting through the next twenty-four hours, or surviving until next week.

There are times when it is cause for great celebration if you begin a new month and you are still in one piece. If you have ever been in a life-threatening situation you understand that the word *success* is relative. It's important to pass this knowledge along to your followers, because when change is taking place you don't want them to be misinterpreting "expecting to succeed."

Succeeding One Day At A Time

When Bill W. and Dr. Bob founded Alcoholics Anonymous they had no idea that their work would change the world. When Dr. Bob (AA uses only first names, for anonymity) had practically ruined his entire life, he reached out to Bill W., a New York stock broker, for help in maintaining his sobriety. Both were alcoholics who wanted desperately to change their lives. On June 10, 1935, AA was founded in Akron, Ohio. From that Midwest steel town came a movement that circled the globe and spawned many other organizations to help addictive behaviors.

The success of AA is generally credited to the simplicity of its twelve-step program whose credo is "love and service." Dr. Bob's final speech to a gathering of AA members in July 1950 in Cleveland, Ohio, reminded them of the simplicity that had brought them so much success. "We understand what love is and we understand what service is. So let's bear those two things in mind." As he drew to a close he said, "And one more thing: None of us would be here today if somebody hadn't taken time to explain things to us, to give a little pat on the back, to take us to a meeting or two, to do numerous little kind and thoughtful acts in our behalf. So let us never get such a degree of smug complacency that we're not willing to extend, or attempt to extend, to our less fortunate brothers that help which has been so beneficial to us."

AA members never say they have recovered: They say they are "recovering." They have expectation of success, but they take it one day at a time. In this world of change, that would not be bad advice for us to share with our followers. Expect to succeed, but there are times when we should take it one day at a time.

KEY #6—"BUILD A PERSONAL COPING STRATEGY."

William G. Dwyer, author of *Strategies for Managing Change*, begins the preface of his book with: "The issue of change is surely the most important matter facing anyone who is responsible for a human organization—be it family, business, school, church, agency, club or association.'' One of the most important responsibilities of a leader is the personal ability to cope with change and its side effects. To prevent burnout and relieve pressures, we need some tools and ideas to keep us in balance. Here are some suggestions that can help:

- Peer communications—You will function more effectively when you have someone to talk to who understands the joys and successes, the difficulties and frustrations of leadership. Find time to be in the company of your peers.
- Physical fitness plays an enormous role in your ability to withstand the pressures and challenges of daily changes. Annual physical examinations, diet awareness, and an exercise program that is compatible with your life-style all give you great return on investment.
- Planning Time—Dr. Perry Buffington writes: "The most effective way to minimize [the negative affect of] change is through planning. The more understanding you have of a soon-to-happen event, the less debilitating change will be. The more you know about a change, the less intimidating it is."

Regular planning sessions help you to be better prepared when change arrives. You may also be better able to predict change because of the information gathering necessary for an effective planning session. Planning time will help prevent or avoid the fire-fighting syndrome that attacks so many hurried people.

- Patience—Develop patience. Even in times of accelerated change, everything takes longer than you think. Don't become a victim of frustration. We live in a world that is always advertising perfection as an attainable goal. There *is* no perfection in this world, so we must take perfection out of the equation of life and strive to do our best while being patient.
- Perspective—Keeping change in perspective is a major task for modern leaders. You can't become overly excited or depressed by events. This doesn't mean that we should fail to enjoy life. Go for the best you can imagine, fulfill your potential. But while you are enjoying life, keep your priorities and reactions in balance. Psychologists tell us that for every emotion there

is a corresponding emotion. You don't want to go through life like a yo-yo. As a leader you will take everyone else with you on that roller-coaster ride, and when you do you'll obliterate productivity.

If, as the Bible says, there is a season for everything, then we will always have winter, but spring is just around the corner to give us balance.

The sixth-century Chinese philosopher, Lao-tzu, advised us to be like the willow tree, whose roots go deeper than other trees. When the storm comes, the willow tree bends with the winds of time and change and remains standing, while the other trees crack and break. The ability to keep change in perspective represents the strong roots of the leader who calms and strengthens followers while showing them how to bend with change.

HELPING OTHERS CHANGE

Very little is more rewarding to a leader than watching people blossom and grow. To see their faces when they accomplish a new task and to share their excitement when they do what they thought was impossible—these are the rewards of a change master-leader. When you help other people change, grow, and discover their own potential, you have added to the quality of their life. You have made a difference and served them well as leader.

————————Creating The Impossible————————

Bob Hurley is the basketball coach at St. Anthony's School in Jersey City, New Jersey. The school is in a working class inner-city area. It has no gym, which creates an interesting problem for the basketball team. How do they practice? How on earth can someone be expected to develop these youngsters into top-notch players without even a gym.

Bob Hurley and the kids have found the answer. They practice wherever they can find a basketball hoop. They set up a hoop on the street, they go to a local outdoor court. Team members work their hearts out for themselves and for their coach who has shown them a way to change their life-styles. The team is number one in the state for high school basketball, and Hurley has been named

Coach Of The Year. Many of his players are going on to top-ranked colleges, on scholarships. These boys have tapped their potential, and Bob Hurley has the personal satisfaction of changing lives and making a difference.

Helen Keller Changed Our Perception ——————*Of The Handicapped*——————

Mark Twain wrote of Helen Keller: "She will be as famous a thousand years from now as she is today." So much romance and speculation has built up around Keller that it is sometimes difficult to find the real woman. However, her lyrical books and articles reveal a genius—a warm, compassionate comprehension of things she never saw or heard.

Helen Keller lost her sight and hearing through an illness (possibly measles) in 1882 when she was nineteen months old. Cut off from much of the world, she became a wild, rebellious little animal. The story of how she discovered language through the efforts of a nearly blind teacher has been dramatized several times, most notably in William Gibson's *The Miracle Worker*.

But Keller did more than learn to read and write a language she had never heard. She attended Radcliffe where her studies included French and Greek. She learned to type her assignments with a Braille-keyed typewriter and published *The Story of My Life* in 1903 when she was just twenty-one years old. The book and Keller were a sensation. She became an object of intense public curiosity and bizarre speculations, some endowing her with near supernatural powers. Yet, through such degrading nonsense, Keller retained an aura of dignity, joy, and compassion for others. Her example changed the way society thought about the "handicapped."

Keller actively sought change in her time. She participated in peace rallies, traveled extensively to raise funds for the American Foundation for the Blind, and lobbied in Washington. During World War II, she and her companion, Polly Thompson, visited military hospitals. Later she made a world tour for the blind.

Keller's spirit was so extraordinary that she would probably have reached prominence in some way, even if she had not been stricken. Our good fortune is that her spirit was not lost in the silence and darkness that overtook her. "I have seen more of the

Divine [in her] than has been manifest in anyone I ever met before," said Alexander Graham Bell. No one, after meeting her or reading her books or even hearing of her, could ever again dismiss the human potential of the blind and deaf. Helen Keller changed our image of not only the blind and deaf, but of all handicapped people.

FEAR OF CHANGE

Psychologists tell us that our fear of change comes primarily from the loss of personal identify. When a major change occurs our internal dialogue sounds something like this: "I won't know how to act"—"I won't fit"—"After this change, I won't be me anymore."

These thoughts can be unsettling at the least, and in the extreme, they can be very threatening feelings. We spend most of our lives figuring out who we are, identifying ourselves, and staking a place in the world based on our self-perception. So when someone wants us to abandon our security by altering how we perceive ourselves, we almost always put up barriers.

If you are going to succeed in helping others to change, you must prevent their loss of self-identity by helping them find the answers to these questions:

- Who and what will I become?
- How do I identify myself during and after this change?
- Will this change improve me? If so, how?

When people confront these questions and become aware of positive answers, they are more apt to accept and support change.

CAPABILITY ASSUMPTIONS

A leadership warning: Never assume that all people have the same tolerance level for change. Outside appearance is not a true indicator of what someone is feeling. Some people's bravado is protective armor against feelings of inadequacy or confusion. Your perceptiveness and sensitivity to your followers' feelings are very important because everyone has a different tolerance for amounts, levels, and intensities of change. If you will get to know your people individually you will be better acquainted with their capacity to change. Don't be afraid to ask questions about the changes they've experienced in the past. Remember the Chinese proverb:

He who asks a question is a fool for five minutes. But he who doesn't is a fool for the rest of his life.

Inquire about what has changed in their life recently. How did it affect them? What did they do? Would they have done anything differently in response to the change? These types of questions, put in a friendly, inquiring manner, will give you insights into their adaptability.

If you assume everyone can change and everyone wants to change, you'll have the same problems Jack Wahlig (chapter 6— "Risk Taker") did when he assumed his firm was ready to change. You can cause upheaval and trauma if you are operating under false assumptions.

MAKING CHANGE POSSIBLE

Can you make others change? The answer, of course, is "no." You can not make someone change. People will change only when they are ready. Even external forces sometimes causes only temporary change. While you can't force change, you can help people see the benefit of change. You can create an atmosphere in which change is possible. There are three steps you can take to foster a receptivity and openness to change:

1. *Provide new information to expand your followers' thinking.* A senior executive wanted her managers to learn to use computers. But they were quite resistant. She felt they were wasting too much time delegating work they could do quite easily themselves, if they could use computers.

She researched information about several data bases from which they could get important material that would make their work easier. She showed them the savings computers would bring in cost, employee hours, and time. Then she got their attention with the information. She then went on to the next step.

2. *Provide new ideas to spark their creativity and broaden their horizons.* She had a meeting of her managers and asked them to suppose that they were already proficient at using these exciting data bases. She asked them to explore all the ways they could use the new material. They also discussed what their assistants could do with the time that would now be freed up. They came to the conclusion that perhaps it would be a good idea to look into learning how to use the computer. But they were still not 100 percent sold on the idea.

3. *Provide new experiences to build a desire for and a belief in the value of change.* The executive brought in a computer consultant and explained the situation to him. They worked out a plan for each manager to have some simple hands-on private training and experience at accessing data most important to their work. The experience was a positive step toward ending their resistance to computers. Soon the managers were all wondering what they did before they had computers.

Information, ideas, and experience are the components on which to build an environment that welcomes change.

Sources of Change

If you are to help others change, it is important to know that there are three impetuses that cause people to change: trauma, the passage of time, and design.

1. *Trauma:* There are personal traumas, such as job loss, illness, divorce, and death. These endanger our physical, emotional, intellectual, and spiritual well being. There are also external traumas that can affect us in very personal ways. For example, the assassinations of President John F. Kennedy, Robert Kennedy, and Dr. Martin Luther King, Jr., changed the psyche and spirit of individuals and the nation as a whole. The Vietnam War was a trauma from which we are still trying to recover.

Although the "School of Hard Knocks" has its proponents, trauma is the least desirable method of change. It is highly threatening and very difficult to deal with. During trauma we lose the option of gradual adjustment. We are forced to learn new ways of doing things in less than ideal situations. While there may be some benefit from traumatic change, in the long run the enormous stress and accompanying problems offset most benefits gained from the learning experience.

As leader, one of your jobs is to try and protect your people, whenever possible, from traumatic change. If someone is a workaholic, you need to counsel them on adjusting their priorities or they may cause themselves great physical damage. If you must cancel the work of a group or department, part of your responsibility is to help the individuals prepare for another job. While you can not prevent trauma in people's lives, you *can* be sure that you are not contributing to their trauma.

2. *Passage of Time:* We look at a picture album and see ourselves in outdated clothing and funny hair styles. Yet it seems like only yesterday those styles were in vogue. These and many other changes come upon us almost unnoticed. They seem to be a natural part of life, and we adjust and change accordingly. To help people realize how flexible they are, it is a good idea to point out this kind of change.

If you have a group that is resistant to change, it will help to review all the changes they've gone through in the last few years. Ask them to join in and discuss these changes. Assure them that they are already much better at change than they believed. Some were married or divorced. Babies were born. Parents became incapacitated or died. Homes were bought. Trips were taken. When change is shown as a common event, people can identify with the process more easily. They can see that if they apply the same skills to future change it may not be so bad.

3. *Design:* Leaders, by definition, *must* anticipate and lead productive change. You can *sometimes* prevent traumatic change; you can *rarely* prevent the changes of time. But you must *plan* the intended course of deliberate change. There are several ways to plan and prepare for change.

First: Help your people begin the intended change. Work with them to determine the benefits of the change. Help them see themselves in the changed environment. Support their new identity. Give them some ideas on how to begin the change and give them feedback along the way to the change.

Second: Help them set realistic goals for the change. As the process of change begins, be aware that people often set unrealistic goals. They may select goals to please you, the leader, rather than setting ones for themselves which is a surefire way for them to fail. They may have set the goal too high for their abilities. You must work with them early in the change process to be sure that they are setting realistic goals. You will be doing them a service. They will have a much better chance at successfully completing the necessary change.

Third: Solicit input. Open communication in a nonthreatening setting is essential during the change process. You need to solicit their input and be an especially good listener, hearing not only the words but the messages of body language, facial expressions, voice intonations, and emotional reactions. You need to be responsive to inward and outward reactions.

Last: Support their progress. The successful leader supports change in others through recognition and reward. Your sensitivity to other people's needs and wants will give you the clues as to what recognition and appreciation would be most appropriate to the situation. Even the most motivated people need emotional support, recognition, and reward. In the long run everyone benefits by the open support of the leader.

—Indianapolis—A Change Master Success Story—

In the 1960s the population shift to the suburbs had left downtown Indianapolis impoverished and blighted, just as it had so many other American cities. In the two decades since, Indianapolis has shown what can be done when a group of change master-leaders combine vision, creativity, and hard work in a team effort. Their problems were not unique, but their solutions were.

When the process began Richard Lugar was mayor of Indianapolis. To revitalize the inner city, Lugar formed UNIGOV (Unified Metropolitan Government). Its purpose was to unify the interests of city and county government. County policy had always been to try to satisfy the needs of several different cities. Inherent in this policy were conflicts of political interest and the waste of duplicated efforts and assets. Through UNIGOV, Lugar was able to enact county-wide planning. Eventually the Indianapolis city limits were expanded to the county limits.

This unification gave suburbanites a stake in urban redevelopment and the needs of the city center. Lugar gained popular and financial support for his vision of revitalizing Indianapolis.

The vision continued when William H. Hudnut was elected mayor in 1976. Both Lugar and Hudnut were change masters who shared the same mission that matters. The word people use to describe both of these leaders is *enlightened.*

Mayor Hudnut built a team of people who were also change master-leaders in their own specialties. The team had many qualities in common: Most important was their sensitivity to issues that could make or break the success of the mission—the concerns of the black community, of business and industry, of education. The list went on and on.

Soon after Hudnut's election, he began working with the Greater Indianapolis Progress Committee (GIPC), a community organization that had been formed in the late 1960s to find solutions to a variety of community problems. GIPC and UNIGOV were the primary forces in the early stages of redevelopment. Several other committees were formed along the way, and now Indianapolis has many key organizations for retaining and continuing the work started by Mayors Lugar and Hudnut.

There are two things to note in this change master success story. One is the ability of the committees to work independently and together on the diverse and often difficult needs and interest of the city. The second is the lack of behind the scenes in-fighting for "turf" or power.

The mission of the change master-leaders was so strong, their guiding vision and persistence so focused, that territorial and ego problems simply were not acceptable. The leaders set the tone and were examples that made the change possible.

They put community interest above private interests, worked as a team, and made their vision a reality. Everyone won. The people of Indianapolis are extremely proud of the result of their hard work and commitment. They have a right to be proud. Indianapolis is once again an outstanding place to live and work.

The leaders of Indianapolis made a difference in their community and set an example for many other cities across the nation.

THE ONLY CONSTANT IS CHANGE

My favorite expression about change is, "Every time I figure out where it's at—they move it!"

The only thing any of us knows for sure is that everything will change. As a leader the best you can do is keep change in perspective. Humorist Mark Russell recently put change in perspective. He asked, "Do you ever feel as though you are caught in a speed trap? Are you overwhelmed by change? Any time you think the world is moving too fast, just stop by the post office!"

When change brings success, you hope to keep your ego from getting out of hand. When the change is negative you need your sense of humor to get you through. Your balance is key to helping your followers adapt and change.

The world has gone through more pervasive, permanent, and profound change than ever before in history. To be a change master-leader in this environment will take all the talent and dedication you can muster. But when you set out to make a difference, there is no guarantee that it will be easy. The guarantee is that by serving your people as a change master and by trying to help them learn to change, you *will* be making a difference.

A LEADER IS SENSITIVE
Inspiring Loyalty

"An effective leader is a flexible leader—
someone who can change his or her style of
leadership relative to the needs
of subordinates and the situation."
—OLIVER L. NIEHOUSE

The inclusion of sensitivity in a list of leadership qualities is a relatively recent phenomenon and one subject to misinterpretation. Sensitive leadership is not leadership that lacks strength or courage. It is not softness or the lessening of power. A sensitive leader has a heightened awareness of the issues, values, and people in our changing society. Sensitive leaders focus on the daily world in which they operate, particularly on the people they lead.

Sensitivity doesn't detract from the leadership qualities we have always valued; it adds to them. Sensitivity leads to the wise use of power. Decision making requires a higher degree of sensitivity than ever before because the world is changing so rapidly. Risk taking requires sensitivity to a much wider range of concerns than leaders of the past had to face.

BEING SENSITIVE TO ISSUES AND PEOPLE

Whether you are trying to make a difference in the private sector, public sector, or the volunteer realm, you must be sensitive to broad areas such as economic policy, government regulations, quality of products, excellence of service, and future trends, to name a few. These are important, but of equal importance are the people you are trying to lead. Sensitivity to their needs is crucial to your leadership effectiveness, because without responsive, productive people, the other considerations quickly become secondary. At its best this sensitivity is called "people building."

People building in the work place includes sensitivity to such things as childcare, retirement programs, unions issues, safety in the work place, volunteer motivation, training programs, career opportunities, fair policy, and the example of high ethical standards. We need to look at our leadership style to be sure it is up to date with the values and needs of the people we lead.

SENSITIVITY TO SOCIAL PROBLEMS

People building also means sensitivity to the social problems we face daily. Men and woman all across the country are becoming grass-roots leaders, taking up the causes surrounding the many social problems we are experiencing. They are saying, "It's no longer enough to spend all my energy achieving my personal success. It's time to lend a hand to others."

Everywhere I go to conduct a seminar or give a speech I hear people talking about their need to be fulfilled by something other than their own quality of life. A young woman told me she felt cheated. She said, "I did everything 'they' said I should. I work fourteen hours a day. I give 150 percent to my career. I played the game. But I am beginning to feel cheated. I'm tired and stressed most of the time. My personal life is almost nonexistent. There has got to be more than this. I feel unfulfilled. I keep thinking, 'Is this all there is?' "

A man in his mid-thirties told me, "I have most of the 'goodies' anyone would want. But recently I've begun to feel empty. Is my life about acquiring more and more toys and things? I'd like to feel as though I did something that mattered. I'd like to make a contribution."

I hear these types of comments over and over again. Together we are realizing that there is more to life than material gain, status, power, and instant gratification. People everywhere are saying, "Wait a minute—you can't sink half a ship. I can't ignore those who need help, letting them slip into the shadows. If I do, I hurt myself, too. We're on the ship of life together and if they go down, so do I.'' You may say, but isn't that just another form of "me-ism"? People helping others just to save themselves? The answer is yes, there is a degree of "me-ism' in saving others to save yourself. But it doesn't matter how it happens. When people start to help others, when they have the courage to look beyond the surface, when they become sensitive to the pain and suffering of their fellow citizens, they change! They begin to make a difference.

It is very painful to open your heart and mind to suffering. How do you feel when you drive down the street on a cold, rainy night and see a person sleeping in a doorway? What does it do to you when you pass a young girl, obviously strung out on drugs, hustling for a trick on the street corner? When you are sitting in your comfortable living room watching the nightly news and they show a young family down on their luck living in their car, how do you feel? To a sensitive person these are very painful experiences.

WHAT CAN I DO?

It is not easy to take a hard look at ourselves and admit that we have not done our share. Once your sensitivity is heightened it can be overwhelming. There is so much to be done. You might say to yourself, "Where do I begin. How can I make a difference? How on earth can one person do anything about these massive problems?"

I want to tell you that *you* matter, *you* can make a difference. You can allow your innate sensitivity to deepen your caring about people and issues right in your community. You do not have to feel helpless or overwhelmed by the immensity of the problems. You can take your sensitivity and put it to good use on a mission that will give you the fulfillment you deserve. The more sensitive you become, the better able you are to motivate and influence others to help you make that difference.

Clara McBride Hale is an eighty-four-year-old black woman. When her husband died leaving her with two young children to raise, she decided to take in other children as a source of income. She did such a good job that many parents left their children with her full time, and Clara ended up raising forty children. She proudly says, "Every one of them went to college and graduated." In 1969, just when she decided to retire, her daughter sent her a baby born addicted to drugs. Clara was off on a new career. Since then she has given refuge to over 600 addicted babies. She has set an example of personal leadership that has encouraged others to become involved.

———————*"The Godfather Of Volunteerism"*———————

Charles Moskos is a professor of Sociology at Northwestern University and he has an idea whose time may have come. On January 29, 1989, five United States senators introduced his ideas to Congress in a bill known as "The Citizenship and National Service Act." This bill would create a Citizens Corps. Young people between the ages of eighteen and twenty-six would be eligible to serve either in the military or on some community-service project. If they choose a community service project they would earn $100 per week while they served. They would commit to at least one year and a maximum of two years of service. Each year would give them a credit of $10,000 or a total of $20,00 to put toward a college education, job training, or a down payment on a house.

The idea has several benefits. First, the idea that citizenship carries obligations would be reinforced. The volunteer corps would re-establish the crucial link between public benefits and civic obligation. Second, the crushing debt that students carry after graduation would be greatly eliminated because they would earn the money first. Third, many of the pressing social needs our country faces would be reduced. Nearly one million young people would work in nonprofit associations and public agencies in the areas of education, health care, childcare, conservation, criminal justice, as well as in libraries and museums, or as citizen-soldiers in the all-volunteer military forces.

A *New York Times* article on the bill said, "If they did nothing but supervise after-school childcare at schools and libraries and provide housekeeping help to keep old people out of nursing homes, the nation would easily recoup its investment."

The idea of youth service is not new. But the current enthusiasm is new. It has become a bi-partisan issue. There is new excitement and sensitivity to the fact "that youth service seeks to revive a civic philosophy, that recognizes obligations as well as rights and accepts duties as well as rewards."

Imagine the enormous benefit we would all receive from college graduates who had first-hand experience with the social issues that are overwhelming us.

In discussing the benefits of his program, Charles Moskos referred to the college president who felt out of touch with the social issues facing the country and took a sabbatical to get some first-hand experience. Professor Moskos said, "When I read about a college president who went off to wash dishes and do laboring work for a year, I said, 'This is crazy.' See, if you had done this when you were twenty-two, you wouldn't have to have felt that way when you were forty-eight."

Grass-Roots Sensitivity

There have been many people whose sensitivity and passion for their mission has motivated others to join them in their fight to make a better world. These movements are often called grass-roots movements, and they are led by men and women whose sensitivity and passion attract others to their cause. Their efforts have had far-reaching and long-lasting results. One of these people had a major effect on our working environment.

Alice Hamilton was born in New York City in 1869 and attended medical universities in Michigan and Germany. She became a professor of pathology at Northwestern's Woman's Medical School in Chicago. There her sensitivity to others led her to work extensively at Chicago's famous settlement house, Hull House.

Her observations during a typhoid epidemic—that flies spread the disease—changed health department procedures. It was also at Hull House that she met disabled and dying workers who had been poisoned by the chemicals and fumes of factories and mills. People were dying by the thousands from toxins and hazardous working conditions, but no one in industry, government, or the medical profession was doing anything about it. Hamilton learned that industrial medicine was a recognized branch of medicine in England and Germany, and that the governments there routinely inspected factories.

Scholarly and ladylike, Hamilton made her determined way past hostile managers into the darkest corners of factories and sweat shops, gathering samples of the choking dust and nauseating fumes. Hamilton's work led Illinois to pass the first state laws on occupational safety and workmen's compensation. As a special investigator for the U.S. Bureau of Labor, she went into lead mines, coal mines, and the munitions industry. Owners were understandably furious, denouncing her as a "socialist." She wrote three major books on industrial poisons and dangerous working conditions.

Hamilton's concern for her fellow humans, both as patients and people, took her from teaching evening classes for immigrants at Hull House to working with the Health Committee of the League of Nations. Alice Hamilton's sensitivity and courageous leadership had a major effect on the safety and health of every worker in America. She made a difference that has affected us all.

THE "SOFT" FACTORS

Even though we have had depressions, recessions, and productivity slowdowns in this century, we are still a nation that expects to grow, change, and achieve at an unprecedented rate. To fulfill this expectation, we need more and more leaders with a highly developed concern for the people-issues as well as the bottom line.

Daniel Yankelovich, futurist and best-selling author, suggests that "capital investment is not the only way to high productivity. 'Soft' factors, such as sensitivity to the values of each person, inspiring dedication, pride in working in a results-oriented environment are key factors in quality and productivity."

—Corporate Sensitivity—The Motorola Example—

There are many companies and organizations where sensitivity to the people-issues is an example for us all. One of the finest is the Motorola Corporation. Bill Weisz is their vice chairman and officer of the board.

When Bill stepped up to accept *New Management Magazine*'s 1985 "Company of the Year" award, he said, "We are a participative management company and each and every Motorolan has a responsibility for making our company a success. All 100,000 [Motorola employees] deserve to share in this honor."

Motorola began in 1928 as an automobile-radio manufacturer with a $500 investment. Today, it is worth $5.5 billion and is broadly diversified in high-technology electronics. One of the major reasons Motorola has become so successful is a corporate culture that matches people skills and attitudes to maximize capacities to tackle the changing marketplace.

When Bill Weisz addressed two hundred Motorola officers, he emphasized the culture that has made Motorola such a success. Referring to the different segments of the company, he said:

> In your organization, you are the CEO, whatever level of the company you are in. Our fundamental policy has always been to decentralize authority and implement our current organizational-effectiveness programs that support the shared value of the dignity of the individual. The most important job of management is to create the environment and the atmosphere in which each and every person can contribute to the maximum of his or her own capability.
>
> Even in the crush of current events, we must pay proper attention to people motivation and management. We believe in the "we approach," not "we versus they." We believe in setting high standards, high expectations. We insist on a healthy spirit of discontent. We believe in creativity and innovation as being fundamental to our business. We believe in customer satisfaction. We believe that managers cannot manage from their offices; they must get out with their people. We believe in being a good corporate citizen and in contributing to the economic and social well being of every community and country in which we operate.

In August of 1987 Motorola ran a full-page advertisement in two Japanese newspapers, thanking the companies they did business with and telling them how much they appreciated the partnership. Motorola's sensitivity was demonstrated by the words: "Our ring of partnership is growing. Let's take the next step together." Motorola was the first American company ever to run such an ad, and it was a huge success.

In April of 1988 Motorola sponsored "Arbor Day" for all its employees. Each employee at the headquarters in Schaumburg, Illinois, was invited to join Chairman Bill Galvin and other executive and senior managers in planting more than 6,600 seedlings around the edge of the property, beautifying not only the Motorola facilities but the nearby community. Motorola executives could have had the maintenance people plant the trees. But they didn't. They were sensitive to the fact their people enjoyed being involved and wanted to make a difference. Each person who planted a seedling felt that they personally contributed to both company and community.

Motorola employees know that they are valued not only for what they can do for the company but as individuals. Bill Galvin, Bill Weisz, and the other leaders of the company clearly understand the "soft" factors. They know that people who are valued return value. These same people see the connection between their own goals and the organization's goals, and they are willing to work hard to achieve them.

FUTURE TRENDS

We live in a world economy, a world market, and a world community. That does not mean that we must lose our national identity. But it does mean that if you are to lead, and make a difference, you will have to think, act, and perceive things from a world perspective. Otherwise you'll be unprepared to function and progress in the challenging years ahead.

Your sensitivity to future trends has two important values. First, it keeps you at the forefront of any field, and second, it gives you the insight to create a vision for your people to follow.

Peter F. Drucker wrote, "Any business that does not learn how to innovate within the next few years will not be around by the year 2000." Thomas R. Horton, president of the American Management Association, wrote, "The CEOs I interviewed are pulling their companies into the future. Aware of changes in customer demand, alert to new technological developments, they constantly look for ways to reach out in new directions."

If we are to heed Drucker's warning and Horton's advice, we must recognize the direct ratio between the sensitivity and support you give and the commitment and cooperation you receive. Sensitivity is a major part of the motivational chemistry that will help you build and maintain a successful organization.

RENEWAL: PERSONAL, ORGANIZATIONAL, SOCIETAL

Sensitivity is an integral part of the other eleven leadership qualities. For example, as a team builder you are sensitive to the skills of others. You match the right people with the right jobs, allowing them to grow and learn in an area that is interesting to them. If you set an example of risk taking, followers gain confidence in their ability to be innovative and creative. By addressing the expanding needs of followers and encouraging their personal renewal, you make a difference by revitalizing your organization and society.

Robert K. Greenleaf, author of *The Servant As A Leader,* wrote: "Some institutions achieve distinction for a short time by the intelligent use of people. An institution that has firmly established the context of people-first moves from people-using to people-building." That means sensitivity to the factors that influence the leader, the followers, and the external environment in which they operate.

In the introduction of this book I referred to the difference between management and leadership. In the chart below, let's look at some of the basic management skills and see how they have evolved into leadership skills for "renewal" and "people-building."

Evolving Skills

Management Skill	to	Leadership Skill
Directing	to	Supporting
Creative thinking	to	Inspiring creativity
Decision making	to	Delegating
Listening skills	to	Ensuring understanding
Constructive criticism	to	Enhancing others
Problem solving	to	Resolving conflict
Implementing technology	to	Humanizing technology

Each of these leadership skills enables you to help people invest in themselves and discover their own best, both personally and professionally. These same skills move you away from doing things *to* people and toward doing things *with* people.

CYCLES AND RENEWAL

Organization cycles are described by Bernard M. Bass: "Effective firms in a rapidly *changing,* complex environment are generally more participative or consultative, involving lower-level managers in department decisions. [Also] effective firms in relatively *stable* environments generally concentrate decision making and influence at the top levels of management."

As a modern leader you'll add to the renewal process if you remain sensitive to change. You can't fall into a comfort zone, taking either the stable or changing environment for granted. The world is in such flux that in a very short period of time you can cycle back and forth between rapidly changing environments and stable ones. Being flexible is your key for surviving.

Bass reminds us that "All the processes of leading include the understanding that group members are people with human concerns and reactions."

THE POWER OF PMA

"A leader must sound an optimistic note
against a chorus of pessimists."
—ANONYMOUS

Your sensitivity to the power of a *Positive Mental Attitude*—PMA—can never be overvalued. Your cheerfulness helps people defeat cynicism, fear, futility, and despair. PMA can inspire a shared vision and help you enlist others to make a difference. It can calm turmoil, confusion, and chaos. Your ability to uplift people's spirits when they feel overburdened or negative is one of the most powerful motivational tools you can possess.

PASSING ON YOUR PMA

Your attitude sets the example that helps your people motivate themselves. PMA is very contagious. Others can catch it and use it to make a difference in their own lives.

Do you know someone who seems to have certain skills, but their self-esteem is so low it keeps them from maximizing those skills? Consider the old axiom: "Tell a person they are a winner long enough and they will start acting like one."

————*The Black Boy From Louisville*————

Louisville, Kentucky, Patrolman Joe Martin collected coins from parking meters during the day. In his private time he was director of boxing for the Louisville Recreation Department. He wanted to help the young boys of Louisville increase their self-image and learn to be good boxers. One night an eighty-nine-pound, twelve-year-old black boy came to the gym in tears. He was so angry he could hardly speak. Joe asked him what was wrong, and the boy told him that someone had stolen his new bicycle. He said he wanted to whip somebody. Joe asked him, "Do you know how to fight?" and young Cassius Clay said, "No, but I'd fight them anyway!"

That was the beginning. Young Cassius would come to the gym and work his heart out. Joe saw his talent and soon began saying, "You're the greatest—you're the greatest." Cassius wanted to live up to Joe's expectations; he put his heart into being a boxer. He liked being the "greatest." He reveled in working his young body into peak-fighting shape. He began believing he was the "greatest." Joe and Cassius were together for 106 fights. Their crowning glory was the Olympics. Cassius Clay was indeed "the greatest." Now, as Mohammed Ali, if you ask him about his boxing, he will still say, "I'm the greatest!".

Everyone wants a cheerleader, someone to believe in them, to help them have a can-do attitude. What can you do to let others know you believe they can be a winner? In what way can you be sensitive to their low self-image? How can you help them tap their potential as Joe Martin did for young Cassius Clay?

At the same time you can't be naive about PMA. Not everyone wants to have a positive, happy life. There are some people who enjoy being negative. They have so much invested in this view of the world that your PMA will never make a dent in their attitude. If you have such a person in your organization, try to keep them in jobs where their bad attitude doesn't affect too many other people. And *never, never,* put these people in contact with those you are trying to serve. It's a sure way to destroy your organization.

Most people want to be happy, so ignore the few exceptions and concentrate on the positive.

————————*Hope Leads The Way*————————

Charles Sawyer wrote:

> "Of all the forces that make for a better world,
> none is so indispensable, none so powerful as
> hope. Without hope men are only half alive.
> With hope they dream and think and work."

How would you feel if you got up one morning and ran five miles in under twenty-five minutes, and the next day your doctor told you that you have multiple sclerosis? What would you do with your hopes and dreams? How would you recover from the shock and try to put your life in some kind of order?

In 1969 Olympic skier, Jimmie Huega, was faced with these perplexing and painful questions. He learned that MS, as multiple sclerosis is commonly known, is a painful, crippling disease with no known cure. It would scramble communications between his brain and body until his vision and muscle control were gone. There was nothing he could do to stop the inevitable.

Jimmie, like many other MS victims, waited with mounting despair. For seven years he watched his Olympian capabilities slip slowly away. He wanted to be physically active, but most doctors advise MS patients to avoid exercise, fearing it will hasten the progress of the disease. He became so disabled that he could barely get out of bed. The end seemed predictable and near.

There is an almost mystical spirit that a few special people are given. Jimmie has that spirit. One day as he lay in his darkened room he looked over at his bicycle. He thought about how much he had loved to ride. He remembered the feeling of freedom as he rode along with the wind against his face, the refreshed energy at the end of the ride. That mystical spirit awoke in Jimmie Huega.

He decided he had to take responsibility for restoring his own body. He dragged himself out of bed and with true Olympian spirit he managed to get his bicycle outside. He got on and rode a hundred yards before he toppled to the ground. It was the moment that turned his life around: He began to hope again. He decided that he would not wait passively for total incapacity and death. At that very point he began the long climb back.

Over the next few years, Jimmie restored much of the strength and agility his body had lost, using a vigorous self-prescribed program of physical and psychological exercises. During this time he was acquiring the personal leadership qualities that would help him make a difference.

He found his mission—he would help other MS patients fight the effects of the disease. In 1984 he organized the Jimmie Huega Center near Vail, Colorado. He calls his program "reanimation philosophy." In addition to psychological and emotional support, the center offers extensive testing, physical therapy, and education about MS.

The center is staffed almost entirely by volunteers. The people of Vail have taken up his cause, too. They contribute many services, including testing facilities and free hotel rooms for visiting patients.

Jimmie Huega's reanimation philosophy offers hope and a sense of control to people who have lost both. The success of the center's program has given him an even larger vision. He wants to extend his philosophy to other areas where people are "challenged—physically, emotionally, or socially."

Jimmie is a hope giver. His sensitivity to the pain and despair of MS victims fired the passion for his mission. He is a powerful example for all of us. He is making a difference. We would do well to compare ourselves to him and ask, "Am I a hopeful person?" If not, "What has happened to me in my past that makes me a negative thinker?" "What can I do to be more optimistic and hopeful?" "How can I be a more positive, hope-filled leader?" As Charles Sawyer wrote, we are only half alive without hope.

ATTITUDE VS BEHAVIOR

There is a difference between behavior and attitude.

* Behavior is what we say and do.
* Attitude is what we feel or believe.

Behavior is what first evokes a response in others. But behaviors come from attitudes. So as a leader it is important to work on your own attitudes first. When you clarify how you feel, it will show in your behavior.

Having a PMA doesn't mean you ignore realities and difficulties. It simply means that you try to find the opportunity in problems. You have an optimistic view when others see only the negative. "PMA won't get you everything," says motivational speaker Zig Ziglar, "but it makes everything you've got a whole lot better."

Analyze your positive mental attitude and have the courage to ask, "What example am I setting?" "What difference am I making?"

Edith Wharton wrote, "There are two ways of spreading light:

to be the candle or the mirror that reflects it." Your positive attitude is both the candle and the mirror. You light the way for others and your positive attitude is reflected in the hearts and minds of your followers.

USING SENSITIVITY TO IMPROVE PERFORMANCE

"[Leaders] earn respect when they are open to
ideas, sensitive to the self-esteem of followers,
and can accurately articulate the ideas to their
own superiors."
—ROBERT TANNENBAUM AND
WARREN H. SCHMIDT

When you want to improve the performance of your people and earn their respect, there are several basic ideas about sensitivity that will help keep you on track.

Be clear about what is important to you. What is your mission? How will you make a difference? Part of the support you receive depends on how clearly you communicate those goals and how sensitive you are to the way others view them. Their performance is enhanced when your vision is clear and they can see how they fit into it. If their contribution is clarified, they will be more enthusiastic about your goal.

Help people identify who they are, not just what they do. In *Chapter House Dune,* Frank Herbert wrote about becoming what you do: "If you fitted yourself too tightly to one thing, other abilities atrophied. We become what we do."

When we meet people we ask, "What do you do?" We pigeonhole people into identifying themselves in terms of their work. It would be healthier for us all if we would ask, "Who are you?" "In what do you believe?" What interesting conversations we would have.

When I see an automotive ad on television that says, "You are what you drive," I'm insulted for all of us. Do the automakers really think we are so shallow that our identity is wrapped up in a piece of machinery? Let's get away from describing ourselves in terms of what we do and look closer at who we are. It takes courage to reidentify yourself, but the results are well worth the effort.

As a leader, if you help others broaden their self-image, you will be doing them a great service. You'll be making a difference.

Recognize where people are, not where you would like them to be, where you think they should be, or, where you think their potential lies. Starting from a realistic point helps you determine how performance can be improved. If you match your leadership style to someone's current performance level, you will achieve much better results than you will by trying to make that person fit your preconception.

In his book, *The Situational Leader,* Dr. Paul Hersey points out that the wise leader uses follower "readiness" as a tool to motivate and influence followers. He writes, *"Readiness* is the extent to which a follower has the ability and willingness to accomplish a specific task. Both qualities are essential and levels vary constantly."

If you think about your followers, you will quickly be able to categorize them in one of four stages of readiness:

- Some are able and willing. These folks are easiest to lead. Their skills and desire match. They are easily motivated and can be role models for the other types.
- Some are able but not willing. This is an attitude challenge. Here your job is to find out what is stopping their willingness. Do they fear failure? Do they need some special recognition to press their willingness button? What can you do to build their confidence, their skill, their commitment?
- Some are willing but not able. Skills and competencies are involved here. These people need specific training in special tasks. They might be the source of great strength in your organization if you can tap their potential by enhancing their abilities.
- Some are neither willing nor able. These people are your biggest challenge, because you must work on both attitude and skills simultaneously. If you have many of these people in your organization, you need to review your interview process. Perhaps the weakness lies in who is doing the interviewing and hiring. It takes a special skill to know what kind of people to select. Or you may need to institute a special basic-training course to work on these attitude and aptitude problems. Either way this group is your biggest challenge.

It is important to note that people can move from one type of readiness to another, depending on the situation. That's why it is so important for you to have the sensitivity necessary to interpret correctly where a person is in terms of their readiness. Again, being sensitive and flexible is the key to your success in serving as leader.

Empathy makes a difference. G. J. Tankersley wrote, "Empathy is the ability to share other people's feelings, to see things, even if you don't agree with them, from their point of view. This is important in virtually all phases of human interaction, and extremely important in any large organization. You can't underestimate the need to handle interpersonal relations well, and empathy is the quality that counts most in that."

While Tankersley's point is well made, you must be careful that you don't let your sensitivity overpower you. Try to find the balance between genuine concern and overidentifying with others, between being available and being prevailed upon. The more people oriented and sensitive you become, the more likely you are to get too close to your followers. You need objectivity in dealing with people and problems. The best way to find the balance you need is not to become "social friends" with followers. Keep your personal friendships in your private life. It is very difficult to step in and give directions, correct people, or arbitrate an argument with friends. We all have many occupational acquaintances, and that is healthy. When we become overly empathic or too close to them, we lose our ability to lead effectively.

Constructive support. When trying to improve performance, be sure to criticize positively. Give "constructive support" and concentrate on the job, not on the character of the worker. Describe what you want, not how to do it. Remember what Rosabeth Moss Kanter said: "Work responsibilities should be described in terms of results, with flexibility in the way they are achieved." The second most important part of this process is to be courteous, especially under pressure. There is never justification for undignified behavior toward anyone. Remember the term "common courtesy." Unfortunately, courtesy isn't always common anymore, but one of the finest ways to exemplify sensitivity is through your personal politeness.

Peter Drucker says, "Every organization needs performance in three major areas: direct results, building and reaffirmation of values, and developing people for tomorrow. All three must be built into the contribution of every executive.'' Sensitivity is essential for building values, developing people, and improving performance.

SENSITIVITY AND LEADERSHIP STYLE

Leadership style isn't what *you* think your style is: It's what *others* perceive it to be. Like beauty, leadership style is in the eye of the beholder. You may see yourself as having a particular style (and you may be right), but if you are sensitive, you'll compare your own perception with that of your followers.

When I discussed leadership sensitivity with Bill Weisz (vice chairman and officer of the board of Motorola), he said sensitivity was very important "because different situations require different kinds of leaders. Leadership in essence is almost like playing golf. You use the right club at the right point. You don't use the driver on the putting green or the putter off the tee.

In any given situation at any given time, a good leader has the capability of modulating his activities, depending on what the situation requires. A leader who is singularly focused and treats every situation in the same way may not be a good leader, even though the thing he is very good at is the best thing for the situation. If you're good at sensitivity to others, you should be able to understand what that means.''

President Eisenhower used to say that he could demonstrate leadership style with a piece of string. He'd lay the string on a table and say, ''Pull it and it'll follow you wherever you wish. Push it and it will go nowhere at all. It's that way when it comes to leading people.''

While few of us will be leaders on as high a level as Eisenhower, it is important that we, too, realize that our leadership style is felt in the heart as well as the intellect of our own followers. If you want loyal followers, you must be very careful that your style of leading reflects the sensitivity necessary to earn that loyalty.

—*The Sparta Brush Story—Tragedy and Triumph*—

Joe Larson was owner and president of the Sparta Brush Company for thirty years. Located in Sparta, Wisconsin, the company had built the reputation as a top manufacturer in the relatively narrow business market of brushes used in restaurants, dairies, janitorial work, and home use. Sparta Brush had an excellent reputation for employee loyalty and pride. Joe Larson's leadership style exemplified sensitivity to the needs and values of his employees. He understood that his people wanted to be proud of the product they produced. They wanted a sense of belonging to a team. Sparta employees knew that their brushes had the highest credibility in the industry and that Joe offered them a place to build a career and a life. "We were reaching together for a common goal," says Joe. "The magic of relationships is what makes a company work."

November 1979 began a series of tragedies that would have crippled a company with less loyal and dedicated employees. That month Joe's wife of forty years, Esther, died suddenly. Joe had just begun to recover from the shock when six months later his son Jack, executive vice president of manufacturing, suffered a heart attack and was told he could work only two or three hours a day. But Joe and his team of loyal employees kept right on going, pulling together to pick up the extra work Jack could not do.

Without warning, a third tragic blow came several weeks later on the Fourth of July weekend. Joe was at home enjoying the holiday when he received a phone call from the police telling him that his factory was on fire. Joe raced to the scene, but by the time he got there Sparta Brush lay in ashes. A lifetime of work and dreams was gone in a matter of minutes.

The cumulative effect of those six months would be enough to stop almost anyone. But Joe Larson is a man of great faith and he often recalls what he describes as "the miracle." By eight o'clock the next morning, his fifty employees were arriving at the Sparta plant with brooms, shovels, and pickup trucks. They said, "We'll start again. Let's get to work."

"No one complained," said Joe. "They pitched in and began to dig. We were able to save a few pieces of machinery. They scraped, cleaned, and worked like the devil. That very day we were able to piece together some desks and chairs, and moved into a vacant auto dealership. We worked as a team to call all our suppliers and customers. In one week we had temporary production and in four months we rebuilt the factory, *adding* 10,000 square feet." Joe is also proud of the customers who stood by him in those hard times: "And you know, we never lost one customer in those four months!"

One of Joe's favorite sayings is, "It's not what happens that matters, but how you respond." Joe Larson is one of the most respected people in his industry. As a leader, his style demonstrated sensitivity to his people—his employees, his customers and suppliers alike. When the need was there they returned his lesson of leadership by showing their sensitivity to him. His message of excellence, integrity, and true sense of service made the difference between success and failure when the going got rough.

SENSITIVITY TO EXPECTATIONS

Shakespeare wrote in *Henry V*, "For now sits Expectation in the air."

Everyone within your organization has certain expectations. It is critical that you know what they are or you'll be leading blind. If you are sensitive to the expectations of your followers, it increases your ability to motivate and influence them. It increases your ability to make a difference.

The four major expectations that people have are:

- *Income*—How much can I expect to earn, now and in the future?
- *Advancement*—How far can I expect to go within this organization?
- *Education*—How much education should I expect to acquire or will I receive while involved with this organization?
- *Relationships*—What kind of relationships should I expect to be involved in?

When you set policy or make decisions, it is important to be sensitive to these four expectations.

Income expectations come in the form of questions such as:

—What can I expect to earn at my present position?
—Can raises be expected periodically or only under certain conditions? What are those conditions?
—How are the other people in the organization compensated for equal or similar work?
—If there are retirement plans or stock sharing or investing,

what are the conditions and what affects my receiving these benefits?

Consider your organization and develop this list further so that you can anticipate the income expectation of your people.
Advancement expectations include:

—When will I be promoted and under what circumstances?
—Is there room for promotion or are we in a stagnant market?
—If there is room for promotion, what do I have to do to receive an advance?
—Who else has been promoted and under what circumstance? Does it have a bearing on me?

If you promote people on merit, you need to set the guidelines very clearly. If you promote on seniority or tenure you will need to take a hard look at the fairness involved in this system. Just because someone has been around a long time does not automatically mean he or she should be promoted. It may be time to reconsider the system you use.
Educational expectations can mean:

—What do you expect your people to do as far as their own education or training programs?
—Do you provide training or education within the organization?
—What can they expect to receive from you to help them be more proficient at their jobs?
—If they take time off to go to school, do you help them?
Training has become one of the hottest issues in the people-building business. Technology demands that people be trained and retrained, educated and reeducated. Lack of a clear leadership policy on education can cause confusion and lack of commitment to the organization.
Relationship expectations concern the give-and-take between the worker and the leader, managers or supervisors. People want harmonious working situations. They expect the leader to create and maintain relationships that foster these situations. They expect certain things from the team in which they function. They have expectations about relationships with other teams and organizations. They want to know, "What are the rules and the leader's expectations of the team relationships?" A clear-cut mission or purpose

statement about what the organization believes will help to satisfy relationship expectations.

Author Simone Weil wrote about expectation: "At the bottom of the heart of every human being from earliest infancy until the tomb there is something that goes on indomitably expecting. It is this above all that is sacred in every human being." The sensitive leader has a sacred responsibility to help followers define expectations. Today people expect to achieve, so as a leader you must use your sensitivity to help them keep these expectations in perspective.

OPPOSITE SIDE OF THE COIN

At the same time, the leader must look at expectations from the opposite side of the coin. Drop your expectations, discard preconceived ideas, and unlearn what you "know." Don't limit your horizons. Lao-tzu, the ancient Chinese philosopher, wrote in the *Tao of Power:* "Without expectation, one will always perceive the subtlety; and with expectation, one will always perceive the boundary." There is a saying that we can never exceed our own expectations. The sensitive leader needs to be able to do two things: To deal with people's expectations and at the same time to see beyond those expectations.

General John Long and I were discussing the importance of leadership qualities. He had said he thought sensitivity was one of the most important. I asked why and he replied, "because basically I believe that the vast majority of people are good, or want to be. If you believe that and you want to give the best you have, then anything you do in a leadership role is going to require other people.

People need to accomplish something. You've got to get the best out of them. You've got to cause these human beings to give you and the organization their best. If you accept that [responsibility], you have to be sensitive to people's needs, their desires, their expectations, their culture, gender, race, education—everything.

You have to be sensitive to people's expectations, what they expect of you and what you expect of them, no matter what their 'station in life.' Meet those expectations. Your word and actions must show people that you are committed to them as individuals, and that what you expect back is a team that will support your goals and your organization's goals."

LEARNING FROM THE PAST, LIVING IN THE PRESENT

People are constantly changing. By studying the past, you are better prepared to grapple with the problems of today. The lessons history has to teach can prepare you to handle the negative human responses of fear, envy, vanity, and self-deception, as well as the positive ones of joy, enthusiasm, pride, and self-confidence.

When you are faced with the problems and challenges of leadership, history can have a calming effect. In their book, *Lessons Of History,* Will and Ariel Durant wrote:

> Known history shows little alteration in the conduct of mankind. The Greeks of Plato's time behaved very much like the French of modern centuries; and the Romans behaved like the English. Means and instrumentalities change; motives and ends remain the same: to act or rest, to acquire or give, to fight or retreat, to seek association or privacy, to mate or reject, to offer or resent parental care. Nor does human nature alter between classes; by and large the poor have the same impulses as the rich, with only less opportunity or skill to implement them.

To serve your people you must resist self-deception about what is going on, good or bad, and must not confuse individual, personal character with "human nature," guts with courage, success with integrity, or winning with happiness. Continually re-examine your perceptions with sensitivity and courage. Leaders with highly developed sensitivity are aware of the forces that affect themselves, their people, and the environment. They have the skill to adjust their style to fit the situation. They are not overburdened by expectations or other people's perceptions, but use their sensitivity as a positive tool to build people and to tap into the wealth of the human spirit.

Don't be afraid to use sensitivity as a leadership tool. The more sensitive you become, the broader your perceptions will become. The broader your perceptions, the wider the range of possibilities you'll see. And the more possibilities you see, the more you will be able to serve and make a difference.

A LEADER IS A RISK TAKER
Expanding The Possible

"What is life, but one long risk?"
—DOROTHY CANFIELD FISHER

TEN REASONS NOT TO TAKE RISKS:

- "We've never done it before."
- "Nobody has ever done it before."
- "It's too radical a change."
- "The staff will never try it."
- "Customers won't like it."
- "We're not ready for it."
- "You're right, but . . ."
- "Good thought, but impractical."
- "We will never be able to do it."
- "It's impossible."

Risk taking is an indispensable part of leadership. When we look at leaders who are making a difference, we see that they have the courage to begin, while others are waiting for a better time, a safer situation, or assured results. They are willing to take risks because they know that being overcautious and indecisive kills opportunity. It's an irony that we are always in search of novelty, yet we can be deeply uncomfortable with taking risks.

What good would big thinking be if it stopped short of taking risks that turn dreams into reality? How could a change master be effective without taking risks? Many decisions would never be made if the leader wasn't also a risk taker.

"The world we live in today," Wilfred A. Peterson points out, "first existed as ideas in the minds of men . . . bridges, sky-scrapers, automobiles, airplanes, religions, philosophies, governments, symphonies, paintings, poems . . . everything." But these ideas didn't remain mental images. They were put into action. Risks were taken to turn thoughts into reality.

If we are to stay strong and healthy into the twenty-first century, we must use our risk-taking abilities to create an environment that supports and encourages innovation and creativity. We must constantly renew ourselves and our followers. When the leader acts as a role model for risk taking, everyone benefits.

The Ultimate Risk

The *Los Angeles Times* wrote: "It's hard to argue with someone who is willing to risk even death to make a point." They were referring to the 1988 water-only fast of Cesar Chavez, president of the United Farm Workers. Chavez said he was fasting to "identify himself with the many farm-worker families who suffer from the scourge of pesticide poisoning in agriculture communities." During the fast he lost thirty-three pounds, nineteen percent of his total body weight. He endured great nausea and intense stomach cramps. Why did he put himself through this? The answer is in the prayer-song that thirteen-year-old Lori Salinas wrote and sang at the Mass the night he ended his fast. Lori lives in McFarland, California, an area with a high incidence of childhood cancer, which is attributed to agricultural pesticides. Lori, who has numerous tumors around her thyroid gland, stood and sang:

"You, Cesar Chavez, have given us a helping hand and have listened to our crying souls. Someday, I hope to march with you and tell the world how much you love us and care for us like our Lord Jesus Christ. I listen to the feelings of our heart as I look into your eyes; I see the pain in your heart which we are suffering."

Cesar Chavez has been a hero to the farm workers since the early 1960s when he gave up a well-paid job to organize the farm workers. He and his wife supplemented their income by working in the fields, right alongside the people they were defending. His sacrifice inspired workers to go on strike for their rights and to withstand the threats and sacrifices they had to make in order to organize. Cesar Chavez's risk taking changed the lives of many thousands of farm workers.

RISKING DANGER AND RIDICULE

A dictionary definition of risk is "the possibility of suffering harm or loss."

Throughout history our risk-taking leaders have left us with inspiring examples of fearlessness in the face of ridicule, harassment, deprivation, even death.

Frederick Douglass, a slave, bought his freedom and became editor and publisher of his own newspaper, the *North Star*. He traveled extensively in the United States and abroad, making our Constitution a reality by exercising his freedom of speech during a time when people could be owned, bought, and sold. Douglass risked his life and helped lead our nation out of the dark ages of slavery.

On March 30, 1981, Sarah Brady became an activist, and she didn't even know it. She did not know that the event of that day would catapult her into the national spotlight as an advocate of handgun control. That was the day her forty-four-year-old husband, James Brady, White House Press Secretary for President Ronald Reagan, was shot in the head by a would-be assassin. Both he and the president were the victims of a Saturday night special.

During Jim's recovery period Sarah took their son Scott to visit friends. While riding in their friend's truck, Scott picked up what appeared to be a toy gun and pointed it at himself. To Sarah's horror it turned out to be a loaded handgun, just like the one used to shoot the president and Jim.

That day Sarah joined Handgun Control, Inc., a grass-roots organization whose goals are to establish a nationwide licensing of gun owners, background checks on prospective buyers, and mandatory training for anyone buying a gun.

Gun control is one of the most controversial issues we face today. There are those who praise Sarah, and others who harass and ridicule her efforts. She realizes that it is very risky to speak out against the National Rifle Association and to ask people to think of how their own interest might affect others. But Sarah is a determined leader in the gun-control movement. She wants to make a difference, and no one can sway her from her mission.

Even if personal danger is not an issue, ridicule is a potent weapon, one that most people will go to any lengths to avoid. There may be times when your leadership is ridiculed. Making a difference may mean standing up for your beliefs and accepting criticism.

The AIDS epidemic has caused irrational fear and prejudice in many people. Working with AIDS victims is criticized and condemned by those who do not understand or who do not want to understand the disease. Many people who volunteer to work with AIDS victims are ostracized and ridiculed. So when Alan Tolleson, a freshman at Richland Community College near Dallas, decided to be an AIDS volunteer, he was taking a big risk. He had been watching television one night and saw a program about dying AIDS victims. He was deeply moved by the suffering and indignities he saw. He said, "I started thinking about what I could do to help." He now volunteers at the AIDS Resource Center in Dallas. His first one-on-one "buddy" assignment (visiting and counseling AIDS patients in their homes) was with a forty-year-old man who had lost his job and had just gotten out of the hospital. Alan says Robert just needed someone to talk to. "I've become more caring toward people in general. It makes me feel good to help someone in need."

Kara and Meredith Blank work on the Teen AIDS Hotline in Rockville, Maryland. The sisters began working at the hotline to fulfill a community-service requirement at their school. But once they started, they didn't want to stop. Meredith and Kara believe they are making a difference. "This is one case where kids can save the lives of adults," say the girls. Kara, Meredith and Alan are the new generation of risk-taking leaders who are making a difference.

THE PERSONAL BENEFITS OF RISK TAKING

There are three personal benefits of risk taking that will enhance your leadership capabilities. They are increased awareness, expanded knowledge, and increased excitement.

Awareness: One of the greatest personal benefits of risk taking is that it increases your awareness. Risk taking opens your eyes and often your mind. When you take risks, you may realize that you are not as good as you thought you were. On the other hand you might discover that you are better than you thought. These are important experiences for leaders. The better you know yourself, the wiser you become. Awareness of both your limitations and your potential enhances humility. "Awareness is not a giver of solace," said Robert K. Greenleaf, "it is just the opposite. It is a disturber and an awakener."

If you go through life with a closed agenda about how things are and how they should be, you block out opportunities to broaden your leadership and to make a difference. Awareness and new perceptions give you immeasurable resources for the future. Your sensitivity to others' values and needs increases. You have more courage to take actions.

Knowledge: Another benefit of risk taking is that it can teach you valuable lessons. Even if the risk turns out badly, you will learn more about your willingness and ability to take risks. Thomas Alva Edison said, "A failure teaches you that something can't be done—that way." Taking risks is the best way—often the *only* way—to add to your knowledge of what works and what doesn't. It's important to know whether the statement, "It can't be done," is right or wrong. Charles Brower said, "You learn more from your defeats than from your victories."

Knowledge itself has some built-in risks. As it expands, you may learn things about yourself that you don't like. You may discover areas of your personality that need work. You may have to take action, make changes, and grow. Knowledge robs you of the luxury of ignorance. If you are honest and don't kid yourself, you can use your new self-perceptions to strengthen your effectiveness as a leader.

Excitement: "Thrill-seeking" doesn't always have positive connotations, but without excitement, exaltation, even ecstasy, your existence would be very flat. Being involved with people or organizations that are doing exciting, positive things through risk taking can be one of life's greatest pleasures. We all like to be involved with strong teams and systems that make a difference in the world. Making a contribution, receiving recognition, and growing are the kinds of excitement that are the prime benefits of risk taking.

———A Life Of Excitement—A Life of Risk———

William Crapo (Billy) Durant led one of the most exciting and risk-filled lives of any businessman in history. He believed that "he who takes the greatest risk deserves the biggest prize." Billy Durant was small in physical size but a giant in his faith and hope in the American Dream. Even though he had no formal education, he was a genius at marketing. He knew how to communicate his ideas and to persuade others to follow his lead. Billy Durant's story stands out as the epitome of risk taking.

In 1886 he borrowed $2,000 from his friends, bought an interest in a carriage factory, and became the chief salesman. Within four years he had built the business into one of the largest carriage makers in the U.S., producing 150,000 carriages per year.

In 1903 Durant heard of a "screwball" inventor named David Buick who was experimenting with a piston engine. Durant purchased the Flint wagon works which was on the verge of bankruptcy. He renamed it the Buick Motor Company and brought David Buick in to manufacture automobiles.

Durant had a vision of becoming the world's largest automaker. So with borrowed money he soon added Cadillac and Oldsmobile to his company. He combined them with Buick and changed the company's name to General Motors.

However the bankers didn't like Durant's risky attitude. So they forced him to resign as president in exchange for a $10 million loan needed to continue General Motors.

Durant began looking for other ventures. One year later he met Louis Chevrolet who had designed a low-priced car. Durant scraped together $100,000 dollars and organized the Chevrolet Company.

Two years later, with the profits from Chevrolet, Durant began buying up General Motors voting trust certificates. In 1915 he made an offer to General Motors stockholders to exchange five shares of Chevrolet for each share of G.M. The stockholders decided to accept his offer. He walked into a meeting of the G.M. Board and announced he had enough GM stock to take over. Billy Durant was back in control of his beloved General Motors.

By 1920, five years after gaining control of GM, he had personal holdings of $105 million in G.M. The stock market began to falter and automobile stocks were hit the hardest. Billy, the risk taker, tried to hold up the value of the stock with his own money.Still the G.M. stock continued to fall. In a few short months Billy Durant's fortune disappeared and he was $20 million in debt. To pay his debts he sold his stock, gave up control, and walked out dead broke.

He decided that since the market had ruined him, it could be the source of his comeback. He formed a partnership with his friends and began to "play the stock market." Throughout the '20s The Durant Syndicate bought and sold with a frenzy as prices went up, up, and up. Finally in 1929 Billy Durant decided to withdraw from the stock market. He predicted that Federal Reserve Policy would cause a "crash." In May 1929, five months before the stock market crash, Billy Durant sold all his stock at a profit of $40 million. However, being the optimistic risk taker that he was, he decided in 1930 that the market had "bottomed out" and he began buying back his stocks. He was convinced that the market would again climb to new heights and he would have "untold wealth."

He was wrong. The market continued to decline, and in 1936, at the age of seventy-five, William Crapo Durant walked into court and declared bankruptcy. In March 1947, at age eighty-six, he died flat broke.

Near the end of his life Billy Durant said, "Money? What is money? It is only loaned to a man. He comes into the world with nothing and he leaves with nothing." The philosophy of a fool you say? Perhaps. But Billy Durant's risk taking led the way for many conveniences you and I enjoy today. The next time you are driving on the highway, look out your car window and you'll see Billy Durant's risks. Then go home and go to your refrigerator for a cool drink. In both cases you'll feel the impact of the excitement and risk taking of William Crapo "Billy" Durant.

YOUR RISK QUOTIENT (RQ)

What kind of risks should you as a leader be willing to take? Where do you draw the line between daring and foolhardiness, between calculated risk and egocentric destructiveness? How do you know when to be moderate and when to go for it?

Little risks, big risks, everyday risks, lifetime risks—you face them daily. Boldness in risk taking is an acquired skill, achieved over a period of time, during which you build self-confidence and wean your self of the need for self-defeating safety. In the words of an anonymous adage: "To lose in the name of moderation is no virtue. If you must lose, do it in the name of boldness."

The risk quotient is calculated this way:

$$S + V \div S = RQ$$

(Self-confidence plus vision divided by need for safety = risk quotient.)

When you have a risk to take, first check your self-confidence. "Can I do this?" Then check your vision. Look ahead to the results, see the benefit, and say, "If this turns out well I will gain - - - -." Finally, question your need for safety. "How far am I willing to go? What amount of danger or ridicule can I take? How safe do I need to be?" When you put these questions through your mental calculator, the answer will be your risk quotient. Look at any risk you have taken recently and run it through the equation. What was your risk quotient? Could you have gone a little further? Or were you stretched out to your limit?

Unlike rubber bands, we humans become stronger through constant stretching. If we stretch a rubber band too far, it will either break or weaken and lose its elasticity. When *we* stretch beyond what may seem to be our limits—when we take daring risks—we may not succeed, but we become stronger. We never go back to the same shape we were in previously.

Be willing to take the initiative. Set new standards and explore new horizons. Push your risk quotient to the maximum. Blaze a trail that makes a difference.

—Trail Blazer Number 1—The Sky's the Limit—

There were many women aviation pioneers, but the one that most captured the nation's heart, imagination, and headlines was Amelia Earhart. Millions of women all over the world had a new role model—a modest, completely feminine adventurer who challenged her own limits as well as those of everyone around her.

In 1920, when she was twenty-three years old, premed student Earhart took her first airplane ride in Glendale, California. Obviously the experience impressed her because two years later she was flying her own plane in air shows. In 1928, Earhart became the first woman to cross the Atlantic by air—but only as a passenger. She kept the log for a male pilot. Four years later, in 1932, she finally soloed from Newfoundland to Ireland, 2026 miles in just under fifteen hours.

She continued to set speed and distance records until in 1937 her plane disappeared during an attempt to fly around the world. A massive search found no trace of her plane. Rumors still persist that she is alive somewhere on a Pacific Island—proof of the power of her personality. It is hard to accept the fact that anyone so vital could fall from the sky like a mere mortal. In just five short years of fame, Earhart had shattered forever the image of the inferior, ineffectual female. She gave us a new image of the trail-blazer risk taker female leader.

—Trail Blazer Number 2—Cutting A New Edge—

Many risk takers have been called "crackpots" at some time. King Camp Gillette was one such man. He risked ridicule and changed the way we think about one of our most common tools. He had what everyone called a cockeyed invention. They said his idea was insane. He could find no investors. No mechanic would take on the project to make a prototype. Experienced cutlers, metal workers, and even experts at the Massachusetts Institute of Technology said it just couldn't be done: No one could make a razor sharp enough to give a good clean shave and cheap enough to be thrown away when it was dull. It took Gillette four years to produce the first disposable blade and six more to get it on the market. The first year Gillette sold fifty-one blades at $5 each. The second year, he sold 90,844 blades. Gillette changed the concept of shaving forever. In 1948 Gillette told *Advertising & Selling* magazine that, "If I had been a technically trained engineer, I would have quit."

SET THE EXAMPLE

If you accept the premise that leaders lead primarily by example, then you must send a strong message to your followers that says, "It is okay to make a mistake while learning to take risks." If you don't send that message, you will cripple them with the burden of perfection. When you can admit your own failures and mistakes and say things like, "Wow, I blew it, gang—I'm sorry, let's try again," then you build a bond between you and your followers.

The leader who must always be right sends the message that he has low self-esteem and low self-confidence. A leader who won't accept responsibility for mistakes and failures loses credibility. Some people view admitting failure as a weakness. They think that as leader they must be perfect. But the opposite is true. By not admitting their errors or failures, these leaders let followers believe it is not acceptable to make a mistake.

An employee of a medium-sized manufacturing company recently admitted, "Where I worked before, the boss was never wrong and there was so much pressure to be right that I was afraid to try. I played it safe. I avoided risks."

This kind of wasted energy, negative feeling, and poor morale is devastating to any organization.

—Admitting A Mistake Brought Great Results—

Jack Wahlig is chairman of the board of McGaldrey & Pullen, one of the nation's largest accounting and consulting firms. A 1987 Lou Harris client-perception poll ranked his company among the top four of the nation's largest fifteen CPA firms.

When Wahlig became managing partner in 1982, the firm had been growing steadily for more than fifty years. "It was a mature, stable firm," says Wahlig, "and the natural tendency was to say, 'If it ain't broke, don't fix it.'

"But we could sense that our marketplace and our business environment was changing. So we made a concerted effort to look into the future—to identify the type of firm our clients would like to be served by and the type of firm that would meet our people's needs. We identified what we were and what we thought we wanted to be; then we charged boldly off into the future.

"It didn't work. We were telling our people, 'Hey, here's what we want to be in the future, let's go there.' But we were asking people to take so many risks and make such rapid change that the organization just froze.

"Then, the unthinkable happened. We didn't make more money for a couple of years. You've got to understand that this is a firm of accountants who believe there's a passage in the Bible that says,

'Your income will be greater every year than it was the year before.'

"At any rate, the lack of income growth really tore the fabric of our organization. We knew we had to change to stay competitive in the late '80s and into the '90s, and we even had a pretty good idea of the direction of that change. But, due to the lack of short-term growth, many were plagued with doubts.

"Fall of 1985 was our make-it-or-break-it time. That summer, the board had sent me to visit all seventy offices to meet with all our people, to sit down and talk with each of our nearly 400 partners, to gather grass-roots input about what kind of a firm we wanted to be. I came back with what I thought was a pretty strong consensus about the firm's direction, and it called for massive change.

"Change of this magnitude was going to require risk takers. So, we reorganized and promoted some of the brightest young people into management. We realized we were facing nothing less than a fundamental shift in our world—from what had once been successful in the past to what we thought stood the best chance of success in the future. We had to make a culture shift.

"We diagrammed it this way:

What Was	What Will Be
We are a CPA firm	We are a CPA AND CONSULTING firm
We REACT to your requests	We INITIATE—We work with you to diagnose and meet your needs PROACTIVELY
We have these SERVICES	What are your NEEDS?
Our contact is the CFO	Our contact is the CEO (plus members of top management). We are CONFIDENT COUNSELORS
We do work on a PROJECT basis	We work with you in a DEVELOPMENTAL PROCESS

HISTORICAL SERVICES are our major fee producer	CONSULTING SERVICES will become a significant fee producer
One INDIVIDUAL has all the skills to serve a client	It will require a TEAM to best serve the client

"It was heady stuff, but once our young new management team, risk takers all, realized the magnitude of the change involved, they also realized that such massive change had to be made incrementally. We realized that people don't change very well if you put them outside their comfort zone. You've got to expand that comfort zone gradually.

"So we went back to the boards. We documented how our marketplace and our competitive environment mandated the culture shift. We identified the behaviors and attitudes that had to change and the skills we had to acquire.

"Now, instead of just telling people they had to change, we could show them a picture of the future—a road map to the destination. We began to think of what we were doing as providing a bridge between what our firm was and what it would become.

"As you can see, this bridge spans a pretty deep gorge. It's only made of old rope and a few irregular planks. It sags in the middle and sways from side to side with every step you take.

"Very few of our people were comfortable crossing that bridge. Only ten to fifteen percent would even try without coaxing.

"So we had to build support systems—safety nets and auxiliary ropes to reassure those with less tolerance for risk. We had to lead them, step by step, saying 'Come on. You won't fall. We're going to help you.'

"Just describing the goals, and keeping everybody focused on them, helped a lot. We set quantifiable benchmarks each year for the next three years and let everyone know whenever we passed major milestones. The progress being made by the high risk takers encouraged the low risk takers to push on.

"As a firm, we're almost to the center of the bridge now. Sure, that's where it sags and sways the most. But we're all pretty sure it'll hold our weight now—nobody's looking back anymore. We're all looking forward, holding on tightly and striding carefully toward what our firm will be.

"We might have done okay back on the other side of the gorge, but you can't be sure. What is becoming clear is that the bridge ropes are sturdier and the planks are getting stronger the closer we get to the future.

"Our people's jobs are more challenging and enjoyable. Our growth and profitability have improved, thus creating more opportunities for our people. And we have more satisfied clients, both in quantity and in the degree of their satisfaction.

"Ultimately, that's what all the risk taking was about—figuring out how to better handle challenges of the 1990s."

THE BENEFITS OF FEAR

It is healthy to have a bit of fear when taking a risk. To be totally fearless is to be ignorant. There are some things in this world that you *should be afraid of.*

Fear can affect you in several ways: It can neutralize you, paralyze you, or it can provide a tremendous rush of energy. Harness that power and it can be a tremendous force in expanding your risk-taking ability. Fear sharpens our perceptions, quickens reactions, and alerts the mind and senses.

There are several ways you can use fear to increase your ability as a risk taker.

TEST YOUR OWN LIMITS

Test your physical limits by taking up a new sport or getting into shape with a new fitness program.

Test your emotional limits by facing a family problem or an intensely personal problem that you have been avoiding.

Test your intellectual limits. It takes commitment to learn something new. Try studying a foreign language. Some experts predict that in the years ahead, effective leaders will need to speak three languages: English, Spanish, and computer. Try reading R. Buckminster Fuller's *Critical Path* or Will and Ariel Durant's ten volumes on civilization. They will test your intellectual limits.

LEARN FROM YOUR PAST

What risks have you taken in the past and how did they turn out? Regardless of your age, think back as far as possible to examine your risk-taking pattern. What was the first really risky thing you can remember doing? How did you feel about what was going on in your life at that time? Did the risk involve others, as in team sports or a school project? Or did you go it alone? How did it turn out? Can you learn anything from these experiences that might give you some clues to your willingness and ability to take risks?

MEASURE THE RISK

How do you decide when to take risks? You start by measuring the risk and weighing it against possible gains and losses. The more you know about the risk, the better prepared you are to take it.

Some techniques for risk analysis are:

1. *Identify the risk.* What is the real risk? This may seem like an easy question to answer, but people don't always know exactly what they are afraid of. Taking the risk apart, piece by piece, will give you a clearer picture of the real risk. A study by the University of Chicago Graduate School of Business found that how the problem is expressed has a profound effect on how the risk is perceived. They described the same problem to two different groups. The first

group was told that the project had an eighty percent chance of success. They voted to go ahead. The second group was told it had a twenty percent chance of failure. They turned thumbs down. Be sure that your unconscious bias isn't framing the question for you.

2. *Identify benefits and liabilities.* Make a list. The biggest payoff is usually opportunity. Risk and opportunity go hand in hand. "Reasons first, answers second" is the first rule of risk taking. If you have enough reasons to take the risk, you will find answers. If not, you won't. Those reasons are the benefits associated with the risk. Paul Moody, author of *Decision Making,* wrote, "Ultimately, the choice of any risk depends on the relative chance of a payoff or loss."

But self-interest isn't the only reason for taking risks. The most rewarding risks are those we take on behalf of others. These risks help you grow as a person and build loyalty among your followers. The term is "belling the cat"—to undertake a great risk for friends and associates. The expression comes from the old story in which a mouse suggested that someone should hang a bell around the neck of the cat so the mice would know when she was coming. The only problem was, "Who will bell the cat?"

————*The Woman Who Belled the Cat*————

Susan B. Anthony was born into a well-to-do Quaker family that produced strong-minded women. In the Victorian era, when ideal womanhood was supposed to resemble a flower both in appearance and intelligence, Anthony was a militant. By 1850 she was active in the movement to give property rights to women, and a group of advocates met frequently at her family home in Rochester, New York. In 1852 she was a delegate to a Sons of Temperance meeting in Albany. But when she arose to address the group, she was denied the platform because "the sisters were not invited there to speak but to listen and learn." This insult inspired Anthony and a group of suffragettes to form the Woman's State Temperance Society of New York.

Anthony spent her life campaigning for women's rights and Negro suffrage, as well as temperance. She was a radical abolitionist before the Civil War. Her campaign to include women in the Fourteenth Amendment was unsuccessful, but before her death in 1920, at the age of eighty-six, she saw the Nineteenth Amendment successfully ratified. Susan B. Anthony "belled the cat" for generations of women.

3. *Create a worst-case scenario.* To measure the possible impact of the risk, describe how bad the outcome could be. Create a worst-case scenario. This will not make you a pessimist. It will help you to be realistic about the possible outcome of the risk. Measuring outcomes gives you confidence. You know what could happen. You can decide what you would do if the worst occurred. Have a plan B in case plan A fails. Give yourself an escape hatch.

4. *Select role models.* Pick out others whose risk-taking skills and experience provide guidelines for your project. Role models help alleviate the fear of risk taking and demonstrate the limits you can hope to reach.

General John E. Long has inspired and motivated Army personnel for many years. He is a risk taker and a very strong example for his staff to follow. He is a role model to many of our best army men and women. When we were discussing the twelve leadership qualities he said that risk taking was one of the most important.

> *Risk taking [is important]* because it is part of my profession. It's an inescapable fact that leaders must be able to determine the best course of action for each situation. Sometimes that means breaking rules or flying in the face of an accepted way of doing things. Sometimes you have to force action if you believe you're right. The leader says, "I'm the leader. I will take total responsibility for this. You are going to help me. It's the right thing to do, even if it doesn't fit the model. We will take the risk.
>
> Because risks can offer greater rewards, they get things done faster. And they can be the most fun. I don't relate [risk taking] to my profession in war time, in the Army or Navy. All military leaders are committed to the risks of war. I'm not talking about that. What I am talking about are the everyday risks and decisions. If you followed every regulation, instruction, rule, tradition, and accepted procedure within the bureaucracy of the Army or the federal government, you might never take a risk. There would be nothing you could do really well.
>
> You must have the courage and ability to take that risk, to say, "I will do that because it's right, and I will take any consequences. I believe

that if we do it well, my superiors and subordinates will accept that it was the right thing to do."

Leaders have to do that. Every organization needs risk takers. Taking risks relieves tension and stress. Then you can go out and get things done, and that, in turn, lessens risks. I don't mean that you shouldn't have sound advice or make joint decisions or consult others. But you simply have to take risks.

5. *Create personal definitions.* How do you describe *risk* and *failure?* How do you describe their opposites, *safety* and *success?* It is important that your personal definitions of these words are as clear as possible. Otherwise outside forces—the expectations of others, of society, or circumstances—can yank you in all directions. You may find yourself judging risk taking by other people's standards.

As you forge your definitions, consider these relevant quotes:

> "Failure is not fatal. Failure should be our
> teacher, not our undertaker. It should challenge
> us to new heights of accomplishments, not pull
> us to new depths of despair. From honest
> failure can come valuable experience."
> —WILLIAM ARTHUR WARD

> "Try not to become a man of success, but
> rather try to become a man of value."
> —ALBERT EINSTEIN

Words are important in defining risk. As leaders we need to be especially careful when we use words like *winning, losing, failure,* and *success.* No one wins all the time and winning isn't always the goal. In our success-driven society it is easy to lose sight of the benefits of risk taking—like growth in difficult times, like new insights, like becoming more valuable because we have gone through the risk-taking process and learned some hard lessons. We need to use a vocabulary that gives balance to our risk-taking attitude.

HELPING OTHERS TAKE RISKS

Many people would like to take more risks, but they are afraid they will be criticized. They don't want to look foolish and stupid. Perhaps they don't know how to give themselves positive reinforcement or rewards for risk taking. They may even fear that if they do something well, they will be expected to do it again and they don't want the pressure. Helping these people take risks is a vital job of a leader. You need followers who will try something new rather than stick with the comfortable. You can help them be more receptive to risk taking when you give them encouragement.

When you were a baby getting ready to walk, your parents probably cheered you on. The first time you tried to take a step, you were standing there on your wobbly little legs, clutching a table leg or chair. Then you took that first step—and down you went, right on your face. Your parents didn't say, "Well, that's it, dummy! Walk today or crawl the rest of your life." Instead they helped you up and encouraged you to try again. There is a part inside of each of your followers that needs that same kind of encouragement. Some people may have more confidence about taking risks, but everyone needs support in the process.

TWO STRATEGIES TO SUPPORT RISK

There are two ways to help others take risks. The first is to cultivate their sense of "ownership"—in your organization, project, idea, or goal. Rodman L. Drake, CEO of Cresap, McCormick & Paget, says, "Participation and ownership are the factors that create risk taking; You cannot reorient a culture to risk taking if you have not also created the organizational elements to support this."

Ownership comes from taking part in decisions, being able to accept and succeed at delegated tasks, being part of a team, and being inspired by a leader who can communicate a mission and a sense of purpose.

The second way is to give others permission to make mistakes as they learn. Let people fail in small ways as they build the skill to win in big ways. Take perfection out of the equation of risk taking. We have all grown up with the expression, "Anything worth doing is worth doing well." Let's turn that around and say, "Anything worth doing is worth doing poorly at first, as long as you give it 100 percent effort.''

This is not an excuse for poor performance. It is a way to take the pressure off yourself and others while trying something for the first time. You learn by trying, making mistakes, and trying again. Followers that give 100 percent deserve solid encouragement, even when they make mistakes.

Cultivating ownership, eliminating the need for perfection, and allowing people to fail in order to learn are the bases for helping others to be risk takers who can make a difference.

GO FOR THE GOLD

A golden thread runs through the life of great leaders. It is the willingness to take risks. The world advances because some people are willing to take worthwhile risks. Followers want to be associated with these risk takers, the excitement they generate, their vision, and their concrete contributions. "Life is either a daring adventure," wrote Helen Keller, "or it is nothing."

Arthur M. Schlesinger, Jr., wrote in *The Decline of Heroes*, "If we are to survive, we must have ideas, vision, and courage. These things are rarely produced by committees. Everything that matters in our intellectual and moral life begins with an individual confronting his own mind and conscience in a room by himself."

Do you have the courage to confront yourself? Do you take risks and encourage initiative? If you do, you announce that you and your organization value action and contribution. You are telling people, "You don't have to be afraid to take risks and be creative here. We welcome your efforts."

Sailing the ship of leadership is risky. The waters are turbulent, the shore out of sight. The navigational tools for finding your way to a new destination include many skills and attitudes, but without risk taking you'll never find the new passage to your mission. With it, miracles can happen. Whole new worlds can be discovered.

American author and social critic Lillian Smith said, "To believe in something not yet proved and to underwrite it with our lives: it is the only way we can leave the future open."

Your future will be bright if you have the courage to take risks that make the difference between success and failure in fulfilling your mission that matters.

A LEADER IS A DECISION MAKER
Releasing Potential

"Decision is the spark that ignites action.
Until a decision is made, nothing happens."
—WILFRED A. PETERSON

For weeks past they had been producing forecasts and charts almost hourly. Now their predictions were not favorable. Weather over the Channel and France would worsen steadily, bringing low ceilings, which would cancel out air activity, also high winds and rough seas, which would hinder beach landings. If the weather continued bad, the whole operation might have to be set back for weeks until the tides and moon again would be right for landings.

For only one day in any month would be really suitable. The moon must be full—to let airborne troops operate effectively, to give our fighter-cover and anti-aircraft a chance to keep the Luftwaffe away, and to make difficult the operation of the Nazis' light-shy but very effective E-boats. The tide had to be at low ebb three hours before dawn to expose underwater obstacles for demolition and make the beach right for H-Hour landing.

On Sunday evening, June 4, the Prime Minister [Churchill] and [General] Smuts—later joined by General de Gaulle—dropped in on Eisenhower and sat for a long time discussing aspects of the momentous decision that was Eisenhower's alone to make.

The High Commanders and their Chiefs of Staff decided to hold one last conference at 4:30 A.M. on Monday, June 5, for the final word. The weather was a gamble, General Eisenhower admitted, but it was up to himself and the High Command to rise to it or turn away.

When each of the High Commanders had given their opinions, General Eisenhower smiled, but only briefly. This was the moment the people of the Allied nations had sweated and toiled for. Looking down the table at his commanders, his face more serious than it ever has been or is likely to be again, he said quietly, "Okay, let 'er rip."

Those around the table rose quickly and hurried from the room to set the operation in motion. Ike called after them, "Good luck."

He was the last to emerge from the room. He was walking heavily, and those who saw him remarked later that each of the eight stars on his shoulders seemed to weigh a ton.*

*Excerpted with permission from: "The Great Invasion" by Allan A. Michie, Reader's Digest August 1944. Copyright © 1944 by The Reader's Digest Assn., Inc.

Deciding to risk sending thousands to their deaths is something few of us can begin to contemplate. Let's hope that none of us ever has to face a decision of that magnitude. General Eisenhower was indeed a leader. One of his strongest leadership qualities was his ability to make decisions. While you may not hold the lives of thousands in your hands, you can and do affect people with your decisions. If your leadership is to make a difference, you must be able to decide.

THE IMPORTANCE OF DECISION MAKING

One of the most important tools you have is the ability to release potential and make something happen. Courageous decision making does that. Author-philosopher Wilfred A. Peterson says, "Decision is the courageous facing of issues, knowing that if they are not faced, problems will remain forever unanswered."

When we are indecisive we forfeit everyone's future and we waste time, energy, talent, money, and opportunity. The most effective leaders are vitally aware of this and would rather make a wrong decision than none at all.

Peterson also wrote, "Decision often concentrates resolve. Decision awakens the spirit in man. It gives him a goal, a purpose, a reason for being alive. Once a major decision is made, carrying it out becomes a matter of will and courage and dedication. The great decision comes first, the great work follows.''

Deciding to decide can be the hardest part of the process. Going through the intellectual and emotional gymnastics of deciding is not always easy. It can keep you up all night, weighing the pros and cons. It can take your energy and attention from other important matters. It can be a difficult, stress-filled time. But getting caught in the trap of indecision is just as bad, because *not* deciding is a decision. When you delay, time, fate, and circumstance will decide for you, and you may not like the outcome.

PROCRASTINATION

"One of these days is none of these days."
HENRY GEORGE BOHN

"Procrastination is the art of keeping up with yesterday."
DON MARQUIS

As a leader you don't have the luxury of procrastination. It is death on the time-payment plan. You must have the courage to risk a wrong decision rather than make no decision at all. Few decisions are so critical that they can not be corrected. Beware when you hear:

- "Let's put it in writing before we decide."
- "We should test it first."
- "A committee should study it."
- "Let's give it more thought."
- "Let's all sleep on it."
- "Let's shelve it for the time being."

These could be legitimate suggestions. On the other hand, they may be excuses to avoid deciding. It may be time for you to take over and *decide!*

FIRE FIGHTING

How often have you found yourself saying, "We could have avoided this if . . ." How often have you heard, "But *I* thought we decided that . . ." If you live and operate in a continual crisis environment of fire fighting, it is partly because of the lack of timely, clear decisions. Many crisis situations can be prevented by adequate, accurate planning. While every disaster can't be prevented, many can be minimized with prompt, unclouded decisions.

A Life of Decisions

He has been called the Evangelist of our time. Even in a time of scandalous television evangelism, cynicism, and loss of religious belief, Billy Graham is considered Mr. Clean. His life has been exemplary, his message never compromised. Early in his ministry he made a decision never to put himself in a position where he could be tempted. He knew that youth was easily enticed, so he removed himself from all allurements. His decision to live beyond reproach does not make him a Goody Two-shoes. It makes him a deeply committed man who tries to live as close to the message he preaches as possible.

Graham has preached to over 100 million people around the world in his Campaigns, in which he asks people to make an immediate spiritual *decision* to accept Jesus Christ as Lord and Savior. His message is simple: "Decide for Christ." His radio show is the "Hour of Decision." His monthly magazine is entitled *Decisions.*

Billy Graham is regularly on the list of the Ten Most Admired Men In the World. Whether you agree with his approach to religion or his religion itself, it is hard to argue that Billy Graham has made some very wise decisions. He is a powerful leader who has a powerful message: *Decide!*

MISSED OPPORTUNITIES

Standing in the shadow of decision is regret—regret over things not done, needs not met, opportunities missed, and experiences bypassed. You cannot afford to say, "I should have," or "If only I had." Your ability and willingness to make decisions is often the difference between mediocrity and greatness. It is the difference between making a difference and just having good intentions. You cannot sacrifice a decision to regret—be it real or anticipated.

Some of life's greatest decisions are made quietly, without fanfare. As Agnes De Mille wrote, "No trumpets sound when the important decisions of life are made." But to take advantage of opportunities you must be willing and able to make decisions.

VALUES AND STYLE

We all go into the decision-making process with different values and concerns, such as return on investment, quality of work, customer acceptance, effect on competition, and social responsibility. Your *attitude*—which is a reflection of your values—about decision making is as important as your *aptitude*. So it is necessary to stop occasionally and survey your values and your style of decision making.

Consider these questions about your decision-making attitude (values) and aptitude (style).

- Do I consider how my people will be affected by my decision?
- How important are the opinions of others in my decision making?
- Will those whose advice is taken feel positive? If so, about what?
- What about those who were not asked for input? How will they feel?
- Am I clear about what action has to be taken and who has to take it? Do I think about whether or not they are able?
- Have I drawn from a wide range of opinions and information to make this decision?
- What are my assumptions about my decision-making style?
- Am I flexible enough to change my decision-making style?

Robert Tannenbaum and Warren H. Schmidt wrote a classic essay describing leadership decision-making patterns and various common behaviors. At one extreme are the leaders who feel that decision making is entirely their own responsibility. They don't want others to share in the process. At the other extreme are those who always seek opinions, consensus, and shared responsibility with followers.

Leadership styles cover the full range of extremes and everything in between. There is no right or wrong, but you must be clear in letting followers know your style. A leader who makes all the decisions but claims they are group decisions lacks credibility and honesty. If you make decisions without consulting others, tell them. If the group is expected to participate, lay down ground rules, format, and expectations. Whatever you do, be honest about your decision-making style. Your honesty will eliminate a lot of confusion, miscommunication, and incongruency.

If you build a reputation for action and set an example of decisiveness, you give people the courage to make their own decisions. Some leaders think that decisions should be made at the lowest competent level of an organization. This is effective delegation and helps others develop their decision-making abilities. You build trust when you let others decide.

Raising Money For The Gym

A church group I belonged to was working on raising money to build a gymnasium for the youth of the congregation. We went to the pastor with many suggestions on how to fund the project. We asked him to decide which he felt was best. In his wisdom he told us, "These are all good ideas, but I think the decision should be yours. After all, you are going to be the ones doing the work. Let me know which you choose." With that he ushered a very surprised group of people out the front door of the rectory.

None of us had ever been involved in such a large fund-raising project before and we did not know where to begin. Our committee chair suggested that we break up into groups and come back a week later with ideas. Then the entire committee could decide where to begin.

In that week's time our group met twice to discuss how to approach the rather awesome task. In the first meeting we soon realized that we did not have enough information to make intelligent suggestions. We decided to assign each member the job of contacting two organizations who had done fund-raising in our community and to inquire how they had done it. By the second meeting we were almost overloaded with ideas and concepts. Each person had become creative and had taken the initiative to go beyond what was expected.

When the entire group met again we discovered that each group had taken the same kind of initiative that we had. By having to make the decision ourselves, our pastor had helped us all tap our potential. We brought him a clear, well-defined list of ideas and he approved them all. The gym was built and I remember how we felt on the day it opened when the kids came running in. We each took pride in a job well done, but most importantly we knew that our decisions had truly made a difference.

Whatever decision-making style you choose, Peter Drucker, in *The Effective Executive,* says that leaders "take a strategic approach rather than just problem solving. They are interested in impact rather than technique, in soundness rather than cleverness."

TEN PREPARING-TO-DECIDE QUESTIONS

One of the most important steps in decision making is preparing to decide. To be effective, you need information and insight into the decision to be made. For simple daily decisions this checklist can be done mentally in just a few minutes. For major decisions you will need paper, pencil, and a quiet place to concentrate.

1. *Is the objective of the decision clearly defined?* Make your objectives as clear as possible or you may be led astray. Solicit facts and opinions. Be prepared to deal with emotions as well as logic. Solicit feelings and thoughts about both the decision and the implementation of the decision. It is important to know how people "feel" because the emotional appeal of a solution may outweigh its practical shortcomings.

Test alternatives, seek disagreement, have a devil's advocate. Do whatever it takes to clearly determine the goal of the decision. You may find the issue is so large that you need to analyze it in parts, or that the entire decision cannot be made at once. Look at the *why,* not just the *what* of the decision. Get beyond what may be just a symptom of a deeper problem.

> "Thinking you knew something was a sure way
> to blind yourself. It was not growing up that
> slowly applied brakes to learning, but an
> accumulation of 'things I know.' "
> FRANK HERBERT,
> *Chapter House Dune*

To sharpen your thinking, turn off what you "know" and ask yourself, is any of my thinking biased? Learning to think in terms of degree is important, because rarely are things 100 percent clearcut. "What" is perceived depends on "who" is doing the perceiving. When you go through the process of questioning your thinking, you'll be surprised, as humorist Will Rogers said, at "how much you know that ain't so."

2. *Who should make the decision?* Are you really the person who should be deciding? An important quality of leadership is to accept responsibility for making a final decision. Coach Tom Landry told me that he felt being a decision maker was high on the list of important leadership qualities, "because in, my business, it's essential to be a decision maker. You have to make decisions all the time—whether a rookie player is good enough to play in the NFL, or whether a veteran player will continue to be a contributor to your team. When the coaching staff prepares a game plan each week, the head coach must have the final decision as to what ideas will be used. Finally, the head coach must make the critical decisions that affect the outcome of the game itself."

If you are the head coach of your team, you should make decisions. But if you have any doubt about making the decision by yourself, think about why you feel others might need to be involved. What if you neglect to delegate part or all of the decisions? What are the ramifications if you decide alone?

Consider the situation of a new executive who wanted to change a corporate culture that had been in place for a long time:

> People here don't like to make clear, individual decisions because if they do, then they're held accountable. They prefer to form a committee, talk around things, and spread the risk. If the decision works out well, fine. If not, then heads don't roll.
>
> But I want them to become more responsible and accountable. We need to get this company moving, and each person must now make their own decisions. Assuming responsibility for those decisions will make them responsible for how the problems are solved. It will give them more "ownership" of the outcome and that's one of my goals.

By not delegating part or all of the decision, you may be sending a message that allows others to avoid responsibility or accountability. There are, of course, times when you must take full responsibility and make the decision. But it is always worthwhile to stop and consider the question: "Who should make this decision?"

3. *What time factors are involved?* Do you have deadlines or

time frames you must work within? Are they reasonable? Paul Moody, author of *Decision Making*, refers to the time/cost tradeoff: The cost of gathering data increases with the time spent. At some point, it becomes too costly to delay making the decision. You need to consider this early on in your preparations to deciding.

When immediate decisions need to be made and there is no time for intensive research, fact-finding, or committee-meeting, you must just flip a coin. You decide immediately without the luxury of going through a checklist, because the crisis requires action *now!*

When that happens, you reach down inside for courage. Use all of your past decision-making experience and go with your instincts. Quick decisions affect relationships, both up and down the scale of responsibility. After a quick decision it may be necessary to devote some time and energy to unruffling the feathers of those people who feel they should have been consulted. If you don't, you run the risk of alienating people who may be important in a future situation. So consider your time frames and always give yourself more time than you need. It always takes longer than you think!

4. *Do you have enough information to make the decision?* Leadership decisions, particularly important ones, usually consist of a set of smaller decisions made over a period of time. At the beginning of the decision-making process, reflect on your personal experience so you can profit from previous successes and failures. Get all the facts. Pay attention to detail. This is no time to let those important little items fall through the cracks. They may come back later and destroy or damage your decision.

Have a healthy distrust of the communication chain. The higher your position, the easier it is to depend solely on others to supply the important information you need. Get all, or at least part, of your information in person. In *In Search of Excellence*, Peters and Waterman describe this as MBWA: Management By Walking Around. In decision making there is also LBAA: Leadership By Asking Around.

Stop and think before deciding, but remember Peters's and Waterman's finding that American companies suffer from overanalyzing. At some point you must stop the paralysis of analysis and take action. To become good decision makers, we must learn *how* to think, not just *what* to think. Leaders' actions must come from thinking proactively, not reactively.

Do it now. Get the product out, spend the money, get more volunteers, solve the problem—get on with it! Realize decision making is never "perfect." You will never have *all* the information you need.

An excellent example of a difficult proactive decision was laid out for us in the tragic drama of the Tylenol poisoning cases. James Burke, CEO of Johnson & Johnson, had to make several incredibly hard decisions. He had to decide how to protect us from the menace of tampering. He had to decide whether or not to withdraw Tylenol completely from the market or come up with a new product name. He could not wait for a long process of examination. He had to decide with what information he had. He appeared on television and told us about his decisions. Few CEOs have been faced with such difficult social and business decisions. But James Burke came through with flying colors on both challenges. He set an excellent example of decisiveness and forthrightness. What would you have done in his place? Whom would you have consulted? Could you have acted as quickly as James Burke did?

The Do It Now Kids

Dr. Helen Caldicott, an antinuclear activist, was speaking to an assembly of high school students at the Milton Academy in Massachusetts. As the youngsters were listening attentively, two of them got up and said, "We need more education on nuclear arms. We need to do something." That statement was the beginning of an amazing story of proactive teenagers, who are taking a stand and making a difference.

A small group of students and faculty began discussing what they could do about the lack of education on nuclear arms. They conceived a huge plan. They would conduct a petition drive among 25,515 American high schools. The petition would call for a television show to be broadcast nationally. It would be called The National Forum. Its purpose—to discuss and better educate people on nuclear arms.

This do it now group of activist teenage leaders and faculty went to work. They received endorsement for their campaign from Presidents Carter and Ford. They raised $40,000 to fund their enterprise. They wrote to high school principals and student council presidents in all fifty states. They collected 320,000 signatures from more than 1,000 high schools from every state and Puerto Rico.

5. *Have you done a force-field analysis?* Paul Moody, in his book *Decision Making,* says that every situation is controlled by the forces (people, circumstances, policies, etc.) acting upon it. What forces will be acting in favor of your decision? What forces will be acting against your decision? By identifying these, you make better decisions and can better plan the course of action to be taken once the decision is made.

It can be relatively simple to list the "for" and "against" forces on a sheet of paper, then rank them in order, so you can spot priorities. When you've listed them in order, consider these things:

- What specialists will you need, either to make the decision or for the follow-through?
- Have you considered all feasible courses of action and weighed them in terms of resources needed, resources available, and probable outcomes?
- Have you prepared for and made provisions for contingencies?
- Have you made the follow-up plan that deals with the forces working with or against the decision as simple as possible?

Looking at your force-field analysis, consider delaying the decision. Leaders must know when not to decide. Knowing when to delay is as important as knowing when to decide. Do not be unduly pressured by others to take action when you have a gut reaction that says "wait." One of the most difficult parts of General Eisenhower's critical decision was waiting until just the right moment to launch the invasion. He must have had nerves of steel to sit patiently and wait for the weather to clear.

—————————*Jesus Knew When to Wait*—————————

A woman was brought before Jesus by a mob and flung at his feet. "The law says she should be stoned," they challenged him. "What do *you* say?" Obviously the crowd was questioning his leadership. Jesus was a well-known "trouble-maker" who had been disputing laws that went back to the time of Moses. What would he do now?

Jesus could have decided to lecture his audience about the benefits of compassion. Or he could have decided to place himself between the woman and the stones as they were hurled as an example of being his brother's keeper. He could have even decided to respect the ancient law and let her be killed.

Rather than making a hasty decision he sat quietly thinking. After some time he began to write something in the dirt at his feet (an excellent example, by the way, of using a delaying tactic while you assess a critical situation and let your creativity take over). And what he decided to do clearly demonstrated at least five other qualities of leadership: sensitivity, ethics, risk taking, courage, and the ability to communicate. He said, "Let him who is without sin cast the first stone." That decision in the form of a statement was worth waiting for.

6. *What risks are involved in this decision?* Risk taking is covered in another chapter, but it bears mentioning here. Are you willing to accept the responsibility for the potential payoffs or losses in terms of human relations, finances, time, effort, or commitment? Payoffs and losses are clearly intertwined in every decision.

There have been some risky decisions in recent years that proved beneficial to millions of people. They started as small decisions that took on a life of their own. One of the best examples of a person who made a risky decision was that of Rosa Parks. She is called the "mother of the civil rights movement." One day in 1955, while riding home from work on a bus in Montgomery, Alabama, she refused to get up and give her seat to a white man. She was simply too tired and *decided* that "enough is enough." After the bus company had her arrested, a local minister by the name of Martin Luther King, Jr., led a bus boycott that spearheaded the whole civil rights struggle of the 1960s. Mrs. Parks is living testimony that people can make a significant impact on society with small, but risky, decisions.

7. *Is your action plan ready to be implemented?* Your action plan requires no less careful thought than the decision itself. If you rush ahead without thinking through the various steps, you'll likely stub your toe. Making a decision before you are ready to act upon it is a waste of time, energy, and money. Be sure that you have at least moderate resources ready to carry out your action plan once the decision is made.

Ask the questions that will give you the information needed for your plan:

- Who must do what to or for whom?
- How soon?
- How much?
- How long will it take?
- If it doesn't work, what is Plan B?

Once you have the answers to the questions, you can then outline the steps to be taken for implementation.

8. *How will you track the outcome of your decision?* Feedback is vital to your decision-making process. You need to be receptive to positive *or* negative feedback. Experience is a good teacher only when the data you get from your actions is interpreted. Your data can be written out in statistical form or it can be obtained by brainstorming with the people affected by or involved in the decision. A flow chart that controls and tracks the flow of information can be a valuable tool in analyzing feedback.

9. *Plan to review.* There are four key reasons why you need to review your decisions and the process by which you made them.

First, the environment in which your decision is made is not permanent. Time and circumstances change things, and the leader cannot afford to operate from outdated decisions.

Second, the decision may not have the results you expected. It may have unforeseen consequences and therefore need refinement.

Third, as Rosabeth Moss Kanter wrote, "The more important the decision, the less precise the tools to deal with it . . . and the longer it will take before anyone knows if it was right."

The fourth key reason for reviewing your decision is that it provides an opportunity for you to consult those affected by the decision. If you are the central decision maker you will build loyalty and team spirit when those involved are consulted.

10. *Consider the consequences.* Morgan W. McCall and Robert E. Kaplan wrote in *Whatever It Takes: Decision Makers at Work:*

> There are at least three types of consequences of decisions. First are the effects of decision on the formation of precedent, both for the organization and the individual manager; second are the impacts on relationships resulting from participation in or exclusion from the decision cycle; and third, decision-making success or failure becomes a track record.

Let's look at each type of consequence.

Decisions accumulate; problems tend to recur. Therefore, in

time, satisfactory decisions set precedents for guiding future action. In short, the organization moves toward making the handling of problems routine. Strategic direction is often the result of a series of decisions made over time, each of which influences the succeeding decision.

If you want to make a difference and influence future decisions in a positive way, you need to remember that any decision has multiple consequences. Evaluating a decision depends on which consequences are being considered and by whom. Not everyone will interpret the decision in the same light, and not everyone will value them in the same way. Your decision will affect people and their relationships to each other.

There can be a considerable time lag between decisions and results, so the people who have to live with the results may not be the same people who made the decision. New leaders must face the results of their predecessor's programs, good or bad. The public tends to hold political incumbents responsible for the results of decisions made by their predecessors. At the national level, this is particularly challenging for a new president in his first year or two in office. It takes time to institute programs, and he may be cleaning up or benefiting from the previous administration. Your decisions will be your legacy to those who follow you.

Those are the ten preparing-to-decide questions. They will help you make a difference, regardless of your current level of leadership. It will be worth the investment of time and energy to give them serious consideration when faced with your next decision.

GUIDEPOSTS FOR COMMITTEES AND GROUP DECISIONS

"Nothing is ever accomplished by a committee
unless it consists of three members—one of
whom happens to be sick and the other absent.
—HENDRIK VAN LOON

Decision: "What a man makes when he can't
find anybody to serve on a committee."
—FLETCHER KNEBEL

We have all heard the numerous jokes about committees and group decisions. Unfortunately, like many social comments, they are true. As leaders, we recognize that individuals, not committees, have vision, courage, and insight. You don't want your people to use committees or groups as excuses to hedge their bets and diminish their responsibilities. You want them to be courageous in both decision making and implementation. Studies show that the pride and social attitudes of workers who have a part in decision making have improved productivity. It is worthwhile to include them in group-decision making because they have more "ownership" in the results.

J. Donald Waters wrote, "To many people, unfortunately, discussion is virtually a substitute for activity. They imagine that to say a thing is tantamount to accomplishment. The effective leader knows, of course, that an encyclopedia of good ideas is no substitute for even the least of them actually put into practice."

If you need to have a group involved, here are some simple guide posts to help:

- *Keep the group small.* When it comes to decision making small is "better." If the group is large, create subgroups.
- *Have your facts ready.* The group decision will be shaped by what the group accepts as truth, so be prepared with accurate facts and information. Do your homework.
- *Encourage the free exchange of ideas and feelings.* Be sure that everyone participates in the discussion of issues and the assignment of tasks. This improves productivity.
- *Seek opinions.* Don't go in with preconceived ideas about what you think is "best." Stay open. As Frank Herbert wrote in *Chapter House Dune:* "The more people on the committee, the more preconceptions applied to the problem."
- *Keep clarifying.* Keep sight of the objective so you don't create new problems?
- *Keep summarizing.* You will keep everyone on track if you summarize as you go. Summarize both the decision you make and your plans for implementation.
- *Use the right people.* Include group members that are appropriate to the decision: otherwise you risk wasting time, money, and resources. If you include the wrong people, you will put

them in an uncomfortable position because they will not be equipped to participate in the decision-making process. That is a sure way to foster bet-hedging and the unwillingness to be responsible and accountable.

Not everyone has the same level of decision-making skills. You must measure the readiness of your followers carefully before asking them to make decisions. When they measure up, be sure to give credit where credit is due. It is easy to overrate the importance of a decision while underrating the work that follows.

VALUES AND DECISIONS

Making a difference is not something that just happens; someone, somewhere has to make a decision based on certain value judgments. There are corporate leaders who have decided to spearhead some creative and wonderful programs that benefit individuals, cities, and the country as a whole. Their corporations are giving back to a society that has given them so much opportunity.

American Express decided to do their part. In November 1986, they collected three cents for every restaurant meal charged on their credit cards in New York City restaurants. The money was then donated to Citymeals-on-Wheels, a program that delivers food to the elderly and homebound. Amex collected more than 1.6 million three-penny chit donations.

Searle and Company, drug manufactures in Skokie, Illinois, wanted to make a difference. They knew that many of the heart drugs they produced were very expensive but vital to the survival of the patient. The doctors that prescribed the drugs said, "I'm sitting across from my patient and I just know they won't fill the prescription because they can't afford it." The board of directors said, "We have to do something." They decided to design a program to help alleviate the financial burden of the poorer heart patient. When a doctor prescribes one of their heart drugs to a poor person, that patient can then receive the drug free of charge, for life if necessary. In 1988 Searle provided 100,000 of these prescriptions.

——CEOs Who Decided To Do It Personally——

Many top CEOs find it easy to pick up the check book and convince themselves that they are doing their part. While it is very important to make financial contributions, there is something special that happens when you decide to make a difference in person. Here are two executives who understand the power of the example they set and the responsibility they have to their fellow citizens.

Walter Falk is president of Metropolitan Mortgage of Miami, Florida. Over thirty years ago he decided to make a difference in the Jewish community in the Miami area. He wanted to demonstrate his religious belief in helping others. He found his vehicle in the Greater Miami Jewish Federation. Walter is a founder of their home for the aged, which serves indigent elderly people of the Jewish faith. The Federation is doing pioneering research into Alzheimer's disease and is a forerunner of advance care for senior citizens. Walter says, "To make a difference giving money is not enough; you have to give your time."

Former secretary of the Treasury, William E. Simon, is now chairman of the Wesray Corporation in Morristown, New Jersey. With a personal worth of over $150 million he could easily leave his impact to his check book. But he doesn't. He has a mission that matters. He regularly counsels teenage drug addicts and runaways at New York's Covenant House, a shelter in Times Square. Even on Christmas he is there. His family joins him in serving food and hope to the young. When they hear him talk about the opportunities in America, when he tells them that they can change their lives—they listen and many believe. Why? Because they want to. They want someone to have faith in them and give them reason to hope. When Bill Simon talks to them they don't see the multimillionaire; they see someone who cares about them and who wants to make a difference in their lives.

These CEOs came down from their towers of power and became everyday leaders. They decided to serve others on a very personal basis. Could you make a decision to serve as they did? Could you set an example of caring for your people?

JUDGMENT AND DECISIONS

The ability to make decisions is important, but it is a quality that must be balanced by informed judgment. President Harry Truman made one of the hardest decisions of modern history, whether or not to drop the atomic bomb. He was famous for the sign on his desk, "The Buck Stops Here." Yet before the buck stopped, he solicited a wide variety of opinions. He was a good listener but reserved final judgment on what to do.

Successful leaders seek advice from all corners but still need objectivity to make a decision. They possess the will to decide and the will to live with their decisions, regardless of the results. They hold themselves fully accountable for the consequences of their own decisions. They exercise decisiveness informed by balanced judgment.

Every decision is a judgment—a choice between alternatives. One of the payoffs of being a decision maker is that each decision helps to develop good judgment.

An old mountaineer from West Virginia was celebrated for his wisdom. "Uncle Zed," a young man asked him, "how did you get so wise?"

"Weren't hard," said the old man. "I've got good judgment. Good judgment comes from experience, and experience—well, that comes from making bad judgments."

Leaders have always made decisions and plans that affect future generations. Remember that people depend on a leader to make wise decisions, to be willing to face difficult issues, and to prepare for the future. They want a leader who serves them by making decisions that will release their creativity, solve problems, and help them build their organization.

Have the courage to make long-term decisions so that you can make a difference to larger numbers of people. Don't settle for a Band-Aid quick fix. Prepare for the future. Keep your mental landscape clear. Step back and view your decisions from an imaginary mountain top. Keep your feet firmly planted in the valley of day-to-day life. Decide to make a difference.

A LEADER USES POWER WISELY

Mastering Influence

"We thought because we had power, we had wisdom."
—STEPHEN VINCENT BENET,
Litany for Dictatorships

How wise are you in using power to make a difference?

A POWER QUIZ

1. You are the head of an office and the final authority. One of your managers is using her power unwisely, in an autocratic manner. The other employees are becoming demotivated and rebellious. How do you use your power to solve this problem?

2. You are chairperson of a volunteer committee in your community. Your business and personal reputation will be enhanced or hurt by how you handle the project of the committee. One of your committee members feels he should have been given your position. He is directly assaulting and undermining your authority through gossip and innuendo; he is setting people against each other and refusing to cooperate. You can't fire him because it is a volunteer group. This community-service project is highly visible and important. You are expected to get people to work together and get the task done. What do you do? How do you use your power wisely to solve the problem?

3. You are CEO of your company. There is an opening on the executive staff and you know exactly the employee who would do

the best job. You submit the name to the board of directors, but they make excuses, hinting that they would prefer someone of the opposite sex, or of a different race, religion, nationality, or educational background. What do you do? How far do you push? Can you reach a compromise without compromising your ethics?

To make a difference you'll be called upon to use power in many different situations. The more you know about power, the more effective you'll be in using this elusive leadership quality called power.

WHAT IS POWER?

The thesaurus gives us these synonyms for power: direct authority, influence, strength, hierarchy, rank, superiority, clout, prestige, sway, mastery, and persuasion. We recognize power when we see it in action. We know a powerful person when we are with them, and we know that we need power to lead. Yet the exact nature of power can be elusive. Prime Minister Margaret Thatcher noted that "being powerful is like being a lady. If you have to tell people that you are, you aren't."

Power is the prime mover of people and events. It is inherent in leadership. You can not lead effectively without it. The leaders who have made the greatest contribution used power wisely.

─────────*A Powerful Mission*─────────

Phil Sokolof of Omaha, Nebraska, is irritating a lot of people and causing a lot of trouble, trouble, that is, to food manufacturers who use coconut and palm oils known as "tropicals" in their foods.

Twenty-three years ago Phil had a heart attack. His cholesterol level was over 300! His doctor told him if he didn't cut the cholesterol in his diet he would probably have another heart attack and could die. Phil changed his eating habits immediately. He began studying and found that 315 percent of the fat consumed in the average American diet is cholesterol. There are many foods that cause the body to manufacture cholesterol and he could not affect them all. So he decided to concentrate his efforts on tropicals.

Phil makes his living as the owner of a successful metal-manufacturing plant; eliminating tropicals became his personal mission. He began writing letters to companies that use the oils. He took out ads in newspapers and magazines telling the public about the danger to their health. He put the pressure on by making telephone calls to food manufacturers and asking what they planned to do about the problem. He spent over $2 million of his personal income on his campaign. He became a one-man crusade—and it worked! His mission that matters has received national publicity and has begun to change the use of tropicals in our foods. Phil Sokolof understands the power of public pressure and persistence. His leadership has affected an issue never before confronted.

While eliminating these oils would not eliminate cholesterol and heart disease, Phil took a large problem and concentrated on the part he *could* affect.

WISDOM AND POWER

Your judicious use of power takes wisdom and restraint. Lao-tzu wrote in 600 B.C.:

> Water is fluid, soft, and yielding. But water will
> wear away rock, which is rigid and cannot
> yield. As a rule, whatever is fluid, soft, and
> yielding will overcome whatever is rigid and
> hard. This is another paradox: what is
> soft is strong.

If you are going to lead you'll need to be strong but gentle, strong enough to tackle the tough issues and gentle enough to keep the solutions humane. You'll need to be demanding enough to challenge others not to settle for easy answers and patient enough to know that all progress takes longer than you think. When Harvey Mackay described the jockey Willie Shoemaker in his book *Swim with the Sharks,* he summed up the essence of power and leadership: "He's the best in the business because he has the lightest touch on the reins. They say the horse never knows he's there—unless he's needed."

Do you have a "light touch on the reins?" Do you use power so well your followers only feel it when needed? Cultivating the wisdom to use power wisely takes time and energy, but the benefits are well worth the effort.

USING POWER WISELY: THE BENEFITS

With power you can accomplish a lot, without it very little. You can possess the other eleven leadership qualities and still not succeed unless you understand power.

Power well used is like strong glue. It holds the other qualities together. It energizes people and resources. When you use power well, you show people that you can be trusted. They know you are sensitive and won't take advantage of them. When followers trust you, you'll gain their loyalty and respect.

EMPOWERING OTHERS

Shared power can achieve great results. When you empower others they have more confidence, they are more efficient. They will be better team members. They will gain self-reliance from their power and may become big thinkers with a mission of their own. Your unselfish example sets important precedents and makes a significant difference in how your people develop as future leaders.

In her book *The Change Masters,* Rosabeth Moss Kanter points out that when you share power there are three "basic commodities" that allow people to take action:

> *"Information* (data, technical knowledge, political intelligence, expertise); *resources* (funds, materials, space, time); and *support* (endorsement, backing, approval, legitimacy)."

What a wonderful feeling it is to know that the information you share enables others to maximize their potential. Shared resources encourage their creativity and innovation. And most importantly your support causes them to take action.

Contrary to what some people think, sharing power increases your power. There are those who covet power. They think that giving power away diminishes their own. If you are a wise leader you understand that the people you empower will help you reach your goals to make a difference. The more you empower others, the bigger you become in their eyes. There is a law in the universe that says, power shared, returns. Power withheld, diminishes.

──────The Power to Escape Slavery──────

Leontine T. C. Kelly understands the value of shared power. As a bishop in The United Methodist Church she is the first black woman bishop of a major American religious denomination. She remembers how as a child in school she struggled with the contradiction of slave owners withholding the power of freedom from the slaves, while teaching them Christianity. Understanding their abuse of power and religious hypocrisy was difficult for her.

One day as she and a group of children were playing in her home in Cincinnati they discovered that the basement of her house had been a station in the underground railway used by slaves to escape to freedom. It went from her house to the basement of the church. When Leontine asked her father about the railway he said, "The real witness of Christianity was in the cellar."

The lesson of the railway and her father's words were not wasted on her young mind. Today as she preaches the Gospel she says, "For me, the crux of the Gospel message is the way we share power. I don't have to exert power in such a way that other people feel they are less than who they are because of who I am."

Bishop Kelly's sensitivity to the use of power, and her understanding that shared power (regardless of race) empowers everyone, is a binding force in her congregation.

POWER OF PERSUASION

Wise leaders like Bishop Kelly don't shrink from power or seek it unnecessarily. They know that having clout often intimidates others, so they use their power carefully to promote cooperation and mutual respect. A key to wise use of power is: "The higher up you go, the more gently down you reach." You may at some point be forced to use your power to correct a situation. You may have to bring the hammer down, but if you do, wrap it in velvet.

Never underestimate your power. People react to your actions and words. Their performance is greatly affected by how you use power. Eisenhower said: "You do not lead by hitting people over the head. That's assault." Indira Gandhi said, "You cannot shake hands with a clenched fist." Truly powerful leaders "pull rank" only in emergencies. Their normal method of leading is persuasion. They lead by mutual respect and cooperation. They use their power to direct and help others to achieve their full potential to make a difference.

ABUSE OF POWER

When you abuse power you force others to cultivate defense systems. This is very destructive because when people are constantly defending themselves they are not free to be creative or to expand their talents. They're not able to achieve self-fulfillment. They won't take risks or make decisions for fear of your retribution.

I interviewed a group of people working for a large advertising firm whose president misused his power.

Question: Why do you all fear your boss?

Answer: (accompanied by snide chuckles) Are you kidding, we've all felt the sting when he thinks we are trying to take away some of his power. He wants to be the only hero with the clients.

Question: Can you give me an example?

Answer: Sure. We had a new client who asked us to come up with ideas for the first stage of a campaign. We needed extra information and called the client. Well, that did it. Our boss was furious that we didn't run everything by him first. He asked us to do the job, and when we did he didn't trust us to do it.

Question: Have you tried to talk to him about how you feel?

Answer: Yes, but he says it's his company and he expects us to do it his way, period. He refuses to give us the trust and freedom to do what we were hired to do. He is afraid we'll somehow diminish him in the eyes of the clients and take way his power.

Question: So what are you going to do?

Answer: (with nervous body language) Several of us have had it. We have feelers out. We'll leave as soon as we have some place to go.

Question: What about the rest of you?

Answer: We don't know what we'll do. The money is good here, but it's tough working for a tyrant.

I later found out that the turnover was extremely high in this firm. The president was known as a very creative person and had an excellent reputation with clients, so he attracted talented newcomers to the industry. However, very few stayed long. Their enthusiasm, creativity, and career goals were crushed under the egocentric need of the abusive president.

He used his power to establish and control a closed system in which his people had little input or choice. This kind of abusive power fosters hostile, introverted subordinates who begrudge even a minimum effort. Leaders who make a difference are confident of their power and have no need to take out their insecurities, anger, or unhappiness on their subordinates.

QUASI-POWER

Sometimes we are mistaken in believing that wealthy or famous people automatically have leadership qualities. Today fame and status come and go like the changing winds. True personal power must be judged on a longer track record. Today's headliner can be tomorrow's has-been. The much-lauded financial whiz or political genius can pass quickly into oblivion, never having understood or acquired personal power.

We all know people in leadership positions who should not be there—people who, according to the Peter Principle, have been promoted to their "highest level of incompetency." These people possess *quasi-power*, the outward appearance of power without the reality.

How do you distinguish quasi-power from real power? The characteristics are relatively easy to spot. People with quasi-power don't admit mistakes, rarely apologize, and would never ask forgiveness. They are frequently rude and discourteous. It is written: "Rudeness is a little person's imitation of power." Quasi-power taken to the extreme enters the kingdom of the power pigs.

POWER PIGS

Power pigs and their piglets are everywhere. They flourish in every sector of our society. They go to the trough of avarice, subversion, dominance, greed, ego, arrogance, self-interest, and force. They thrive on yielding raw power.

Power pigs exist for one purpose and one purpose only—to accumulate and wield as much raw power as possible. Intoxicated and obsessed with their own importance, they attract unsuspecting piglet followers, because they usually possess all the trappings of power. It's important to be able to recognize a power pig when you encounter one, otherwise you might get trapped. If you can see them for what they are—self-serving egomaniacs who are abusing power—you'll be able to protect yourself from their seduction.

"I love raw power!"

They have an abundance of the five deadly power-pig traits. To be sure you have not become a power pig, review the traits and see where you stand.

FIVE DEADLY POWER-PIG TRAITS
- Arrogance—Overvaluing yourself, having a condescending attitude toward others.
- Vanity—Intensely craving admiration and applause; having excessive pride in yourself and your accomplishments.
- Disloyalty—Violating the trust of your followers; being unfaithful to your values.
- Intemperance—Immoderately or excessively indulging your appetites and passions.
- Presumption—Assuming superiority and privilege where it is not warranted.

Check yourself periodically to be sure that you never slip into these weak, destructive behaviors of power pigdom.

We've seen power pigs come and go. They almost always destroy themselves. Unfortunately they also destroy many piglets who, with a model of power wisely used, might make a difference.

When we watch quasi-power and power pigs in action it may seem unfair that these people receive the rewards of real power without having any. It's important to understand that these people have insatiable appetites and these rewards never satisfy them. They are not fulfilled as true servant-leaders are.

Power can bring out the very best and the very worst in us. It's up to each of us to stand guard at the door of our desire for power. "Power tends to corrupt," Lord Acton noted, "and absolute power corrupts absolutely." Frank Herbert, author of *Chapter House Dune,* wrote: "It is not that power corrupts, but that it is magnetic to the corruptible. . . . We should grant power over our affairs only to those who are reluctant to hold it, and then only under conditions that increase the reluctance."

PERSONAL POWER AND POSITION POWER

There are two kinds of power: the power that comes from holding a particular position and the power that comes from within. Personal power is the real "horse power" in making a difference. It's the magnet that draws people to you. It is the energizer that gets things done.

If you ever have to choose between the two, always choose personal power, because no matter what happens, if you have personal power, you'll be able to handle change and difficulty. Making a difference is not always easy. As we've discussed in other chapters, you can run into all sorts of difficulties. You can encounter road block after road block as you try to change something or overcome established systems. Your personal power will outlast position power every time.

When people only have position power and situations change, they are often left out in the cold because they had little personal strength to call upon. "How the mighty have fallen" is a constant human theme since biblical times. It's been the subject of Greek tragedies and Hollywood potboilers alike. Position power is minimally effective without personal power. However the combination of these two powers can be a mighty force that accomplishes great things.

Unexpected Position Power

Some people who are thrust unexpectedly into positions of power develop remarkable personal power. George VI of Britain was a younger brother, shy and a stutterer, who never expected to be king. Yet when his dashing older brother, Edward VIII, abdicated to marry Mrs. Wallis Simpson, he suddenly found himself on the throne. His quiet, confident leadership through World War II was an inspiration to all Britons.

When President Roosevelt died and Harry Truman suddenly became president, he had to lead a nation fighting a world at war. No other president had ever been in his position. His personal power showed in many ways, not the least of which was his ability to gather information and make difficult decisions. He boldly accepted responsibility and the sign on his desk became famous. It read "The Buck Stops Here." His calm nature and uninhibited way of expressing his opinions was a stabilizing force to a grieving nation.

When Dan White assassinated Mayor George Moscone and Supervisor Harvey Milk, San Francisco was nearly torn apart. Diane Feinstein was head of the board of supervisors and automatically became mayor. Her communication skills and sensitivity to the explosive situation helped to quiet the passions of San Francisco's diverse group of citizens. Feinstein's eleven years as mayor were imprinted with her ability to use her personal power wisely.

Both Truman and Feinstein earned the respect of their constituencies. As Irvin Federman noted, "Your job gives you authority—your behavior earns you respect."

VOLUNTEERISM AND POWER

Using your personal power in a volunteer group is one of the biggest challenges you will ever encounter. You don't have the same power base as you would if the volunteers were employees. Volunteers have very different motivations and priorities than their paid counterparts. Your powers of persuasion, communications, motivation, and direction must be highly developed. People volunteer because they are excited or passionate about something.

Since they do not receive pay for their effort they want to feel that they are making a difference. They want recognition for their time, effort, and energy. As a leader your willingness and ability to share your personal power is critical to the success of the group.

Your sensitivity to the use or abuse of power will never be tested more than in a volunteer organization.

INFORMAL POWER

Machiavelli wrote, "It is not titles that honor men, but men who honor titles." There are people who have no imposing title or formal authority, yet they command great personal power. They have an aura about them that attracts, excites, and directs others in ways that go beyond any job description. You know people who do the same thing on a smaller scale. They entice others to their causes through sheer personal power.

————Eleanor Roosevelt————

One woman who used informal power to make a difference was Eleanor Roosevelt, wife of President Franklin D. Roosevelt. She quietly exercised her enormous personal power as a persistent and an indefatigable fighter for causes. Mrs. Roosevelt was a one-woman war on poverty during the Depression. She visited coal mines, hospitals, and squatters' camps all over the nation. She traveled around the world, speaking with kings, presidents, and the destitute with equal enthusiasm and compassion. During her husband's presidency, she acted as unofficial ambassador to the world and devil's advocate to his conscience and the conscience of a nation. Despite painful shyness, she used her personal power to champion the poor and powerless.

After her husband's death, with no official capacity, Eleanor Roosevelt continued to be a spokesperson for dozens of causes. When President Truman appointed her to a new League of Nations, Henry Cabot Lodge gave her what was considered an inconsequential committee concerned with human rights. Lodge did not realize that he gave Roosevelt a perfect platform from which to launch a worldwide fight for fairness and quality.

She was ignored and minimized. Every place she turned she encountered barriers that would have discouraged a less passionate person. She cajoled and compromised. She pleaded and demanded. Everyone she came into contact with felt the power of her convictions. Her work on the "Bill of Human Rights" for the newly formed United Nations came to fruition after four years of arduous effort. To date, this document has been used as the basis for the constitutions of sixty nations! Eleanor Roosevelt's personal power made a major difference in our world.

It is our job, both as leaders and followers, to learn to distinguish between personal power and position power. We must take the time necessary to build personal power so that when our position changes, we are still leading by example and using our power wisely.

Life After The White House

There have been many of our presidents and First Ladies who have used their power after leaving the White House to champion worthy causes.

When Gerald Ford left the White House he undertook many projects. During the 1989 presidential election, he teamed up with Jimmy Carter and wrote a white paper on the most pressing issues facing the new president. They agreed that they would go to visit the new president and present their white paper. If the Democrats won, Carter would make the presentation; if the Republicans won, Ford would be the spokesperson. When asked about his leadership style, Ford said: "I have spent my whole life trying to pull people together. I've always tried to create a team environment, whether it was in athletics, on board a ship in the navy, or in politics. I think that's the only way to get the job done."

Mrs. Ford has been called the "Unsinkable Betty Ford." Her courage and determination have been an inspiration to the American people. She survived breast cancer and conquered alcoholism and drug dependency. She has had arthritis since age forty-six. Since leaving the White House she has used her personal power to advance the causes most dear to her. She raised $6.9 million dollars to fund the Betty Ford Center, an eighty-bed hospital for recovery from chemical dependency. She is an honorary trustee for the National Arthritis Foundation, and speaks for the Susan G. Komen Foundation in Dallas to raise funds promoting early detection and prevention of breast cancer.

President and Mrs. Ford did not leave their personal power in the White House, they continue to lead and make a difference.

President and Mrs. Carter have always been leaders and progressive thinkers. Since leaving the White House, they have continued to use their power wisely.

When Jimmy and Rosalynn Carter went home to Plains, Georgia, leaving behind life in the world spotlight, it was not an easy adjustment. It tested their relationship. They had to decide, "What now?" The strength of their commitment to each other and to the plight of people around the world soon found them right back in the thick of things.

The Carters wanted to use their skills and resources to continue to work on issues that were important to them and would make an appreciable difference in the world. In 1982, they founded the Carter Center in Atlanta, Georgia, a nonpartisan public-policy institution that seeks to improve the quality of life of people in this country and around the world.

Through The Carter Center, President Carter continues his global peace-making efforts, active intervention in human rights cases, and interest in national and international health issues. The center is comprised of a consortium of nonprofit organizations, and combines academic research under the auspices of Emory University with outreach or demonstration programs. President Carter also shares his insight and experience with the next generation through his role as Distinguished Professor at Emory.

Today under the Carters' leadership, Carter Center staff are teaching the hungry in Africa to feed themselves. They are making significant progress in the worldwide immunization of children and the eradication of such debilitating diseases as guinea worm and river blindness. Working with Soviet scholars and officials, they are helping us better understand the changes taking place in that country. And over the last six years, some of the world's most respected leaders and thinkers have gathered at the center to address conflict and other issues in the Middle East, Latin America, and other countries.

"I have never been afraid of taking a chance or facing the possibility of defeat, and I've always done the best I could," says President Carter. "It is important not to accept unnecessary limits in our lives. The most severe limit is most often the one we place on ourselves by not striving for greatness. It is irresponsible not to attempt to use our talent, ability, and opportunities to benefit others."

As First Lady, Mrs. Carter chaired the President's Commission on Mental Health, created by her husband. She has continued this vital work and each year hosts The Rosalynn Carter Symposia on Mental Health Policy, a series of meetings that brings together mental-health experts from all over the country to study mental-health issues and determine how to provide better care for those suffering from mental and emotional illnesses.

In addition to her mental-health advocacy, Mrs. Carter is involved in human rights, peace, and women's issues at the Carter Center, and with other organizations such as The Friendship Force, an international nonprofit citizens exchange program.

President and Mrs. Carter also share and support many common interests. They are intimately involved in Habitat for Humanity, a grass-roots nonprofit organization that builds homes for the needy in the United States and underdeveloped countries. While at home in Plains, they both teach Sunday School at Maranatha Baptist Church.

In their spare time, the Carters have also managed to write five books, including one they wrote together. Jimmy and Rosalynn Carter are among the finest examples of the wise use of power.

KEYS TO ENHANCE YOUR POWER

Lao-tzu wrote:

> The best of all leaders is the one who helps
> people so that eventually they don't need him.
> Then comes the one they love and admire.
> Then comes the one they fear. The worst is the
> one who lets people push him around. Where
> there is no trust, people will act in bad faith.
> The best leader doesn't say much, but what he
> says carries weight. When he is finished with
> his work, the people say, "It happened
> naturally."

Let's consider some ways to enhance our ability to use power wisely so that our followers can say, "It happened naturally."

TEACH OTHERS TO USE POWER

When you teach others to use power wisely, you'll transform them into partners. In *Change Masters,* Rosabeth Moss Kanter identified the power skills you can teach others to master. They are: problem definition, coalition building, and mobilization.

We have seen many examples of people attacking the wrong problem. They can't see situations clearly, so the solutions are flawed and the results don't work. Teach people to go through the Who What When Where and Why process of evaluating problems. Review the dilemma from an intellectual as well as an emotional standpoint. Clearly defining problems for our followers gives them the power to come to correct decisions and solutions.

When you teach team-building skills to help people establish a coalition or a network of support, you give them one of the major qualities of leadership. In chapter 10, "A Leader is A Team Builder," you will find many ways to enhance skills for soliciting and maximizing a coalition of people.

The third part of teaching power is showing how to mobilize others. Motivating and inspiring people to action will enable others to tap the energy and desire to make a difference. You will have created a partnership between you and your followers because you were willing to teach and share power.

———*The Hugh O'Brian Story—HOBY*———

Actor Hugh O'Brian's films and television series have brought him fame and celebrity status. But when you ask him what is the most rewarding part of his life, he will quickly tell you it has been his work with young people. Hugh has taught leadership skills to thousands of young people from around the world. He could have coveted his famed and fortune; instead he shared his power and created a vast partnership of commitment to American ideals.

In 1958 Hugh visited Dr. Albert Schweitzer in Africa. During one of their conversations Dr. Schweitzer made a statement that would change Hugh's life and the lives of thousands of young people around the world. Schweitzer said, "The most important thing in education is to make young people think for themselves."

Hugh returned from the trip motivated by Dr. Schweitzer's words and decided to put them into action. He founded HOBY—Hugh

O'Brian Youth Foundation. He understood the power of his celebrity status and knew that he could use it to make a difference. His name unlocked doors and people paid attention to what he had to say. His excitement and commitment to the concept of youth leadership attracted many other important people. He solicited donations to support his fledgling foundation. His dream began to come true.

From 1958 to 1967 HOBY's leadership seminars took place in Los Angeles for high school sophomores from California. In 1968 Hugh expanded the scope of the foundation to include national and international participation. Today young people come from all fifty states, the District of Columbia and twenty-one other countries. First they are chosen from their high schools to participate in state HOBY seminars, and then one boy and one girl from each local seminar is selected to attend the International program held each summer at absolutely no cost to participating high schools or students. HOBY takes great pride in the fact that all funding is provided by the private sector: corporations, foundations and individuals. HOBY is unique in that Hugh has never asked for, nor will he accept, government support.

The purpose statement of the foundation expresses Hugh's vision and the power of his commitment.

> In the belief that America's greatest resource is its youth, Hugh O'Brian established the Foundation in 1958. Its purpose is to seek out, recognize, and reward leadership potential in high school sophomores. HOBY's format for its programs is basically simple: Bring together a select group of high school sophomores with demonstrated leadership qualities with a group of distinguished leaders in business, education, government and the professions, and let the two interact. Through annual all-expenses-paid seminars at the state and international levels, these tenth-graders get a realistic look at what makes the "American Incentive System" tick, thus better enabling them to think for themselves. The give-and-take, question-and-answer format shows students that they are important, that their thoughts and actions can make a difference, and that learning how to think can be just as important as what you think.

Hugh O'Brian's power has built teams of people benefiting youth around the world.

DECREASE "POWER TOWERS"

Power towers are the trappings of authority that separate the powerful from the masses. They can be squadrons of secretaries and bodyguards, chauffeured limousines with smoke-glass windows, private elevators to the executive suite, or massive, elevated forbidding desks floating in seas of ankle-deep carpeting.

If you wish to remove the power towers that separate you from those you want to lead, look at the physical design of your working area. If it interferes with open communication, redesign it with less emphasis on symbols of power and separation. That doesn't necessarily mean that you put your desk in the center of the work area with free access for every employee and customer, although some executives do this.

Doug Tomkins, president of Esprit de Corps, has a tiny glassed-in office in the center of the clothing firm's headquarters. Anyone can look in and drop in at any time. He has not diminished his power by decreasing the power-tower syndrome. He feels it gives him access to the vital working area of the company.

GET OUT WHERE THE PEOPLE ARE

We've discussed participative leadership style in other chapters, but it deserves mentioning again here. The wisest leader is one who takes the time to communicate directly with people. It's not uncommon for people to be hesitant about approaching their leader. Be sure that people are not intimidated or punished when they come to you with honest opinions or criticisms. Insecure leaders hide behind their titles, office doors, financial successes, or autocratic demeanors. Be accessible to your followers and go where they are to make sure you understand their problems and challenges.

Accessibility Supported Her Power

One woman who was always available to her people was Lillian Lynch of AT&T. She had an open-door policy and she managed by walking around. By the time she retired she had moved from the bottom ranks of operator service to one of the highest positions ever held by a female at AT&T. She was vice president of Operator Service for a ten-state region. She had enormous power, and her reputation for kindness and wisdom held her in the highest esteem of all her staff. Lillian's followers would, as the saying goes, "walk on fire" for her.

Lillian's managers would laugh at the pandemonium she would cause when visiting the various operator offices. When she walked in the door, all the operators would immediately begin talking to her and seeking her attention. She would stop at each individual operator's position and have a few minutes of personal conversation. Everyone was always amazed that she remembered names and special bits of information. She would ask each operator about a family member or a vacation experience they had. Her accessibility was one of the most important factors in her considerable personal power.

COMPROMISE

A good leader's self-worth does not depend on winning every time. Secure leaders can compromise because they know that they do not have the only correct answer or solution to any problem. They recognize the multiple benefits of compromising—greater self-esteem and support among followers as well as future cooperation.

During Dwight Eisenhower's presidency compromise was a key factor in getting things done. Sam Rayburn, Speaker of the House, and Lyndon Johnson, Majority Leader of the Senate, were both very powerful Democrats. Eisenhower knew that to win the support of these two leaders he would need to compromise on certain issues. To implement his policies it would be foolhardy to confront these two power houses openly. Instead he would invite them to his private quarters at the White House where the three of them would sit "sipping whiskey," discussing and compromising on important issues that would affect all their constituents.

SHARE KNOWLEDGE

Knowledge shared is knowledge multiplied.

When you use your power to support and encourage knowledge sharing in your organization, you show people that what they are doing is valuable. By sharing knowledge you empower your followers to act on their own. Shared knowledge enables people to take a risk to expand an idea and to venture to a new horizon.

———Helping Ourselves Means Education———

Encouragement and education can make a difference in someone's life. They did in the life of Carol Sasaki.

When Carol Sasaki stood in the White House to receive the 1986 Volunteer Action Award from President Ronald Reagan she felt like she was in a dream.

As a child Carol was sexually abused and when she was eighteen she was brutally raped. As a result she had no self-esteem, no hope for the future, and she attempted suicide. She managed to survive and met a man with whom she had a child. When he deserted her she was an unmarried woman with a new son to support. She had so little education that she could find only minimum-wage jobs. After taxes and childcare there wasn't enough to live on. So she was stuck on welfare. Carol says, "I wanted an education badly, but I had no idea how to get one. It just seemed as if my chance in life had passed me by."

By accident Carol met a woman administrator of a community college who understood her dilemma; she too had been a welfare mother. She encouraged Carol to investigate grants and assistance programs that would allow her to get the education she wanted so badly. In 1983 Carol enrolled at Washington State University, and she was on her way. At age thirty she received her bachelor's degree in liberal arts.

If this were a story of courage and perseverance we could stop here and be inspired by what Carol achieved. But what makes her different, what makes her a leader who has made a difference, is the reason President Ronald Reagan gave her the Volunteer Action Award in 1986.

Early in her pursuit of a college education Carol realized that if she could share what she'd learned about financing an education she could help other welfare mothers. Soon she was holding informal workshops in her home. Carol called her group HOME—Helping Ourselves Means Education. By the time she stood on the White House steps, HOME had grown like wildfire. Now, over 20,000 people from every state in the Union are learning how to get off welfare and to have control over their life. Carol says, "Welfare mothers are not lazy, they're stuck." She says HOME is a sorority for poor people. Carol made a difference because she shared her knowledge and communicated hope to others.

BE AVAILABLE FOR COMMUNICATION AND CRITICISM

When you isolate yourself, the flow of information and criticism to you dwindles. Maintaining communication and information gathering should be a major task for a leader. Leaders can't grow if they allow their power to isolate them. Nor can they grow if they are surrounded by "yes" people.

Isolation can come about because of followers' overwhelming affection for a leader. This affection blinds the followers and they can no longer see where a leader needs to grow. Their good intentions can create a false sense of security in a leader. The entire organization may hold the leader in such reverence that any criticism seems to question the validity of the group and its members. This lovely kind of incest may sound like utopia to someone seeking power: everyone cheering you on, loving everything you do, modeling themselves after you, building team spirit and ownership. But this kind of myopia can be the very thing that diminishes the effectiveness of the leader. Everyone needs constant monitoring to stay on top.

There are still many old-time organizations where the power position is treated as something holy, where leaders think that they are exempt from being criticized, and that any opposition is an attack on the institution itself. Basically such quasi-leaders are saying, "I know it all." This is one of the quickest ways to start the slide from power. Followers who are afraid to offer opinions about situations that affect them profoundly may react unconstructively out of self-defense or they might even seek vengeance. They may do nothing to help the oppressive leader, or they may quietly derail plans and actions in retaliation.

It takes a very secure leader to accept criticism and make use of it while in a position of power. The dividends for enduring this discomfort are immeasurable. Be sure to solicit criticism and ask for frequent appraisals of your skills and attitudes. Don't be a leader who is afraid of critics. You need open communications for the personal power to retain your position power.

SEEK OPPOSITES

As a leader you must guard against surrounding yourself with too many people similar to yourself. We all like to be around people who resemble us, who have similar beliefs and prejudices. This is comfortable and reassuring. But a real leader avoids this trap and seeks contrast.

Look for people who have the talent you need, not just those who duplicate yours. Having too many supporters with similar strengths and weakness diminishes creativity and innovation. You want people who will give you new perspectives rather than mirror images of your own vision.

DEVELOPING SUCCESSORS

In *Leadership Life Cycle*, John P. Kotter wrote: "In early career, aspiring leaders are challenged to establish power bases. Appropriate use of power characterizes successful mid-career years. The transfer of power to prepared successors marks the successful end of a leader's career."

In the final stage of leadership, wise leaders use power to develop successors, people who could take their place. This is rarely easy. It is like allowing a child to grow up and leave home. As a parent, you stand at the door and wave goodbye, hoping and praying that what you have given them will get them through the obstacle course of life. True servant-leaders give up position power with the same hope: that they have done the best they could and now their replacement will carry on with courage and commitment. If the retiring leader has used power wisely, the chances of a successful succession are great.

The wisdom to use your power well doesn't come overnight. You'll make mistakes and probably have to mend a few fences from time to time. There is no such thing as perfect use of power. People and circumstances require different kinds of power. As you grow you'll learn to be flexible. The most important thing to remember is to be fair, ethical, and judicious in exercising your power.

THE RESPONSIBILITY OF POWER

When you accept the responsibility of power you will quickly find that it is a delicate instrument. Like the sharpest surgical knife, it can destroy and cause pain or heal and create new opportunity.

Peter Drucker wrote, "The leader sees leadership as responsibility rather than rank and privilege." When we view power in terms of developing others, the wisest among us says, "My greatest responsibility is to use all my energy to fulfill the potential of those who follow."

───────────────*The Gray Panthers*───────────────

When Maggie Kuhn, age sixty-five, lost her job because of mandatory retirement she was angry and frustrated. She, like hundreds of thousands of other people, had been cast out by a system that doesn't value experience and maturity. She refused to retire and declared war on ageism, sexism, racism, and all other "isms."

She got together with five others who had suffered a similar indignity. "We decided we needed some kind of collective project just to keep us alive after we retired and we chose the Vietnam War." They formed the Gray Panthers, now a national organization with branches in twenty-four states, representing over 60,000 people.

Since its beginning the Panthers has been a grass-roots movement. They fight for the rights of the elderly and the young, for health care, Medicare, and Social Security. Maggie believes that the young and old should work and be together. The young should help protect the world they have been given and the elderly should work for a better world into which the young will some day come. Her message is simple: "A healthy community is one in which the elderly protect, care for, love and assist the younger ones to provide continuity and hope." Maggie Kuhn and the leaders of the Panthers take their responsibility seriously. They are making a difference by helping those who follow fulfill their potential.

HUMILITY OR ARROGANCE?

Humility is your most powerful asset as a leader. Arrogance is the most destructive quality a leader can have. President Dwight Eisenhower's farewell address to the nation on January 17, 1961, was perhaps his most eloquent message to the American people. Eisenhower talked about the dangers of the military-industrial complex becoming too powerful. He cautioned us to beware of meeting the needs of the moment by mortgaging the future. And he spoke of power and humility:

> America's leadership and prestige depends, not merely upon our unmatched material progress, but on how we use our power in the interest of world peace and human betterment. . . . Any failure traceable to arrogance or [to] lack of comprehension or readiness to sacrifice would inflict upon us grievous hurt both at home and abroad.

In recent years, American arrogance has hit an all-time high. This is not to our benefit at home or abroad. The "ugly American" is not a myth. There have been times when we have behaved badly in our relations with our world partners. If you have traveled or done business abroad, you understand that we have not always been at our best in dealing with other countries. Even if we were the very best at everything we do, that would be even more reason for humility. Anyone with more talent, resources, and power has a tremendous responsibility not to abuse those assets.

Today's leaders must be keenly aware that our dominance in the areas of commerce, military force, and wealth can no longer be taken for granted. The patterns of world power are shifting and we are no longer king of the hill in all things. We won't get into a political and economic analysis of why this is so. The point is not to lay "blame," but to remind us all that, as leaders of at least one person (ourselves), we have a great responsibility to be humble in our use of power, both personal and positional.

Courtesy and humility are essential for the effective use of power. Being gracious elevates a powerful leader to the level of a statesman.

I had the privilege of meeting and spending some time with Helmut Schmidt, former chancellor of West Germany. We were discussing the use of power and he said, "When it comes to leading people or nations, sensitivity is paramount." He pointed out that truly powerful people are humbled by the knowledge of their power.

Only the insecure and unsure require the trappings and constant demonstrations of a demagogue. Truly powerful people have no need to proclaim or flaunt their power. They know that their responsibility is to be a people grower—to believe in the worth of others, to inspire the best in them, and to encourage them to make a difference.

PART OF THE PROBLEM OR PART OF THE SOLUTION

When it comes to the wise use of power, you are either part of the solution or part of the problem. There is no in between. If power is abused and you do nothing, you are part of the problem. If you abuse power yourself, you are certainly part of the problem.

If you and I are to survive and prosper in the next century, we must decide whether to be a passive part of our nation's problems or to take an active role in the solutions. The power of free men and women will be greatly affected by the examples leaders set in solving the complex problems we face. We need a new group of heroes to inspire us to be better than we are, to encourage us to make a difference. Heroes have inspired us to advance and perform far beyond our limited expectations. Arthur M. Schlesinger, Jr., wrote in *The Decline of Heroes:* "A free society cannot get along without heroes, because they are the most vivid means of exhibiting the power of free men."

THE POWER OF SERVICE

Of all the examples we set as leaders, perhaps the wise use of power has the most obvious impact. If the basis of your desire for power is one of service, then your leadership acquires an aura of dignity. Your charisma is increased a thousand fold.

The majority of a good leader's time is spent on people problems and issues. Here your power is essential to direct and empower others to act. Whether you are a young developing leader, an established leader, or a major public figure, the examples you set will have enormous impact on those who watch and make judgments about how they should live and act. The person who understands the "power of power" will do the most menial job when necessary, and since they demonstrate that willingness, they rarely have to do it. When our motives for power are to serve, our followers respond quite differently from when we seek power for self-aggrandizement. True power can be lonely, the responsibilities heavy, and the pleasures few. But when we understand the wisdom of losing ourselves in service to others, we no longer need to seek power. It comes to us automatically.

HAVE THE COURAGE TO EVALUATE YOURSELF

If you are to deserve authority and master the act of influencing others, you will need a regular session of self-evaluation to keep you on track. These four self-evaluation questions will help:

- Why do you want power?
- What will you do with it?
- What will it mean to you once you have it?
- Who will you serve with your power?

When you have personal and position power in balance, when you are humble about your power, and when you are willing to empower others, you can make a difference. Grass-roots leaders and famous leaders alike know that power and greatness are not a goal but a by-product of learning how to serve.

A LEADER COMMUNICATES EFFECTIVELY

Forging Productive Relationships

"What you are speaks so loudly
I cannot hear what you say."
—RALPH WALDO EMERSON

"They that govern the most make the least noise."
—JOHN SELDEN

It is beginning to get dark. You can hear the evening rush-hour traffic overhead. The band of people living under the overpass are getting ready for another night. Some have a few personal possessions to guard, others arrange newspapers and cardboard boxes for shelter. A homeless woman searches through her bag for part of a sandwich she found that morning. A drug addict lies on the ground, his eyes glassy and blank. His right hand is cut and badly needs attention, but he is oblivious.

A young man with broad shoulders and neatly cut black hair leans over him and examines the injured hand. He reaches into his medicine bag and takes out a disinfectant, puts some on a bandage and wraps it around the injured hand. He walks among the others, stopping to talk. He checks an eye here, an ear there. The people trust him. He's been there several times before.

Cuban-born Pedro "Joe" Greer lives in Miami. His father was the first member of his family to finish high school. He became a doctor and treated the poor. Young Joe learned about helping the needy at an early age—he, too, would become a doctor like his father.

When Joe took the Hippocratic oath he vowed to treat people who were ill. Today, he doesn't reserve his skills for those who can pay or those who have insurance. He says the inner city is like a third-world nation. The public health system is not working. Joe says, "I want to help the homeless; they don't have the breaks I did."

In the beginning he served food to gain the confidence of those who needed help. The power of his message spread. Joe soon had over two hundred volunteers, sixty physicians, fifty nurses and medical students helping him.

He found ways to make a bigger impact on the problems of the homeless. He wrote a course for medical students on treating the poor and homeless. He built a seven-room clinic where he treats anyone who comes. He solicited free drug samples from pharmaceutical companies.

As Joe looks at the Freedom Tower, one block from his clinic, he says, "There is something wrong when I have to step over people in the streets. In this society we have so much and we have to give back."

Dr. Joe Greer's actions speak louder than his words. But when he does talk about the clinic or the people he treats, he communicates a powerful and poignant message. Joe says, "A nation should not be judged by its wealth, but by how it treats its poor."

Making a difference requires effective communication. A good communicator has skill (aptitude) and a philosophy (attitude). Your skill can be learned and polished, but *what* you communicate and *why* grows out of your mission, your sensitivity, courage, ethics, and commitment—all the qualities that make you the leader you wish to be.

In this chapter we will consider the *power* of communication; how it affects relationships and how you can use it to enhance your leadership and serve your followers so they can help you make a difference. We'll also look at the less obvious, more subtle elements of communication that play such an important role in forging productive relationships.

GOOD COMMUNICATION SKILLS PAY OFF

The dictionary defines communication as "fostering understanding." Obviously that is an accurate definition, but to lead and make a difference you'll need to take communication skills to the next level: turning understanding into action. If you are a leader who can communicate, you will be able to:

* Motivate and inspire people to take action
* Build cooperation and trust
* Maintain focus on the issues
* Resolve conflict
* Provide accurate information
* Prevent communication breakdowns

We've all been frustrated in knowing that we have not really gotten our message across. We've seen our words and actions misinterpreted; we've seen them cause hard feelings or problems. There is no such thing as perfect communication. But as leaders we must strive to perfect our communication skills to avoid misunderstanding. As a leader you must be able to clear away extraneous issues and get to core ideas. The better we communicate, the better off we are. The better we communicate, the better chance we have to make a difference.

─────────*A Builder of Communicators*─────────

In 1912 the YWCA on 125th Street in New York City refused to risk paying a $2-a-night teacher's salary to an unknown.

Young Dale Carnegie was out of a job and wanted to try teaching communications skills. He was not easily put off. He explained, "People want to be able to stand on their feet and say a few words at a business meeting without fainting from fright."

He arranged to work on a profit-sharing basis with the Y. Fees paid would go first to the expenses for printed matter and postage. Any profit over that would be shared between the Y and Carnegie.

Dale Carnegie soon found that he had tapped an important need. Within a few months he was teaching at YMCAs in New York, Philadelphia, Baltimore, and Wilmington.

In 1944 he began licensing his courses and today more than 140,000 students a year attend Dale Carnegie courses. His classes have helped strengthen the communications skills of many leaders including, Chrysler Chairman Lee Iacocca, Labor Secretary William E. Brock and Mary Kay Ash, founder of Mary Kay Cosmetics.

BECOME A WORDSMITH

"Wordsmith!" Isn't that an intriguing term? It conjures up images of a person who can mold and shape words to influence others. A wordsmith is a person who has the power of language. To be called a wordsmith could be the highest praise any communicator could receive.

The history books are filled with women and men who have influenced history with their words. They led the fight for causes and issues that have shaped our world today. As children, we all learned the words Patrick Henry spoke before the Virginia Convention of Delegates on March 23, 1775. The question was independence from England. The Revolutionary War had begun and Henry said, "Is life so dear, or peace so sweet, as to be purchased at the price of chains and slavery? Forbid it! Almighty God! I know not what course others may take, but as for me, *give me liberty or give me death!*"

The power of an eloquent phrase is immeasurable. When we hear "I have a dream" or "Ask not what your country can do for you," we know immediately that Martin Luther King, Jr., and President John F. Kennedy spoke these words. They are indelibly etched in history.

You may not be addressing delegates considering independence, fighting for civil rights, or making an inaugural address. But your words need to be equally expressive if they are to represent a passionate mission.

If you are willing to work toward a more powerful command of language, make a thesaurus your friend. Either purchase one from the bookstore or have one installed in your software program if it doesn't already have one.

Let's look at what a thesaurus can do for some common words.

- job—becomes: assignment, chore, duty, responsibility, task, business, employment, occupation, position, post, trade, work

- eat—becomes: chew, consume, devour, ingest, dine, feast, sup
- mad—becomes: angry, enraged, furious, incensed, infuriated, irate

Not only can individual words be made to say more, but you can use groups of words to paint pictures. President Franklin Delano Roosevelt used groupings to create images in our minds. He talked about: "The forgotten man," "A new deal for the American People," "The great arsenal of democracy."

When Pearl Harbor was attacked by the Japanese, one of FDR's assistants was helping write the speech to be given to a stunned nation. The assistant wrote, "December 7, 1941: A date which will live in world history." FDR substituted one word for two, and we have one of the classic lines in oratory: "December 7, 1941: A date which will live in infamy."

A communicator of equal skill painted a word picture for us about equality: "I have a dream that one day on the red hills of Georgia the sons of former slaves and the sons of former slave owners will be able to sit down together at the table of brotherhood." That communicator was Dr. Martin Luther King, Jr.

While quotes, slogans, and phrases alone are not enough to lead, they are a powerful part of the arsenal of an effective communicator.

KEEP IT SIMPLE

The Declaration of Independence has only 1,322 words, Lincoln's Gettysburg Address has 268 and the Lord's Prayer has 56 words. It doesn't take volumes to make an impact on people's lives. The leader who understands the art and genius of simplicity has a rare gift.

Oliver Wendell Holmes was invited to give an after-dinner speech. His host gave him the following advice: "What we like is to gather, gobble, gabble, and git—in that order and about that fast." As leaders, we would be wise to get on with it also. Get to the point and then "git." Remember that acronym from the world of sales, *KISS*—"Keep It Simple, Stupid." In leadership, we can use the same letters, but change their meaning to "Keep It Short and Sweet."

LANGUAGE GOBBLEDYGOOK

Let's get away from the gobbledygook we hear every day. A

major California bank, reporting on their financial standing, said: "We have $1 billion in non-accrual loans." What does that mean? It means that they have $1 billion in bad debts caused by greedy and imprudent loans to foreign countries. An airline reported that they showed a profit from "one-time conversion of used equipment." They meant that they had received insurance payments for a plane that crashed. Is this kind of language used to misguide, duck responsibility and accountability, or lessen bad publicity? I think it is.

We have turned our own language against ourselves. People have created language and words to justify their existence and enhance their exclusivity and importance. As leaders, we need to make language more, not less, precise, and to build communication bonds, not erect walls. We need to accept responsibility and accountability for our actions and let people know we do by our honest clear language.

We hear terms every day that are at best ludicrous and at worst deceiving and lacking in ethical standards:

- revenue enhancement and user fees mean more taxes
- negative patient outcome means the patient died
- pre-emptive strike means we shot first
- decrease in the rate of inflation means it's still going up
- found to be redundant means you are laid off
- he was neutralized means murdered

The preceding culinary process aided by the passing of time and the expansion of heat has brought the task to fruition. It would be wise to cease your current activities and respond to your body's need for sustenance—means it's time to eat!

ANOTHER WAY TO SAY IT

I won! It's a boy! We did it! Play ball! Dinner's ready! The art of simplicity doesn't mean speaking in one-syllable words. Or disavowing the language of new technology, or forsaking sensitive eloquent language. Simplicity means not purposely complicating how we interact with others. If you are going to influence others, you need to be honest and clear in your speech. Words put simply can make an essential difference in your ability to lead.

——————A Master Communicator——————

There is no doubt that he is a controversial politician; however, it is hard to refute the command with which the Reverend Jesse Jackson uses language. His evangelical style is part of his impact. But more important is his ability to string words together into phrases that are very nearly poetic. They go right to the heart of the listener. In his speech to the Democratic Convention in 1984 he used some of his most persuasive communication skills. He started right off with a bang:

> This is not a perfect party. We are not a perfect people. Yet, we are called to a perfect mission: Our mission, to feed the hungry, to clothe the naked, to house the homeless, to teach the illiterate, to provide jobs for the jobless, and to choose the human race over the nuclear race.

Few orators of either political party or of any persuasion have the magic to match that of Jesse Jackson.

VERBALIZE YOUR EXPECTATIONS

You are faced with many challenges and problems in all parts of your life. When problems arise they often come from the lack of clearly communicated expectation.

A chief executive who did an amazing job of transforming a rundown company into an outstanding success communicated his expectations for a new positive outlook at the company. He had all department heads submit reports to him every Monday morning, describing all the *good* things that had happened in their departments during the preceding week. The staff soon learned that their efforts were appreciated and recognized. They knew that he expected them to look for new positive solutions and procedures, instead of concentrating on past failures.

We all function better and are more productive when we know what is expected of us. We can made decisions, take risks, build teams, identify our ethics, handle change, and be more committed when we understand the mission, goals, and values of our organization.

————The Clift-Four Seasons Hotel————

One spring day I was walking in downtown San Francisco. I passed one of the city's finest hotels—the Clift-Four Seasons. I turned the corner and within a few feet I saw the employees entrance. Above the door a big brass sign reads: "Through these door pass the most courteous employees in San Francisco."

You might think that passing under that sign every day would blunt the importance of the message for the employees. However, it is obvious when you go to the hotel that the sign is not just a slogan, it's an ingrained philosophy. As a five-star/five-diamond hotel, the Clift Hotel and its famous French Room restaurant have earned their reputation as a premier hotel and restaurant in a city known for great food and hospitality. Every employee from the general manager to the newest housekeeper knows that it is his or her personal responsibility to fulfill what the brass sign proclaims.

Verbalizing expectations can be done in many ways. The Clift Hotel's expectation of its employees is written in brass and repeated verbally to employees at every level and in every department. The expectation is well communicated and makes an important difference to clients and employees.

Question: Can you honestly say that your followers really understand your expectation? Do you think they have pride in fulfilling your expectation?

————In Their Hearts or Over Their Heads————

On May 16, 1902, William Jennings Bryan was attending a banquet during the inauguration of the first president of the Republic of Cuba. In his speech he compared their struggle for independence to that of the United States, and said that he was there to witness the lowering of the American flag and the raising of the new Cuban flag. Regardless of our position on Cuba today, we can learn from his words: ". . . for it is better that the Stars and Stripes should be indelibly impressed upon your hearts than that they should float above your heads."

When you see that the values, missions, and objectives of your organization are "indelibly impressed upon the hearts" of your followers, there is no need to dominate or be autocratic in your leadership style. We cannot force our policies upon others and be sure of obedience. We can only persuade and impress our messages on their hearts. Be sure your expectations are clearly and regularly communicated to your followers, whether there are two or two thousand.

USE YOUR SKILLS TO COMMUNICATE
THREE VITAL MESSAGES

No matter how often you verbalize your expectations you won't be able to cement relationships unless you clearly define and communicate the *what* and *why* of your expectations. What is your mission? What do you want to make a difference about and why?

These messages need to be expressed as often as possible. They will give power to your leadership. They'll vitalize your organization. They are at the heart of your leadership.

#1—Mission: What is the purpose, the mission of this organization? Why are we in existence?

Some organizations state these in very focused terms. Jack Wahlig, chairman of the accounting firm McGaldrey Pullen, communicates his expectations for the firm very clearly. Each employee receives a copy of the company's "Statement of Philosophy, Policy & Ethical Practice Standards" booklet. The opening page states the company mission, methods, and objectives. One of the most important ingredients in their success is the last part which reads:

Beliefs
    We believe: —in our clients
                 —in our people
                 —in innovation
                 —in leadership
                 —in teamwork
                 —in doing what's right
                 —in success

The message at McGaldrey Pullen is loud and clear. They have strong beliefs and they communicate them clearly and often.

#2—*Objectives:* What are the long-term objectives of the organization? What are we going for? What do we want to accomplish?

─────────*IBM Communicates Clearly*─────────

Since 1958 IBM's chairmen have been issuing what they call "Management Briefings." These briefings capture the spirit and substance of the company's philosophy as it has evolved over the last thirty years. Every manager in the company receives a copy of the briefing. It re-emphasizes why IBM is in business and what objectives the company strives for.

The following is the April 24, 1986, briefing sent to IBM's management team by John Ackers, their chairman.

> After receiving the results of our most recent opinion surveys I am happy to report that overall morale is high. I am not happy to report, however, that at an IBM site where morale was not so good, many employees felt that our attention to people management had eroded significantly.
>
> When I asked site management why this had happened, they told me, with the sort of candor I appreciate, that they simply got too focused on getting product out the door.
>
> Our industry is going through some demanding times. I know you're all very busy meeting our business objectives. In this environment, it is tempting to shortchange our responsibility to our people. Don't succumb to that temptation.
>
> Remember that our people are operating under the same pressure, and they too are working very hard to meet the same objectives. It's a manager's job to provide balance between the needs of the individual and the needs of the business.
>
> Whatever challenges we face in 1986, we must not cut corners on people management. That includes basics such as timely performance plans and appraisals, recognition, and thoughtful career development. But it also means sensitivity to the on-going employee/manager communications.
>
> At the same time we also have to strengthen our efforts to stop doing nonessential work that puts unnecessary demands on our people. We must streamline procedures and organizations. In the last few years we've discarded many redundant and unnecessary jobs, reorganized to eliminate layers of management and speed decision making, and reduced

travel and meetings to save both money and people's time. We want to stop what is marginally useful so our people can focus their time and attention on what is truly necessary.

People management is every manager's principal responsibility. But the elimination of unnecessary tasks also must be very high on every manager's priority list. We achieve our business objective, not in spite of, but because of our belief in respect for the individual.

IBM is one of our nation's finest success stories. There are many factors that have created that success. One of the most powerful is their ability to communicate the corporate mission, objectives, and values.

#3—Values: What is the value structure that makes this organization what it is? Where did these values come from? Why are they values we espouse?

Robert K. Greenleaf wrote in *The Servant as Leader:* "There is something subtle communicated to one who is being served and led if, implicit in the contract between servant-leader and led, is the understanding that the search for wholeness is something they share." Shared values bring a wholeness to individuals and organizations so they can weather the storms of change. We are what we value!

People will follow your lead if you communicate to them something in which to believe. They want to find fulfillment in their work. They want to be inspired and feel a part of something that matters. Your ability to touch their hearts and hopes and dreams is the magic of these three vital messages. They will stay longer, try harder, and care more if you give them reason. They will follow you to hell and back if your philosophy speaks to their inner needs and eternal values.

A National Treasure

Marva Collins, founder of the Westside Preparatory School in Chicago, clearly communicates her value structure. She has been called "a miracle worker, a super-teacher," and a "national treasure." She has been praised by many and attacked by some. In the early days of the Reagan administration, she was widely mentioned as a top candidate for the post of Secretary of Education. Several educational institutions have awarded her honorary doctorates. All of this is because she believes in children's desire and ability to learn and she forcefully communicates these beliefs.

Collins was born Black in the deep South during the Depression. As a child growing up in Monroeville, Alabama, she was a voracious reader—but she could not use the local libraries. They were restricted to "Whites Only." Still Collins read everything she could get her hands on.

As a teacher in inner-city Chicago schools, Collins saw the necessity of getting children "to see the intrinsic value of education, so they . . . want to learn for the sake of learning." Not everyone appreciated her efforts. She was a vocal advocate and her criticism of what she saw as lacking in other teachers brought her hate mail. Her special targets were apathetic, ineffective, and ill-prepared teachers who lacked the necessary commitment to inspire children. After fourteen years as a teacher in a Chicago school, an angry and disillusioned Collins quit. She felt frustrated with the system and in her efforts to make a difference. But even with her frustration and disillusionment there was still a fire in her heart. She refused to give up.

In September 1975, with her $5,000 retirement money, Marva Collins began a private school in the basement of Daniel Hale William University. Her first class consisted of her daughter and three neighborhood children. By 1982 the school had 240 elementary students and had moved to its present site on West Chicago Avenue. Collins presides over the school instructors whom she has "retrained" in her philosophy of teaching the 3 Rs and communicating values. She wants them to emulate her childhood teachers who were "strict and strong—there was no foolishness." Her words and actions match.

Collins's ability to transform what were once called "unteachable" ghetto children has won her recognition and awards from the National Education Association, the American Academy of Achievement, and the National Urban League. When I spoke with her I immediately got the impression of a no-nonsense, action-oriented person who knew exactly what she is about. She communicates her mission clearly. What she does is in harmony with what she says and what she teaches. She makes you want to "do something" and she lets you know that she expects you to do it! She is making a difference.

BECOMING AN EYEWITNESS

If you are to make a difference you can't express expectations in the abstract. If you are going to lead effectively, you have to go out among your followers. Building relationships requires first-hand experience and contact with those involved.

If we agree that the main purpose of communication is to build relationships and foster understanding with people, then you must go where people are, feel what they feel, see what they see, and experience what they experience. When you only see others from a distance, you run the risk of seeing them inaccurately or becoming patronizing. If you can get first-hand knowledge of people's values and problems, you can make better decisions, set expectations more clearly, and use your power more wisely.

Robert Kennedy offers a good example of a leader's ability to understand and articulate the needs of others. During his years of public service, Robert Kennedy's personal experiences changed him greatly. He left the comfortable and insulated world of wealth and privilege to go into parts of this country where children existed in wretched poverty. He saw and felt firsthand the pain of those who needed help, the debilitating economic and social effects of segregation and racial prejudice. His personality changed—or rather his abstract understanding of a problem became a vivid, personal experience. His expectations changed. His passion and ability to communicate what he saw and felt in person was very powerful. You could see it in his face and hear it in his voice. He became a magnet to millions of people. He inspired them to try to make a difference.

LISTENING IS MORE THAN HALF OF COMMUNICATING

> "The best way to persuade is with your ears."
> —FORMER SECRETARY OF STATE DEAN RUSK

Learning to listen is more than half the battle for clear communication. When you take a close look at the people problems in any organization, it is usually clear that somewhere, somehow, the leader has missed hearing the true nature of the problem.

Mervin Morris, founder of the Mervyn's department store chain, feels that communication skills and listening are two of the most important leadership qualities (the other being high ethics). This is what he said about communications:

"You have to be a good listener, and you have to be a good communicator. You gather the facts by listening. Then communicate your decisions to those you are leading. Obviously, if you're leading any number of people at all, you have to have a strategic plan and people have to understand what it is. I think everybody wants to know two things. First, "What do you want me to do?" and second, "How am I doing?" Its important for a leader to be very explicit to any subordinate and make sure that the information is communicated to them: What is it you expect of this subordinate? Periodically, you have to communicate to each person how they're doing according to the plan you had for them: "Here was your mission, here was your strategic plan or whatever you want to call it, this is what we agreed your job would be." Periodically, once a year, twice a year, whatever one wishes, people should be reviewed and told how they are doing.

When I say being a good listener—really I should alter that—it's taking time to absorb the facts, verbally or in writing. You could also be reading reports and gathering information, which is just as good as listening. You don't just hear what you *want* to hear; you want to be hearing what is going on. Hearing can be the voice, the body language, or the written word. So listening is not just with both ears; it's with the mind."

God gave us two ears and one mouth, which ought to tell us something about what our ratio of listening to speaking should be! There are two ways to strengthen your listening skills:

The first is *effective questioning*. Isador Isaac Rabi, one of America's most famous physicists, tells the story of his childhood. When he came home from school, his mother would ask him, "Did you ask any good questions today?" Not "Did you learn anything today?" He attributes a great deal of his success to his ability to ask good questions. We can learn from his example. Rather than always looking for answers, we should look for good questions. Remember the proverb that says, "If you know all the answers, you haven't asked all the questions."

——————————*A Media Master*——————————

You switch channels and on your television screen is a face that needs no subtitles for identification. The intense eyes behind the glasses, brown hair, and slight Texas accent belong to a familiar face. He tweaks your conscience, challenges you to learn something new, asks you to reconsider your current way of thinking. Bill Moyers has turned the skill of asking questions into an art form.

His direct, simply stated questions pierce all pretense and barriers. They go straight to the heart of the matter at hand. These penetrating questions are based on his deep desire to explore ideas and values. You may not agree or even like what he says or how he approaches a topic, but if you watch more than two or three minutes it is almost impossible to switch to another channel—he's got you!

Born in Marshall, Texas, he studied to be a theologian as a young man, and ended up in journalism. His appetites and passions were fostered as an administrator for the Peace Corps. When he was press secretary for President Lyndon Johnson he was deeply involved in the "Great Society." He's been a correspondent for CBS and now spends his time at PBS, thinking of new ways to inform and stimulate us. His many award-winning documentaries show his love of country and compassion and concern for people. In a recent interview he said, "I hear an almost inaudible but pervasive discontent with the price we pay for our current materialism. And I hear a fluttering of hope that there might be more to life than bread and circuses."

As we move out of our cycle of materialism, Bill Moyers will be leading the way, challenging us and asking questions that make a difference.

Think of the people you know whom you consider to be true leaders. When you are with them, they invariably ask questions. They are interested in you and your ideas. They are also interested in improving their listening skills, in another way—*seeking feedback.*

How to give feedback is discussed elsewhere, so let's focus on the *benefits* of giving and receiving feedback. Shared goals are instilled in an organization by the leader who exploits every opportunity for giving and receiving feedback. When you ask questions and then involve yourself in the give-and-take of feedback, you build trust and openness with others. Ownership of ideas comes from the shared trust built between leader and follower.

When you are involved in feedback, be sure to ask, "Have I made myself clear?" rather than "Do you understand?" Take responsibility for your own communication skills first. When you do everything in your power to make yourself understood, you improve the chances that someone will really hear and understand your message.

There's an African legend about a bird who could build a perfect nest. All the other birds asked her how she did it, so she started to explain. "First I collect some mud," and one bird cried, "Aha, now I understand," and flew off. As she described each step, another bird would cry, "Aha, now I understand," and fly away. When she finished and looked around, no one was there. If she had been checking for understanding, perhaps her listeners would have stayed for the full message.

SARA

From time to time we must all give or receive unpleasant news. Even if the person communicating bad news is an expert, those on the receiving end will have a reaction that affects their capability to listen well.

As leader of your group how can you handle bad news? How can you ask people to do things they don't want to do? There is an acronym that describes the sequence of responses to unwanted information. It is SARA

S—Shock

A—Anger

R—Rejection

A—Acceptance

When you must ask people to do something unpleasant, their response to the bad news often goes through the SARA stages. Shock is followed by anger and then rejection. As leaders it is our job to recognize and understand this natural sequence of reactions, and to become top-notch salespeople, moving our followers to the fourth and final stage, acceptance. We can do that only when we are superior listeners, using questions and feedback to move people ahead. And when we ourselves are the recipients of bad news, we can recognize this four-stage reaction process and move ourselves to acceptance.

Are you a good listener? Here are some questions to consider:

About your listening attitudes:

- Do you like to listen to other people talk?
- Do you encourage other people to talk?
- Do you listen even if you do not like the person who is talking?
- Do you listen equally well whether the person is man or woman, young or old?
- Do you listen equally well to friend, acquaintance, or stranger?

About the way you listen:

- Do you put what you have been doing out of sight and out of mind?
- Do you look at the person talking to you?
- Do you ignore distractions around you?
- Do you smile, nod your head, and otherwise encourage the person to talk?
- Do you think about what the person is saying?
- Do you try to understand what the person means?
- Do you try to understand why he is saying it?
- Do you let the person finish what he is saying? If he hesitates, do you encourage him to go on?
- Do you restate what he has said and ask him if you got it right?
- Do you withhold judgment about his ideas until he has finished?
- Do you listen regardless of the person's manner of speaking and choice of words?
- Do you listen even though you anticipate what the person is going to say?
- Would your followers describe you as a good listener?

When you have examined these questions, have someone you trust answer these questions about your listening habits. Compare your answers to theirs. You may be surprised at what they see that could improve your ability to be a good listener.

CONFLICT RESOLUTION

Conflict in any group is devastating unless handled immediately. Teams stop functioning, productivity diminishes, and emotions cloud reason when conflict is present. You can't power your way through conflict. Power may get the warring factions to stop momentarily, but then you must use the art of communication to resolve the problem. Your sensitivity is critical. What you say and how you say it really makes a difference.

WHERE CONFLICT BEGINS

Conflict most often arises when someone's power or pursuit of a goal is threatened. Beverly A. Potter wrote about conflict in her book, *Changing Performance on the Job:* "Conflicts emerge when a person believes someone else is interfering with the pursuit of a desired goal." Since openly expressing anger is rarely acceptable, some people who feel their power or goals are threatened will resist dealing directly with the conflict. Instead they turn to manipulation, or even disruptive behavior.

IGNORING CONFLICT

If you want to accomplish anything, you don't have the luxury of ignoring conflict. You must let people know that you expect them to participate in resolving conflicts and that conflict—open or subverted—is not acceptable. If you are to build strong teams who can disagree in a healthy manner and live in harmony, you cannot function under the threat of unresolved conflict.

There is a Chinese parable about two men arguing heatedly in the midst of a crowd. A stranger, noting the depth of their anger, expressed surprise that no blows were being struck. His Chinese friend explained, "The man who strikes first admits that his ideas have given out."

As a leader you need a deep well of ideas to help solve problems and resolve conflict. If you aren't willing to face the problem, the unresolved conflict can undermine your entire organization. If you try to avoid conflict by ignoring it, you will lose credibility. The leader who helps others resolve conflict will be respected, trusted, and supported. Of course, few conflicts can be resolved to everyone's complete satisfaction, but if you are willing to try, your people will be more likely to have positive attitudes about you as leader, about the organization, and about their work.

Several years ago I was hired to conduct a leadership seminar for a group of middle managers. I did my usual needs assessment with the executive who hired me and with a sampling of the group to whom I would be speaking. All seemed well and I began the seminar. As I went through the morning I would give ideas on improving skills or building new ones. Every once in a while I'd notice some strong nonverbal language being exchanged between the managers. They also began asking questions about conflict resolution. It became clear that these were not casual inquiries. There was major conflict brewing within the company. At the lunch break I decided I'd better get to the heart of the problem if I could. I began asking questions privately. At first, people were very reticent in answering. But I soon found out that the president of the company appointed an assistant and gave him an executive title with enormous clout. This man was the antithesis of every leadership quality in this book. He was arrogant and abusive in his manner of giving orders. He treated everyone as slaves. He was a chauvinist and let it be known that macho was the only type of man there was. Those who had to work directly for him were angry and frustrated. They had no court of appeal because the president of the company would listen to no one about the problem. He refused to acknowledge that there were any problems or conflicts. He had a major mutiny on his hands and did not have an inkling of the seriousness of the problem. I am sorry to report that most of the middle managers quit within six months. Many other employees left also, because they could see the writing on the wall. If the president would not acknowledge his managers' unhappiness, what hope was there for them?

This organization was seriously weakened because the leaders did not understand the importance of communication. The president would not listen, the senior executive was dictatorial in his communications. The middle management could not get its message through. Conflict was a predictable result.

KEYS TO RESOLVING CONFLICT

"The most important thing in an argument,
next to being right, is to leave an escape hatch

for your opponent, so that he can gracefully
swing over to your side without too much
apparent loss of face.''
—SYDNEY J. HARRIS

Conflict is never pleasant, but if it isn't handled correctly, it can cause major damage to team spirit and individual performance. When standoffs start, communication usually stops. That is the key to resolving conflict—communication. If you can get people talking, you have a chance to solve the problems, resolve the conflict, and get everybody back to the tasks at hand.

How can you get people talking again, defuse a hostile situation, and swing people to another side of an issue?

First, *collect information.* Everyone has their own perception of reality. Their feelings are as important as facts. Be sure you have analyzed both the feelings and the facts of the conflicting parties. Ask for both. Don't wait for information—pursue it. Ask hard questions, accept bad news, insist on uncensored versions of events. Don't try to zero in on the problem and offer solutions too quickly. Absorb the irrelevant. First, ask questions that reveal the feelings involved, such as:

* On what points do we agree?
* When did this conflict begin?
* ''John, what do you think are the key issues here?''
* What is different now than before the conflict?
* What is still the same?
* Is a value or priority being questioned?
* ''Pat, how do you feel about this?'' (Listen to feelings.)
* ''Bob, from the point of view of your department, how would you handle this?'' (Take the pressure off the individual and stimulate thinking about the good of the larger unit.)
* ''If you were in her place, how would you work this out?'' (Initiate empathy.)
* ''Suppose you were in charge of the whole division/job area— describe the big picture to me.'' (Expand awareness.)

Keep asking questions until you have a clear perception of the actual problem or conflict.

Second, clarify issues and defuse hostility by listening to all sides.

- "Audrey, you're saying that—" (Restate her point in question form. If you are wrong she will correct you.)
- "Bob, if I understand you correctly, you feel that these are the key issues here—"

Keep clarifying and restating until you are sure you are at the heart of the issue.

Skillful leaders use all of their sensitivity to walk the conflict tightrope while reopening the lines of communication between the warring factions. Clarity is vital: You cannot resolve what you don't understand.

Next, move to neutral territory. Take the parties involved out of the conflict area. Go to neutral ground where neither adversary has the advantage. If you must, pull rank to quiet the situation so you can get people talking. Take them to your office or anywhere they regard as your power base, so you are in control of the negotiations. If that is not necessary, sit at a round table, in a nonthreatening arrangement. You are less likely to have people making a power play at a round table.

Then identify common ground. Rarely is a situation so bad that there is absolutely no area of agreement. Review what is agreed on and find small areas of common ground to work within. If the conflict is small, you can go right on to making an action plan for resolution. If the conflict is large or has many parts or people involved, work out little things first to pave the way for the bigger issues. Finding common ground relieves some of the pressure that has built up.

Last, form an action plan. To resolve the problem, be clear about who does what and when. Make an action plan with the accountable parties reporting progress to you. For large groups, give each person some part in the accountability. Be sure you clearly communicate the plan to everyone involved.

If the conflict cannot be resolved and you have done the best you can, it may be time to bring in a third party to act as mediator. You'll have to go back and start the process of questioning and clarifying all over again.

In extreme cases, when even outside mediation does not work, you may have to assert your power. (See chapter 8, "A Leader Uses Power Wisely.") Sometimes you must be authoritative instead of participative. Leadership was never meant to be a popularity contest. There are times when you will have to take a hard stand and adjudicate the problem. Explain that further hostility is not acceptable. Let it be known that if disruption continues, you will take harsher steps for the benefit of the group. You may have to move someone to another department or area, with a clear explanation of why you are taking this action. If there is still further conflict between this person and the members of the new team, you may have to fire the combatant. Someone who cannot or will not resolve conflict can damage an entire group. In this day of change and need for adaptation, you, as leader, simply cannot allow such disruption to continue.

TEST YOUR WILLINGNESS

To strengthen your sensitivity to the issue of conflict resolution you must constantly reassess your ability to mediate the problem. Here are three questions about your willingness to resolve conflict:

1. "How do I respond when faced with conflict?"
2. "What message am I sending in the way I handle conflict?"
3. "Do my actions and words match?"

Conflict can even be healthy and invigorating when it brings out new thoughts and ideas, but unresolved conflict can be like a cancer festering within your group. One of the most damaging things in any organization is to allow people to have pent-up frustration or anger. It is very important for you to sense the initial stirring of conflict so it can be resolved early.

THE MATURITY GAP

Obviously communication goes beyond letting others know what you want. The smallest infant can make others aware of its needs through gurgling and shrieking. Mature communication is infinitely more complex and relies on a delicate balance of intellectual and emotional awareness.

We have an emotional reaction to almost everything, but we can't run our lives on emotion alone. We must temper our emotions and use our intellectual response system. The less time it takes to do so, the greater our maturity. Maturity is emotion tempered by intellect. Either alone doesn't work.

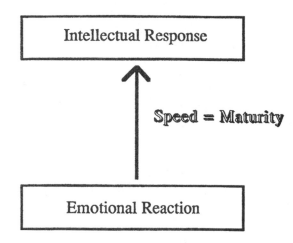

The speed with which we move from emotional reaction to intellectual response is our degree of maturity.

We all have instantaneous emotional reactions for which we are not responsible. Think back to SARA. The shorter the time between the emotional reaction and the intellectual response is one important measurement of emotional maturity.

This kind of maturity is important, because when you are dealing with conflicts you are usually dealing with emotions first. You hope to get to acceptance through mediation and reopening the lines of communication. But you need to be aware of the maturity-gap theory in your communications with others. When you approach people, be aware that they are responding emotionally, and that you may need to give them time to get to acceptance.

As people express themselves, listen to both content and presentation. Both give clues to the emotions and logic with which you are dealing. Listen not only to what is being said, but what *isn't* being said. Don't argue with what is being said. Let people talk. Don't disapprove. If you disagree, draw the person out to find the real meaning of the complaint.

In a world that has grown increasingly impersonal, the sensitivity needed to resolve conflict is vital to the leader's success.

THE WORDS THEY HEAR AND THE ACTIONS THEY SEE

The moral tone of your organization is established and communicated by you, its leader. Your team is held together by the words they hear and the actions they see. When you use your expertise to reinforce the organization's goals, values, ideas, and ideals in the minds and spirit of your followers, communication becomes an art form.

The highest form of communication is example. You serve your followers best when your mission is articulated more by what you do than what you say.

It is said that a picture is worth a thousand words. What pictures do you create for your followers? What messages are you sending and what examples are you setting?

LEADERSHIP QUALITY TEN

A LEADER IS A TEAM BUILDER
Maximizing People Potential

"A successful team is a group of
many hands but of one mind."
—BILL BETHEL

More than any other leadership skill, team building depends on and draws on all of the other qualities. As a team leader, you must have a *mission* to inspire the group. You must be a visionary—a *big thinker*—with plans to carry out that mission, which means you must be an effective *communicator.* You must also be a *risk taker* who creates a working environment free of harsh criticism when mistakes are made.

The effective team leader is *sensitive* to all kinds of factors including the wise use of *power,* the skills of *decision making,* the ability to handle and create *change,* and, of course, you need high *ethics* to set standards and behavior. Your *courage* and *commitment* in the face of difficulties may be the only thing that holds your team together at times. That's why being a team leader is so important. It encompasses all the qualities of a leader. When you are a good team leader you can build teams that make a difference.

One of my clients, a man in the communication industry, told me, "I think team building is probably the most difficult and at the same time the most rewarding of all the responsibilities that I have."

If we made a list of the benefits of being a team leader, I think we'd agree that the biggest is the reward of seeing people grow, watching them solve problems, building their individual skills, and working well with each other. These are the component parts of what I term the Productivity Principle—which means a team of motivated, capable people working together to make a difference.

Shriver and the Peace Corps

One of the most exciting examples of team building in recent years was the formation of the Peace Corps.

John F. Kennedy arrived at Ann Arbor, Michigan, the night of October 14, 1960, and found 10,000 University of Michigan students waiting to greet him. In his extemporaneous speech on the steps of the Student Union building, Kennedy asked the students how many would be willing to donate time to work in Asia, Africa, and Latin America as teachers, doctors, and engineers, sharing the richness of the American dream. Thousands of young people roared their affirmation.

On January 20, 1961, John F. Kennedy was inaugurated as president of the United States. He stood on the steps of the Capitol Building and said, "Ask not what your country can do for you—ask what you can do for your country."

The next day, he asked his brother-in-law Sargent Shriver to design and organize the volunteer corps he had told the students about. In eight short months the Peace Corps, led by Sargent Shriver, went from a concept to reality. Let's look at this amazing example of team building.

On that first day Shriver began bringing in good people to form his team. "My style," said Shriver, "was to get bright, informative, creative people and then pick their brains." He telephoned thirty-four-year-old Harris Wofford, a brilliant law professor at Notre Dame, who had extensive experience in Third-World countries and had long advocated a government-sponsored "peace force." Shriver recognized Wofford as the pivotal person on the team. Then for the next two weeks they interviewed a steady stream of academic, government, business, and religious leaders.

Shriver built the team philosophy from fresh ideas. Opinions flooded in from every corner of the country. Some people felt that the new organization should not be under the federal government because it would be seen as "imperialistic." Some wanted the Peace Corps to include older people, to work within the United

States. Former President Eisenhower ridiculed the entire idea as "a juvenile experiment." Other detractors called it "Kennedy's Kiddie Korps." The only general agreement was that the new agency should start slowly on a small scale.

On February 6th, Shriver brought to President Kennedy a report that was to be the philosophy of the Peace Corps. It was developed by two young men, William Josephson and Warren W. Higgins, who had extensive experience in administering international programs. The report described sending thousands of America's smartest and most dedicated young people to Asia, Africa, and Latin America as working ambassadors of goodwill.

On Friday, February 24th, Shriver delivered his first full report to the president. The plan outlined a broad base of participation and operations. Kennedy signed the Peace Corps into existence.

In May, Shriver had invitations from eight countries for 3,000 volunteers. Recruitment began with the May and June graduating classes at colleges and universities all over the country. On July 24th, forty-three volunteers began training at Harvard. The first Peace Corps volunteers arrived in Lagos, Nigeria, on September 26th.

Less than two years later, the Peace Corps had 7,000 volunteers working in forty-four countries. Today more then 100,000 Americans have been a part of the team that Shriver built.

Kennedy provided the spark, and Sargent Shriver built the team that turned the idea of the Peace Corps into reality. Over the years the Peace Corps has made a difference in hundreds of thousands of lives, in both volunteers and recipients alike. "I'd never done anything political, patriotic, or unselfish because nobody ever asked me to," said one volunteer. "Kennedy and Shriver asked."

Is there someone in your group like that volunteer? Does he or she know how to contribute to your mission? Give them some motivation and courage. People are waiting to be asked to help make a difference.

THE VALUE OF TEAMS

Humans have always formed groups to accomplish goals that could not be reached by any one person. Being a part of a team is highly valued in many societies from the simple to the most sophisticated. Even in a culture like ours that values individuality, the individual's need to be a part of something human, supportive, and reinforcing is strong. We know we can make a bigger difference when we do it together.

If you are a leader who can attract the right people to your team, communicate a mission, and then motivate, train, and direct that team to maximum productivity, you'll be one of the most valued leaders we have to take us into the twenty-first century. Whether you approach leadership as an employee, as a concerned volunteer, a public servant, or a parent, the art of team building will help you maximize your potential to make a difference.

THE TEAM BUILDER IN BUSINESS

If you are a business leader you know that there is a trend toward smaller operating groups, and this trend makes team building more important than ever. As middle management shrinks, you need to strengthen communication lines between upper management and workers and keep those lines open. This means getting different teams to communicate and share knowledge, creating a closer relationship between people with different agendas.

————*A Business Leader Who Knows How*————

I had a conversation with Bill Weisz, vice chairman of Motorola, Inc., about the twelve qualities of leadership. He had these comments:

> After ethics, I'd say *team building,* along with sensitivity, are probably the most important things. When our managers get together, we say, "Your most important job is to create the atmosphere and environment in which everyone can contribute to the maximum of their potential."
>
> You can't do that unless you are a team builder, which implies that you are a participative manager. That's slightly different than being just a team builder. You have to be able to encourage participation horizontally and vertically. You can't do that unless you are sensitive to others. Motorola invented participative management.
>
> To me that combination [of sensitivity and team building] is the most important of the leadership combinations. If you were completely idealistic, you could say that if you really did build this team, build this environment, you wouldn't have to do anything else.

This kind of team building between executive and employee is one of the best ways to instill the loyalty and trust you need in effective teams. Team building of this kind increases productivity and reinforces the human spirit. It results in loyalty, pride of work, and greater quality of products and services.

THE VOLUNTEER TEAM BUILDER

Building a team of volunteers will test all your leadership skills. While the passion and spirit of a volunteer team is often much higher than an occupational team, leading volunteers is more challenging.

In a work team you have people of common skills and background. You are in a position to direct them more authoritatively. The members of a volunteer team are much more diverse. Their interest in the cause or mission may be the only thing they have in common. Egos get bruised more easily in a volunteer group. Your ability to reward and recognize each person's contribution is critical to retaining their support.

————Teaming Up To Clean Up————

In 1982, New York City Mayor Ed Koch formed a grass-roots organization called We Care About New York. He felt that the private sector could make a difference in the prevention of litter and graffiti in New York City.

The idea was well received, but nothing really happened until four years later when Emory Jackson became president of the organization. Emory says:

> In 1986 I brought a team of four with me. They were experts in community organizing, public relations, and advertising. We restructured the organization and announced to over ten thousand civic groups that we needed their help in getting as many people as possible to take broom in hand and start cleaning up.

Emory and his team involved these groups in the year-round cleaning of streets, parks, vacant lots, buildings, highways, and even abandoned buildings. "The response was overwhelmingly positive," said Emory. "We went from 16,000 volunteers in 1986 to over a quarter million in 1988, working in 5,227 neighborhoods and saving the city over 1.4 million dollars. These numbers include pre-schoolers to senior citizens. They include every ethnic and socio-economic group in town.'' The corporate community in the Big Apple contributes nearly one half million dollars annually for such items as booms, shovels, rakes, and trash bags.

Besides helping to change the city's profile from littered to clean, We Care About New York has changed people's lives, as well. A group of homeless men have started a street-cleaning business, contracting their services to several large commercial areas in Brooklyn. Emory's volunteer team is about as diverse as you can get. But he was able to form and direct his team by emphasizing the one thing all team members had in common: civic pride. Emory summarized the program, ''There is immense social pride in teaming up to make a difference. New Yorkers have stepped up to the challenge.''

THE HOW-TO'S OF TEAM BUILDING

To be a leader you can't sit in ivory towers. You must be a coach in the classic sense. To build and sustain your team you must concentrate on the five basics of team building:

- directing
- motivating
- training
- delegating
- gratifying

Let's look at those five basics of team building so you can maximize both your potential as a leader and the potential of your followers.

DIRECTING

When you give people direction, challenge them to use their talents, and give them the autonomy to achieve a goal, you have helped them fulfill their personal potential and that of the team.

MINI-MISSION STATEMENTS

In chapter 1, we discussed the importance of having a mission, using as an example United Technologies. Every organization needs an overall mission or statement of purpose. But each part of the whole—the individual teams—also needs to have a sense of purpose. At the team level, I call these "mini-mission statements," and as a team builder, you must direct their formulation. My husband Bill and I were involved in a successful political campaign whose overall success was due to the clear purpose of the teams working for the candidate. Each team knew exactly how many doors it had to knock on and how many phone calls it had to make. We knew our exact deadlines and each team member had to determine how much time we'd give each day to the campaign. We had team pep rallies, spaghetti suppers, and phone blitzes. Our teams had very clear mini-mission statements.

Gather your team together and get everyone to participate in defining, clarifying, and structuring a team mission statement. It is very important that everyone feels ownership of it. A mission statement created by someone else never has the power to inspire that one you set for yourself does. Here are the basic steps for building a mini-mission statement:

GET ORGANIZED

Think about and list the elements that make up the purpose of the team:

- Why does the team exist? (Make this a general statement.)
- What business are you in?
- Whom do you serve?
- Are your "customers" internal or external?
- What is the most basic reason for this team? (Make this a specific definition.)

I was working with a defense contractor that manufactured high-technology early warning devices for military aircraft. We were working on mini-mission statements for different teams. When we got to the question: What is the most basic reason for their existence, they came up with answers such as, making money, making profits for shareholders, fulfilling government contracts, and those were all true. But when we discussed why the employees were motivated by working on this equipment, we finally got to the most basic reason for their existence: to save the lives of pilots.

As team leader you cannot allow your team members to become blasé about what they do. Pride in a basic service or product can be a prime motivator.

The last question to ask is: What role does the team play in the larger group—the organization, the country, the world?

Mini-mission statements can not be overemphasized. They have the power to unite a team and to keep it together in hard times.

EVALUATE YOUR RESOURCES

Have each person in the team list his or her personal strengths and weaknesses. The group can then have a discussion about how its members can help each other. This doesn't mean criticizing each other. It means recognizing that people are happier and more productive when they are matched to a task for which they have skills. Next, look at the tasks your team performs. Break these tasks down into smaller parts and decide if they are being performed as well as they could be. If not, list what tasks are not being completed. Have the team members discuss who has the skills to work on each task.

IDENTIFY POTENTIAL PROBLEMS

Review the mini-mission statement, then look for areas where problems *might* occur. What challenges might arise? For example, a group that I was working with had a new product due on the market in six months. When we discussed mini-missions, theirs were very clear. They were using their resources well, but they had not clearly identified the potential roadblocks they might meet. They took the time to stop and identify them. They assigned specific people to act as lookouts, and then went back to work, relieved that they were less likely to be surprised by a problem.

FOCUS ON SOLUTIONS

Remember the old formula: "Two minutes on the problem, fifty-eight minutes on the solution." Don't get caught up in numerous meetings and long sessions about the problems. People tend to overdiscuss the issues and sometimes use meetings as a way to avoid action. Once you have defined the problem area, stop discussing it and get on with the solutions. As team leader, this is one place where you may have to exert some control.

SET YOUR ACTION PLAN

The last step of your mini-mission statement is to decide what you can do to correct a problem, advance an idea, or move the team forward to achieve its mission. When forming your action plan, consider individual skills, time frames, budgets, and evaluation criteria. Take the time to plan where you want to go, how you will get there, and how you will know you have arrived.

When everyone discusses these five topics you have a clear direction that the whole team can see.

REWARD AND RECOGNITION

Reward and recognition are the "fertilizer in the garden of human growth," wrote author and Ph.D. William Bridges in his book *Transitions*. It is not enough to direct your team. Your team must want to be directed, they must be motivated to follow your lead. If you are trying to be a gardener in that ground of human growth, it is imperative to recognize the power of rewarding and recognizing people's efforts and talents. Those who feel they are appreciated will be receptive to your direction.

When it comes to any of the team-building principles (directing, motivating, training, delegating, or gratifying) there are two cardinal rules to remember:

Cardinal Rule #1—Praise In Public—Correct In Private. We've all been in the presence of someone who is being corrected in a humiliating fashion. It's embarrassing, for everyone. You want to dig a hole and climb in! If someone does something so terrible that you lose your temper, take a few moments to cool off. Then take the person aside and correct them. Nothing causes more hard feelings than humiliating someone in front of others. What's more, it's not necessary. Sugar always gets you further than vinegar; Translation—you'll get much better results if you allow people to keep their dignity while learning what they did wrong.

On the other hand, nothing builds a person up more than praise in front of others. Public praise has two important benefits: The person being praised feels good, and the listeners benefit by knowing that if they do well the leader will acknowledge them also. Samuel Goldwyn said, "When someone does something good, applaud! You will make two people happy."

Another important thing to remember is that the fastest way to ruin a team is to reward only the best. Find ways to praise all your people. I've worked with sales organizations to structure sales incentives on a tier system that rewards at each level of achievement.

This allows many "winners." If there is just one winner who takes all, it can create hard feelings and actually trigger poor performance. When a superstar outsells everyone, the rest may feel, "What's the point in trying?" We call these sales-incentive programs "games" (everyone on the team gets to play) rather than "contests" (winners and losers).

Cardinal Rule #2: Praise What's Right—Train for What's Wrong. Many successful organizations have long understood this philosophy. Praise whatever people do right and train for what needs improvement.

People are more motivated by the expectation of pleasure (the satisfaction derived from work) than by fear of losing their jobs. Satisfaction comes from being part of an effective team and feeling that you are important to that team.

Whatever your occupation, you can increase pride and help build team spirit by finding ways to offer honest praise and to define good behavior and performance. You will see your team-building success increase proportionally. "It is always easier to dismiss a man than to train him. No great leader ever built a reputation on firing people. Many have built a reputation on developing them" (from the magazine *Bits and Pieces*, November 1982).

MOTIVATING

I can't motivate you and you can't motivate me. Motivation is something that we do for ourselves. However, as a team leader, you can create the environment that fosters personal motivation in your people. You can help them be more professional, no matter what their job description. You can respect them as individuals and help them grow.

When Tom Landry was head coach of the Dallas Cowboy football team, his philosophy of motivation made a big difference to their success: "Sometimes the big difficulty that a lot of us have— in football teams and in companies—is that we meet in boardrooms at top levels and establish this great goal. We motivate at the top level but we forget to go down to where it's going to take effect."

Landry talked about how his team philosophy motivated the Cowboys:

Our team philosophy is to keep the defensive team from recognizing our intentions. If you've ever watched the Cowboys, you know that they are a shifting team; they've been moving up and down, they've been shifting into different formations. That's our philosophy: To defeat the defending team's ability to read our intentions so they can prepare to attack. We develop a philosophy for each of our teams. They know what it is. Then we explain how we're going to achieve it. We list the critical events that must take place. That's how our full plan works here for the Cowboys.

The Dallas Cowboys are considered one of the most professional teams in modern football, and a major part of that professionalism was Coach Tom Landry's understanding of human nature—how to motivate people to be the best that they can be.

BUILDING PROFESSIONALISM

The chain is only as strong as the weakest link. Your team will only be as strong as its weakest member. Building professionalism in even the smallest or least important job increases everyone's motivation.

"A profession is not only a way to make a living," said English essayist John Ruskin, "it is a way to make a life." As a leader, it is important for you to consider what professionalism means in today's world. In the past, the title of "professional" was restricted to those who had certain academic credentials—medicine, law, religion, or advanced educational degrees. However, we all know lawyers, doctors, clergy, and educators who have not earned the right to be called professional. They fall short of the title.

Today we use "standard of performance" as the criteria for the title of professional.

It's not the job you do—but how you do the job that entitles you to be called a professional. To set an example of professionalism ask yourself the following questions:

- Have I defined professionalism for myself?

   You can become so busy in your daily responsibilities that you forget to spend time on your own development. If you want to build a strong effective team, you need to take the time to define professionalism for yourself. Then if you work on the execution of the definition you'll be setting a positive and motivating example for your followers.
- Have I helped my team define professionalism for themselves?

Your team will have a much better chance to succeed if each member knows what it means to be a professional in his or her job. Help them individually and collectively define and outline how they can improve and grow.

* Do my people have clear job descriptions that define responsibility and accountability?

A very important part of defining each team members professional standard is a clear, well-written job description. People can't do what they don't understand.

* Have I set clear performance standards and criteria?

Defining performance standards is your next step after outlining job descriptions.

* Do I have an effective-performance evaluation system?

As people grow and achieve, they require evaluation to guide them. If you are not familiar with performance-evaluation systems, get help. This last step summarizes and clarifies where the members of your team are and where they need to be.

If you set high standards and expect people to meet them, you must be articulate in your communication of these standards. Every member of the team can be a professional if you take the time and effort to help them. There is no better way to serve than to help them be the best that they can be.

PMMFI—PLEASE MAKE ME FEEL IMPORTANT

One of the most powerful motivators is the need to feel that what we do is important. Every one of us has an invisible sign hung around our neck that says: "Please make me feel important" (PMMFI—pronounced "pum-fee.")

We need to feel that we make a difference. We want to be needed, appreciated, and recognized. When you tell people that they have done their jobs well, you create a special kind of pride. People thrive on praise, but lose their commitment when good performance doesn't make any difference. The leader that understands the importance and power of PMMFI will be able to build strong teams of dedicated, loyal people.

PMMFI IN ACTION

Several years ago, I developed a sales and leadership program for CITICORP Savings and Loan, a division of CITIBANK. The culmination of the work was a series of two-day seminars introducing the leadership program to all of the managers responsible for the branches, regions, and divisions.

At the close of the first day, I told them about PMMFI, what it meant, and how to praise people correctly by defining what you are praising.

The second morning, one of the branch managers came in early to talk. She said:

> My branch is very near to this hotel and I went back to the office after the seminar yesterday to check in and see how things were going. There were no customers in the branch and my people were closing out for the day. There is one of my staff members that I have never fully been able to bring in as a team member. I've praised her but I thought I would try your idea of PMMFI.
>
> So I said aloud across the office so that everybody could hear, "I want to thank you very much for closing out at the end of each day so well"—and then I described each of the things that she did well— "because if you didn't do such a good job, I might have to stay and clean up your work, and that would mean taking time away from my family. So I really appreciate you being such a fine team member."
>
> The woman looked at me with shock on her face and big tears started to run down her cheeks. She ran into the ladies' room. I thought, "Well, so much for PMMFI." I went in after her and told her how sorry I was, that I hadn't meant to embarrass her. I just wanted her to know that she is a very valuable team member.
>
> The woman said to me, "Oh, please don't apologize, I just can't remember as an adult ever having anyone praise me like that."

The branch manager told me that they sat down and had a long talk, not only about business and the needs of the branch, but the woman's personal goals as well. She said PMMFI seemed to open a floodgate of emotions and that it had been a very rewarding evening for both of them.

PMMFI is a very powerful tool. You and I never really know our people as well as we think we do. Sometimes, as Thoreau said, "people lead lives of quiet desperation." We don't really know what is going on in the hearts and souls of our people. Sometimes they can put on a wonderful exterior while they are hurting inside, waiting for someone to help them feel better about themselves. Wouldn't it be a wonderful reward to make a difference in their lives by helping them feel better about themselves and bringing them into the team where they can feel a part of something that is worthwhile and fulfilling?

CONSTRUCTIVE SUPPORT—
NOT CONSTRUCTIVE CRITICISM

How do you like being criticized? Most people don't: At best, they don't mind too much if it's done nicely.

The term "constructive criticism" is a contradiction in terms. It does not serve us well as leaders. Criticism is rarely constructive. Constructive criticism is like trying to have an impersonal fist fight: After the first blow, it becomes *very* personal. When people are criticized, they almost never respond with openness and receptivity. Instead they put up barriers and begin defending themselves—the opposite of the desired response.

All of us want our people to improve, change, and grow. So it's time we discard the old term "constructive criticism" and replace it with "constructive support." This is a much better phrase. It creates a bond between you and the other person. Do your team members want to be supported in their growth and progress? Do they want to do better, feel fulfilled through work well done? You bet they do!

If you must tell someone about a mistake or work that needs improvement, you will get a lot further with a supportive approach. You may argue that this is only semantics, "that it's all the same thing in the end." No, it's not. Both what you say and how you say it are important. Your tone of voice can be supportive or confrontative, helpful or critical. It can say either, "I think you are incompetent," or "Let me help you do better."

If you want to make a difference in people's lives, try constructive support a few times and see what happens. I think you will be delighted with the results.

TRAINING

As leaders we must make education a top national priority. It is the key to staying competitive in the world market. Clients often tell me that one of their major problems is finding people who can read and write well enough to fill the jobs. It is said that "if you think education is expensive, try ignorance." As a nation we cannot afford twenty-seven million illiterate citizens. If we don't correct the problem we will pay the price of having an ignorant populace that can not fill the jobs that keep us moving ahead. Each dollar that *isn't* spent on education costs several dollars for social programs to solve the problems of the undereducated.

The training your organization provides its members can go a long way in solving the illiteracy problem.

ADULT LEARNING PRINCIPLES

Since motivation is an internal process that our team members must undergo themselves, your job is to find ways to trigger that process. Training is the key to unlock potential. When people can see a way to improve, they are more easily motivated to do so. Training is the great motivator.

The following are seven adult-learning principles that you, as leader, can implement or direct, either personally or through others.

1. DON'T SKIP THE BASICS

A construction company was building a large new home across the street from us. Every morning the foreman gathered all the workers together and reviewed the plans. I asked him why he did that, and he answered, "I just want to be sure that everyone keeps the whole plan in mind. If we need more supplies or equipment I need to know now, not later. This is just basic stuff."

I thought "basic stuff"—yes, but also important stuff. We are all building something, whether it is a product or a service. Reviewing the basics keeps us on track. More organizations have failed because they didn't review basics often enough, than because they reviewed them too often.

Vince Lombardi, acclaimed coach of the world-famous Green Bay Packers football team, would gather his team together at the start of each football season. Legend has it that he would face his men and hold up a football, saying: "Gentlemen, this is a football." Lombardi knew that, while you don't need to spend enormous amounts of time reviewing things that basic, you need to make sure that people don't lose the sharpness of their basic skills.

2. USE A "NEED TO KNOW" APPROACH

Teach adults what they need to know. For most people, new ideas, techniques, and information must be relevant to their immediate needs. The training must improve their ability to function, or they won't retain it. If you have a clear job description and performance standards for each individual, it will be easy to determine what they know now and what they need to know to improve.

3. STRESS PERSONAL BENEFITS

You can be good at reviewing the basics and using the "need to know" approach, but if you fail to begin each training session with some WIFMs (what's in it for me), your people will not be motivated to retain and use the training. The first thing you do is tie your training to a personal benefit. Each of us wants to know:

- How will this training benefit me?
- How will it increase my competence?
- Is it relevant to my job or life?

4. GIVE HANDS-ON TRAINING

The commonsense approach to training helps demystify issues. Confucius said, "I see and I forget. I hear and I remember. I do and I understand." A western equivalent is, "Experience is the best teacher." While you may not always be able to offer real-life experience in a training setting, simulation and role playing are invaluable.

5. USE SHORT TRAINING SESSIONS

There may not always be a choice, but as often as possible, have short training sessions. Use the formula: learn, study (or experience), then return for feedback and further learning.

6. RECOGNIZE INDIVIDUAL LEARNING RATES AND STYLES

Realize that adults learn at different rates and in different ways. Provide a variety of instructional techniques such as lectures, discussions, and role play.

7. MATCH THE TRAINING TO THE STUDENT

When a new person joins your team, find out what prior training they have had. Take the time to assess their knowledge and experience. Then, when you are planning a training session, you can match the training to the proper student.

It seems that as soon as you have one training session, another is needed. It also seems that there is never enough time to do all the training you should. The best you can do is to stay current with the training needs of the team, schedule top-quality training, and do it as often as possible. Training makes the difference between having people on your team with good intentions and those who can make a difference.

DELEGATING

To be a team builder who really makes a difference, you must be willing and able to delegate. You cannot practice the old saw, "If you want something done right, do it yourself." Teach yourself to delegate the projects and details that others can do or can learn to do.

Seven Steps To Productive Delegating

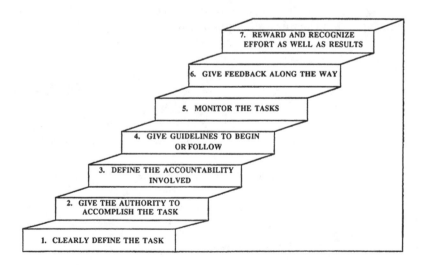

The important thing to remember about delegating is that if you can't or won't delegate, you send a negative message to others: "I don't trust you," or "The job is so important that you are not capable of doing it." Have faith in your people. Be willing to let them make mistakes or even fail while learning. (This is discussed at length in the chapter on risk taking.)

Here are the keys to help you avoid the "do it myself" trap. They'll help you become a leader who delegates effectively.

1. CLEARLY DEFINE THE TASK

When you assign work, don't tell people how to do the job. Instead, describe the results you want. Then give them an opportunity to complete the task on their own. This can even be a short goal-setting session. The better you can describe the benefits of accomplishing the task, the more interest there will be in seeing it through.

2. GIVE THE AUTHORITY TO ACCOMPLISH THE TASK

There is nothing worse than being given a job to do but not the authority to get it done. If you don't trust someone, give the job to someone else or assign it in stages so you can monitor it more closely. Don't demotivate a person by withholding authority.

3. DEFINE THE ACCOUNTABILITY INVOLVED

People want to and must be held accountable for their actions. How else can success or failure be measured? Without a clear description of accountability, people don't know the parameters of the job they are being asked to do. They don't know how far they can or should go. Accountability is crucial in delegating effectively.

The next time you bring a bag of groceries home from the store, look at the bottom of the paper bag. If it was produced by Princeton bag company you'll find some very interesting printing. The one I am looking at reads:

With Pride from The Best People
Princeton
Personally Inspected by Dorothy Carter

The folks at Princeton bag are accountable for their work. They are equally proud to tell us who is responsible for inspecting our bags.

4. GIVE GUIDELINES TO BEGIN OR FOLLOW

Assuming you have matched the right task with the right person, you can increase your delegating success by giving guidelines on how to begin. Some people only need to be given the ball and they are off and running on their own. These high achievers are a joy to have on a team. They will ask for help when they need it, but are able to monitor themselves.

However, not everyone can jump into a situation and immediately be off down the road. Some people are afraid of losing face and won't tell you they don't know how to begin. When you give helpful hints and guidelines for the delegated task, you cover all three groups:

* You reinforce the skill of the high achiever.
* You "save face" for the uncertain.
* You instruct the unskilled.

5. MONITOR THE TASKS

The word is "monitor," not hover. It is frustrating and discouraging to be given a task and then have the leader peering over your shoulder every step of the way. Give people room to operate and the freedom to use their skills and talents. If you think the job is too big or too difficult, break it down into more manageable parts.

6. GIVE FEEDBACK ALONG THE WAY

There are two ways to give feedback: Asking questions and giving advice. Questions help people clarify their thoughts and ideas. "Bob, how do you think this project is going so far?" gives Bob a chance to express himself without being intimidated by your opinion. When Bob feels that his opinion is important, it is a lot easier to help him make a "course adjustment."

Statements can be equally motivating and informative: "Betty, I think you are doing well. May I make a suggestion?" You can let people know you value them and want to help them do better. Feedback is the only way people can judge how they are doing along the way to the desired goal.

7. REWARD AND RECOGNIZE EFFORT AS WELL AS RESULTS

To build a team of people to whom you can delegate difficult tasks, you need to reward and recognize effort as well as results.

There are those motivated folks we spoke of earlier who can run with the ball and find their own joy and motivation along the way to the goal post. Others can't even see the goal post. If you give them a task and say, "Here it is, tiger, go get 'em," they may freeze or panic. However, these people *can* be developed into trusted team members by rewarding and recognizing their efforts along the way to the goal. Bring them along slowly. Help these folks one step at a time. Delegate small tasks to them. Let them build confidence in themselves and in you as the leader. At the same time don't forget to give plenty of recognition and reward to your high achievers. Remember, many of these folks enjoy the journey as much as the reward, but praise from the leader is still necessary to keep them motivated.

GRATIFYING—MAKE IT ENJOYABLE

We rarely succeed at any task unless we enjoy it. One of the most significant tasks you have as a team builder is to create an atmosphere free of tension, fire fighting, and stress, in which your team can enjoy its work. Obviously, everything isn't fun and games. But if you can find ways to tap people's inner excitement, if you can make their work enjoyable, you'll go a long way toward channeling their talents and energies to achieve the goals of the team.

I've met many leaders who understand the value of making work enjoyable. One of the best is Mary Jayne Overman, a team builder par excellence. When she was hired as the new president of Commercial Properties Group, Inc., in Glendale, California, the company was managing forty-one office and industrial properties with a square footage of 1.8 million. During her first year as president, she and her team set an unprecedented leasing record—1 million square feet! By the end of her second year, the Commercial Properties Group managed sixty-two properties in ten states with more than 4 million square feet, 1,600 tenants, and a ninety-two percent occupancy rate. Mary Jayne is one of the finest team builders I've ever met. She makes her team's tasks enjoyable and interesting. She directs and motivates her people. She trains them well and is not afraid to delegate. She says, "I knew where I was going. I had to get everyone to go with me. The vision of what the company could become and where it could go had to be put into something the people could digest and understand and accept. I wanted them to say, 'Okay, I'll join you because I know where you are going and I want to go there too.' "

M.J. (her nickname) directed her team to set mini-missions.

We had to take it one step at a time. We broke everything down into goals and plateaus that allowed [employees] to achieve recognition and feel good about themselves, rather than having to worry about how to deal with the entire picture at once.

We replaced the executive staff, trained the on-site staff, involved the accounting people in the field operation, and went back to the basics. Ours was a theme of "keep it simple," streamline administration, put leaders in charge, and make it happen!

M.J. trained, delegated, and motivated her people to success.

Leading the Commercial Properties Group is more an adventure than work. If you can get people enthusiastic, you get a lot more done. I avoided criticizing the old regime or dissecting the past mistakes. I said, "That was past history—that was yesterday, let's see what tomorrow will bring." Rather than saying "this is all wrong," I started with today and said "this is where we need to be in thirty days."

I try to create little entrepreneurial teams that have their own missions and goals and hurdles so that they are working on their goal, which is part of a larger one. All our success was based on taking what was there and supporting it, believing it, giving everyone permission to think. I was always asking questions: How are you? How do you like this? How is it going? Where are you? What do you want to do in life? Why are you still here? How did you survive this chaos?

As the coach, I had to be sensitive to the team's needs. Any time there is a massive change in someone's life or business, it can create chaos. The team needed to trust me, so I covered the entire country and talked to them all. They were surprised that I was so normal—not presidential. I had solutions to their problems, gave them permission to make decisions, eliminated levels of confusion. I put them in charge and told them where we were going in a very positive way.

I asked team members questions: How can we streamline this? What paperwork can we throw away? How can we get back to the basics of our business? What kind of staffing do you need? How much will it take to fill up the building? I was interested in them as people first, and then I wanted their thoughts on how to streamline the business, how to make money and have more fun. What's the scariest part of the job? What concerns you? What kind of training did you have? What have you heard about me? Will you feel comfortable picking up the phone to call me?

I have a good sense of humor and I use it to tell them about me, about my mistakes, the risks I've taken, the barriers I've overcome. I tell them I don't know all the answers. If you can be real about yourself, it gives them hope that they, too, can succeed. Even now, I'll know when they are troubled about something. I may not know exactly what it is, but when you've been in business for twenty-five years, you have a funny story or example about almost anything. Then their stress level drops and they say to themselves, "I'm okay—she understands." Leaders need a sense of humor and the ability to tell stories so their people know that they are human, too.

Consistent training is very important. It should offer a long-term view with the same message for everyone in the company. At the Commercial Properties Group we communicate directly with field people. Everyone knows the score. We train the entire company on certain skills and philosophies of doing business, on caring for the tenants. We help them realize that without our clients we have no business.

As a child I was taught to treat others the way you want to be treated. So I teach my team to collect information, to make decisions, that it's okay to make mistakes—nothing is terminal. I have learned to be a good listener. I like to free people from routine, have everyone aware of my agendas, keep everyone energized. We dissect the failures briefly with input from everyone, then we get on with solutions. I spend one-on-one time with my people—a phone call, a note. A little reinforcement makes a big difference. I am here to serve others. I like to get people to keep enlarging their scope, not to become static or think they have all the answers. I like to say "yes" a lot, give people choices, and keep everyone on the same track.

WHAT ABOUT YOUR TEAM?

Do your followers have an opportunity to have fun and laugh occasionally? Is the team spirit high? Do they look forward to coming to work or being on the team? Do they want to follow you because they find their work enjoyable and fulfilling?

Team building is the catalyst of all you want to accomplish. As a servant-leader there is no better way to serve your followers than by directing, motivating, training, delegating, and gratifying. These five make up the formula for success. The road to making a difference can be challenging and difficult, but with a team of competent, willing helpers, you will find the journey much more worthwhile.

A LEADER IS COURAGEOUS

Strengthening Resolve

"Few will have the greatness to bend
history itself, but each of us can work to
change a small portion of events . . . it is from
numberless acts of courage and belief
that human history is shaped."
—ROBERT F. KENNEDY

The United States is at a crossroad in its history. We can continue our headlong rush to materialism and financial Darwinism, or we can have the courage to take up the challenge that President George Bush gave: to build a kinder, gentler America. We have a track record of accomplishing impossible feats and we can accomplish this one, too. If we work together, we can maintain our standard of living, increase our productivity, and stop the growing division between the haves and have-nots. It won't be easy. It will take individual sacrifice and national sacrifice. There may be a time when sacrifice will mean giving up an hour or two of your leisure time each week to go out and lend a hand. Sacrifice may mean spending some of your hard-earned money to support a cause you care about. But you'll be sacrificing ego gratification for soul gratification.

The "thousand points of light" President Bush campaigned on are you and me. They are our neighbors, our families, our coworkers—each of us having the courage to face difficult or unpopular issues. We must build our courage so that we can lead, not just manage.

We must balance self-interest with the interests of our nation and our world. Unless we have the courage to include all the people, not just one segment or special interest group, in our leadership, we will never have that "kinder, gentler nation."

The hour of courage is here. The challenge is, what will you do to make a difference?

DEFINING COURAGE

We may define courage as: "The state or quality of mind or spirit that enables one to face danger with self-possession, confidence, and resolution." Danger is obviously relative. It is dangerous to live in the nuclear age. It is dangerous to put yourself on the line and stand up for your beliefs. It is dangerous to get involved in relationships with others. You could get hurt. The world has always been a dangerous place. And the world has always had leaders who led in spite of the dangers.

There's a saying that courage is "fear that has said its prayers." We are all afraid of something. Yet we have all overcome fear and displayed bravery at some time in our lives. But there is more to courage than bravery in the face of danger or hardships. While there is physical courage, mental and moral courage are just as meaningful. Courage also means being able to keep going when the burden is heavy and there is no end in sight. Courage can be the willingness to live one day at a time, doing the best you can. Eleanor Roosevelt said, "You have to accept whatever comes and the only important thing is that you meet it with courage, with the best that you have to give."

Doing your best every day requires courage. The harder you try, the more you will develop the leadership quality recognized as *courage*. Persisting, hanging on, surviving, maintaining stamina through the daily wear and tear are courageous acts. Frances M. Beal said, "To die for the revolution is a one-shot deal; to live for the revolution means taking on the more difficult commitment of changing our day-to-day life patterns." Your courageous leadership will make a difference on that day-to-day basis.

Trying to describe courage and how to build it is like trying to describe love and learning to love. You know a courageous leader when you see one. You recognize the results of their courage and yet you wonder, "How do I become a more courageous leader myself?" The answer is not found in a set of skills, like those one develops for delegating or taking risks. The answer is in *knowing*—knowing what you need to be courageous about. First you discover the "why" of courage. Then the "how" will show itself to you.

————Sojourner Truth and the Law————

The struggle to change social and legal custom is one that requires an extraordinary kind of courage. How much easier, safer and more logical it would be to accept the status quo and concentrate on our own interests! But fortunately, there have always been mavericks with the courage to look beyond how things are.

During the fight against slavery in the nineteenth century, a former slave named Sojourner Truth had the courage to "get behind the law" to gain equality under the law. Born a slave in New York state in 1797, she saw her parents die of neglect and her children sold before she was freed by the state's emancipation law in 1828. She immediately used the law to regain her son from an Alabama plantation.

Later, she was the first black person to file a suit against a white person for slander. (She made further history by winning, even though her adversaries were prominent white people.) In 1843, eighteen years before the beginning of the Civil War, Truth left her job as a domestic to travel the country, speaking at religious and anti-slavery rallies.

Her electrifying presence gained her many followers as she took on many unpopular causes: workers' and women's rights and prison reform, as well as abolition. She was the first black person to test the legal desegregation of the streetcars of Washington, D.C., enduring the pummeling of outraged whites so that she could cry, "I've had a ride!" The Freedom Riders that rode the buses in the 1960s were direct descendants of her courage.

Truth worked tirelessly to aid freed slaves in finding homes, jobs, and opportunities. Labeled "crazy" by her opponents, she became such a legend in her own lifetime that newspaper accounts of her exploits often added twenty or thirty years to her age, making her as old as the nation she was born in. During the Civil War she challenged the Southern sympathizers who wanted to silence her: "If you put me in the guardhouse," she said, "I'll make the United States rock like a cradle."

Tall, imposing, and deeply religious, she never let fear of hardship or danger deter her. When she met Abraham Lincoln, she told him, "I never heard of you before they put you up for president." Lincoln replied, "But I have heard of you."

CHALLENGING A NATION

One hundred years later, we still find courageous men and women leading us in our search for a fair, challenging, compassionate world.

- Ralph Nader's battle for the consumer was far from popular when he began. He was dismissed, denounced, and evaded by the companies, products, and groups that he challenged.
- Gloria Steinem and Betty Friedan rocked the nation in leading the revolution for women's rights. Their challenges to legal inequality reverberated to the most personal corners of our social structure.
- During the early days of the Vietnam War, when the "hawks" were equating disagreement with treason, Senators Wayne Morse from Oregon and Ernest Gruening from Alaska were solitary voices against the war.

All of these people were attacked and vilified for their actions. They could have chosen an easier path, but, diverse as they were, they shared one trait: courage. Their deep beliefs in emotional, intellectual, and spiritual values kept them going when most other people would have given up. Despite almost daily confrontations and harassment, they applied their resources and creative energy against seemingly overwhelming odds.

THE HOWS AND WHYS OF COURAGE

General George C. Patton said courage is "fear holding on another minute." Our most courageous leaders are valiant and undaunted in their approach to life. They "hold on." They venture forth with faith and stamina to set a courageous example for others to follow. You can do the same right in your community, your job, your family. Your grass-roots leadership will inspire others.

You build your courage as a leader when you:

- follow a difficult path in the face of danger
- stand up boldly for your beliefs and values
- sacrifice immediate satisfaction for future gains
- follow your instincts and act on your own unique strengths

There are many ways for you to be a courageous leader who makes a difference. Each of the other eleven qualities in this book offer many opportunities for strengthening your resolve.

BECOMING MORE COURAGEOUS

To be a more effective leader, it is vital that you evaluate your capacity for courage. This is not always easy, but candor in your self-examination will show where you can improve. The more clearly defined your personal list of courageous qualities, the stronger you will become.

Here are descriptions of sixteen kinds of courage. As you consider them, remember that "school" is never out for a leader. At the end of each description, step back and act as your own teacher. Give yourself a grade on willingness and ability:

A = excellent
B = good
C = average
D = below average
F = failing.

1. *The courage to seek the truth.* The truth is not always easy to accept. It is rarely what you want it to be. The truth may even conflict with things you have a great investment in: It may threaten your physical, intellectual, and emotional security. But to lead in the next few decades, you'll need to seek truth.

There is an old story about truth that makes the point very well. A man was elected president of a large company. One of the older directors said, "So now you are president."

"So it seems," the man said.

"Then," said the older man, "you have heard the truth for the last time."

The more power you have and the higher your leadership takes you, the more critical it is to maintain access to the truth. Senator Sam Ervin of South Carolina said, "It is impossible to overmagnify the importance of seeking truth. This is so because truth alone can make us free." Your personal freedom depends on your ability to seek and find truth.

My grade for seeking truth:

Willingness _____

Ability _____

2. *The courage to have faith.* Sam Ervin also said:

> Faith is not a storm cellar to which men and women can flee for refuge from the storms of life. It is, instead, an inner force which gives them the strength to face those storms and their consequences with serenity of spirit. In times of greatest stress, faith has the miraculous power to uplift ordinary men and women to greatness.

Faith uplifted Martin Luther King, Jr., into greatness. He was threatened, harassed, beaten, arrested and jailed. When his house was dynamited he quietly said, "Let us keep moving with the faith that what we are doing is right, and with the even greater faith that God is with us in this struggle." When he led 250,000 people on a civil-rights rally in Washington, D.C., it was an act of faith that reached around the world.

In assessing our courage to have faith, there are many factors to question: What do I have faith about? Do I have faith in my God-given skills, talents, and abilities? Do I have faith in people's desire to lead a productive, contributing life? Do I have faith in the democratic process and in democratic systems of government?

Just to reply, "Yes, I have faith," is not enough. Where is your faith strongest? Weakest? Where do you need to build your courage?

My grade for having faith:

Willingness _____ _____

Ability _____

3. *The courage to seek humility.* Humility may be defined as the "quality of being humble; a modest sense of one's own significance." We must never mistake education for knowledge, specialization for expertise, or a confident façade for understanding and wisdom. Thousands of people learn how to study, take tests,

write impressive papers, and get high grades, yet have little or no skill in leading people.

We possess money and think we have worth. The person who has the privilege of education, who builds people skills, who combines experience with knowledge, and then balances all of that with humility, has the potential to be a great leader. Self-importance and arrogance will destroy the personal power of anyone trying to lead.

Being humble doesn't mean being weak or lacking in courage. Just the opposite. Humility is one of the most powerful tools you can possess. Humility respects and enhances the opinions and skills of others. But it is also the most difficult trait to acquire. Coleridge wrote that the devil's favorite sin "was the pride that apes humility." And T. S. Eliot noted, "Humility is the most difficult of all virtues to achieve."

My grade for seeking humility:

Willingness _____

Ability _____

4. *The courage to live an ethical life.* At the age of nine, Henry Heinz helped his mother in her four-acre vegetable patch and sold their surplus door to door out of a basket. At twelve he made his rounds with a horse and cart. Then he constructed special hot beds, which are highly fertilized and intensely cultivated growing areas. He hired three women to help his mother. By the age of sixteen he was supplying nearby Pittsburgh markets. His precocity and business savvy continued to pay off until, at the age of thirty, he made a disastrous investment. He had agreed to buy cucumbers at a fixed price, but a bumper crop flooded the market, dropping the price and forcing him to sell his relishes at a loss. The business prodigy was now bankrupt. Although he had no legal obligation, Heinz got a notebook and wrote on the cover, "The Moral Obligations Book of Henry J. Heinz, 1875." He repaid all the people who had trusted him, then he started another company, one that became famous for Heinz's 57 Varieties.

All of us keep a "Moral Obligations Book" in our head or our heart. Describe yours. How successful are you at maintaining high ethics? Golda Meir, prime minister of Israel, said, "I can honestly say that I was never affected by the question of the success of an undertaking. If I felt it was the right thing to do, I was for it, regardless of the possible outcome.''

Napoleon Hill, author of the 1928 book, *The Laws Of Success,* wrote that ''moral courage demands that you assume responsibility for your own acts.'' Any ideology that relieves people of personal responsibility, that encourages or requires them to surrender personal morality to others, is dangerous.''

Review chapter 3, ''A Leader Has High Ethics,'' if you need to. In a cynical, sometimes dissolute world, it takes a special kind of courage to resist the temptations and derision of those less ethical. Do you have that kind of courage?

My grade for living an ethical life:

Willingness _____

Ability _____

5. *The courage to be involved.* Apathy and indifference can be more devastating than any natural or manmade disasters. As a leader, can you get people involved? Do you set an example of personal effort and personal involvement? We've read about people ignoring someone in trouble. Have people become so desensitized that they no longer see what their apathy is doing to their community and themselves? One important job a leader has is to attack the apathy of others, to get them involved.

People laughed at Ted Lempert when he said he wanted to get involved. He said he wanted to make a difference; he thought one person still had the ability to change things for the better. When he graduated from Stanford law school and began practicing in his home town, he was drawn into community matters. He told his family and a few friends that he wanted to run for the State Assembly. They were encouraging, but his support stopped there. No one knew about the inner courage and determination he possesssed.

Ted Lempert was only twenty-seven years old. He had always been interested in community affairs. Members of the local political ''machine'' thought, ''How can a young, inexperienced person, with no money and no clout unseat an incumbent with over a quarter of a million dollars in his war chest?'' When he registered as a candidate the odds were 51 to 17 against him. No one including his own party took him seriously.

Ted Lempert began what was an impossible campaign. He decided that old-fashioned door-to-door politics was what his district needed. In March of the election year he began walking the precincts and knocking on doors. As he went door to door he began to ask his neighbors to help. Could they give a little time? Could they give a little money? Could they come down and make some phone calls? What started slowly with no publicity became a campaign that broke all the rules. By August he had personally knocked on 30,000 doors in his districts and by election day he had 700 volunteers knocking on every door in every walkable precinct.

Two and a half weeks before voting day the leaders of his party finally had to admit that maybe the "kid" had an outside chance. His opponent had outspent him 2 to 1, yet the polls showed Ted had closed the gap. He had made believers of a lot of people, including his own party, which finally gave him 300 thousand dollars. In the last two weeks of the campaign he covered the district with radio and other publicity. On election night a jubilant Ted Lempert won the election that could not be won. He became the first Democrat to hold the State Assembly seat from his district since they began keeping records over 100 years ago.

He attributes his victory to his campaign issues of clean government, campaign reform, education, the environment, and the willingness of individuals to become involved.

When I asked him about the power of involvement he said: "People don't think they can make a difference. When they get involved, they're amazed at how much they can accomplish."

You don't have to run for office to be involved in something that matters. But as a leader you must re-examine your willingness and ability to be involved. You can't make a difference without being involved.

My grade for being involved:

Willingness _____

Ability _____

6. *The courage to believe in something.* Thomas Carlyle wrote, "A man lives by believing something, not by debating and arguing many things." One of the toughest questions is, "What do I believe in?" That's because it must naturally be followed by other questions: "Why do I believe this?" and "What would I do to support or protect my belief?"

Do you have the courage to question your beliefs—not to destroy or minimize them, but to reconfirm their meaning and value? Are you sure you haven't bought a package of someone else's ideas that don't mesh with your own values? Having and supporting strong beliefs is much harder than it seems.

Sydney Harris wrote, "I am tired of hearing about men with the 'courage of their convictions.' Nero and Caligula and Attila and Hitler had the courage of their convictions. . . . But not one of them had the courage to examine their convictions or to change them, which is the true test of character."

Do you have the courage to find men and women who will challenge your beliefs? Great leaders can step outside of their comfort zones and decide which convictions and beliefs to hold on to and which to consider modifying. Leaders' words must match their deeds or they lose credibility.

My grade for believing in something:
Willingness _____
Ability _____

7. *The courage to reject cynicism.* We have more than enough cynics in this world. In the name of "truth" and "reality," they try to make the world as barren for us as it is for them. You can't indulge in the luxury of cynicism and still expect to build the trust and optimism needed to inspire effective teams of people who make a difference.

Cynicism is a form of protection, an attitude that prevents disappointment by expecting only the worst from people and events. Having trust in people is a courageous act.

Cynicism, on the other hand, requires no courage. Cynicism doesn't solve problems, expand relationships, or provide positive energy for the tasks we face. You serve your followers well when you set an example of realistic optimism.

My grade on avoiding cynicism:
Willingness _____
Ability _____

8. *The courage to resist social and peer pressure.* One of the most courageous things you can do is identify yourself, know who you are, what you believe in, and where you want to go. This is the first step in resisting social and peer pressure. When you know

who you are, where you are going, and approximately how you wish to get there, then you do not succumb to distractions easily. Have the courage to determine your own values and lifestyle. Don't trade integrity for status or power—it's a very poor bargain. It is helpful to start by describing "success" in very personal terms. Success has become a catchall word. What does it mean to you? The clichés—"happiness," "money," or "helping others"—are not definitions. They are pleasant concepts, but they do not address the real issues. What does happiness mean? Do you need to control your workaholic behavior and spend more time with your family? What does "money" mean? You will never have "enough" money. There is no such thing. When you achieve a level of financial success, the next level beckons and seduces you. "Helping others" is nice. But what others? Where are they? What are their problems?

When defining success you have to go below the surface and start defining general terms. Then you get to the core ideas; that is where you can really begin to make a difference.

Ralph Waldo Emerson wrote:

> To laugh often and much, to win the respect of intelligent people and the affection of children, to earn the appreciation of critics and endure the betrayal of false friends, to appreciate beauty, to find the best in others, to leave this world a bit better, whether by a healthy child, a garden patch, or redeemed social condition, to know that even one life has breathed easier because you have lived, this is to have success.

What is your definition of success?

My grade for resisting social and peer pressure:

    Willingness _____

    Ability _____

9. *The courage to speak out.* The magazine *Bits and Pieces* (December, 1982) reported, "Most of us are proud of our freedom to say what we please. What we wish we had is the courage to say it." Do you have the courage to use the words that encourage others, that reach out to lead, words like brotherhood, family, honor, duty, justice, loyalty, compassion, faith, courage, and God? Do you have the courage to speak out in the face of ridicule, intimidation, even danger?

Martin Niemoeller, the prominent German minister, commented after World War II: "In Germany, they came first for the Communists, and I didn't speak up because I wasn't a Communist. Then they came for the Jews, and I didn't speak up because I wasn't a Jew. They came for the trade unionists, and I didn't speak up because I wasn't a trade unionist. They came for the Catholics, and I didn't speak up because I was a Protestant. Then they came for me, and by that time no one was left to speak up."

"You die one way or the other. Either you speak out and take the risk or you die in the cesspool." Powerful words, spoken by a powerful, determined individual. Barbara Washington is forty-seven years old. She raised eleven children on her own. She lives in Boston's Columbia Point housing project, one of the toughest in the nation. Drugs, guns, and poverty are a way of life. One day she said, that's enough. I've had it. She organized the Columbia Point Anti-Drug Committee. She spoke out and gave others courage to join her. They set up hot lines for anonymous tips. They held anti-drug rallies in the park. In an area where there had been no arrests for drug dealing, Barbara's words and actions are beginning to take effect. She says, "If you get even one off the street, it's better than none. It's important to make a difference." Barbara Washington is a leader in her community, making a difference.

When was the last time you spoke out for what you believe, even though it meant supporting someone you dislike or criticizing someone you admire? Did you have the courage to withstand criticism for your beliefs?

My grade on speaking out:

    Willingness _____

    Ability _____

10. *The courage to be controversial.* Some people deliberately create controversy for their own benefit: to stimulate interest for publicity, as a bargaining device, or to demonstrate their own power. Yet few people feel comfortable in the midst of controversy.

Mary Hart Kimball Massie Todd is controversial. Her opponents called her a Communist. She had the courage to tell them they were wrong. She remembers when integration turned her home of Nashville into a battle ground and she joined blacks at lunch counters. She has worked to abolish the state's poll tax. She has defended juvenile rights. She has been an activist for fifty years. At eighty-three she is still out lobbying lawmakers for aid to the homeless. She says, "I still have some things to do and I'm going to be busy doing them." Mary Todd will continue to have the courage to be controversial; it is a way of life for her.

This is an age of hard issues—not that we haven't been faced with hard issues before. But we have hard issues in greater magnitude than ever before. The sheer numbers of people on this planet and the possibility of exterminating them all within a few hours should impress us. If that possibility seems too overwhelming to grasp, there are still the issues of drug and alcohol abuse, poverty and the homeless, the AIDS epidemic, minority rights, and world hunger. Leaders must be prepared to deal with these tough issues and have ideas on how to help those they lead. Andrew Jackson wrote, "One man with courage makes a majority."

To move toward your mission you'll need the courage to handle the controversy associated with new ideas and solutions that defy conventions. With all the challenges we face—the diminishing ozone layer, pollution of our deepest oceans, the inequitable world food supply, profound issues of social and economic justice— there is no way to avoid controversial solutions.

My grade in handling controversy:

Willingness _____

Ability _____

11. *The courage to assume responsibility.* Assuming responsibility for your own actions requires courage. It also takes courage to assume responsibility for the actions of your followers—their failures as well as their successes. When your followers know you will always be behind them, they will be there for you, too.

Responsibility is inherent in all the qualities of leadership. Lack of responsibility and accountability has caused many of the major problems we live with today. There can never be too much emphasis on being responsible and accountable when it comes to being a leader.

My grade for taking responsibility:

Willingness _____

Ability _____

12. *The courage to lead at home.* Courage to lead at home is as important as leadership in the world beyond. If you are a parent, do you have the courage to offer your children equal discipline and love? In the push and pull of working families, we can not afford to have our leadership role delegated to childcare workers. Ask yourself some tough questions:

* If my child were to become my leader, would I want to follow?
* Does she or he have the values and ability of a leader I could follow?

The point is not to push our children into positions of leadership, but to be sure that we pass our leadership abilities on to those that matter most to us.

Columnist Walter Lippman wrote that "the final test of a leader is that he leaves behind him in other men the conviction and the will to carry on. . . . The genius of a good leader is to leave behind him a situation which commonsense, without the grace of genius, can deal with successfully." When we mentor our own children, we leave our most powerful legacy.

My grade for leading at home:
Willingness _____
Ability _____

13. *The courage to stand for something.* Be a leader who stands *for* something, not just against something. Know what you want, not just what you don't want. It makes a big difference in your approach to life, problems, and people.

It's easy to speak out against things without offering solutions. But simply stating what you are against can lead to trouble. The McCarthy "witch hunts" of the 1950s were a perfect example; everyone was against the perceived threat of Communism. Senator Joseph McCarthy exploited that fear to create a personal power base, ruining people's lives in the process.

How you approach problems is greatly affected by your original premise. If it is negatively oriented ("That's wrong!"), solutions are usually sketchy and often ignored. Some people appear to be leaders because they can state very clearly what they are against. It's important to ask them, "What solutions do you have?" Ask them what do they stand *for*.

My grade for standing for something:
Willingness _____
Ability _____

14. *The courage to persist.* In 1894, the rhetoric teacher at Harrow in England wrote on a sixteen-year-old's report card, "A conspicuous lack of success." Winston Churchill persisted.

In 1902, the poetry editor of *Atlantic Monthly* returned the poems of a twenty-eight-year-old poet with the following note: "Our magazine has no room for your vigorous verse." Robert Frost persisted.

In 1905, the University of Bern rejected a Ph.D. dissertation, saying that it was irrelevant and fanciful. Albert Einstein persisted.

In 1932, a Hollywood studio employee evaluated the screen test of a newly imported Broadway performer: "Short, balding, enormous ears, and bad chin line, can sing and dance a little." Fred Astaire persisted.

One of our greatest weaknesses is our obsession with immediate gratification. We want it *nice* and we want it *now!* That covers everything from the quarterly-earnings report for stock holders to our insatiable appetite for feeling good and having our rewards and toys right now.

The leaders we need for the next critical decades are the ones with the courage to tell us about the long haul—where we will be in thirty or forty years and what will we lose if we don't change our ways. They need to tell the truth and say, "You cannot have it all. The world does not work that way." We need to hear this from the president and special interest groups, from heads of companies and worker organizations, from parents and our children. We must have a longer view of life.

These same leaders need the courage to use the big "S" word: SACRIFICE. You remember Aesop's fable about the ant and the grasshopper. While the grasshopper played during the summer, the ant worked hard to store food. When the snow came, the grasshopper perished. Good leaders capture the attention of the eternally optimistic "grasshopper" in all of us and then appeal to our cautious "ant," making us willing to sacrifice short-term gratifications for long-term benefits.

How many times have you been rejected, criticized, or ridiculed?

How many times has your courage to continue been tested? For how many projects have you had the courage to follow through, to persist over the long haul?

My grade for persistence:

Willingness _____

Ability _____

15. *The courage to serve.* The first astronauts certainly had the courage to serve their fellow Americans and all mankind. Their rockets and space capsules seem pitifully small and primitive now, almost like the early constructions of wire and cloth that bore the first aviators into the air. The computers that sent the early space travelers into the cosmos were less sophisticated than today's average home computer.

The courage to serve others can mean putting ourselves second. In an ego-driven, success-driven society, that takes courage. But only in serving others can we reach the true pinnacle of leading.

How we serve our people directly affects how they serve the people they deal with. Customer service is one of the hottest topics today, and it should be. The real service problems don't begin with the service workers. They begin with the leaders.

Do you ask your employees to provide good service and then tie their hands with policy? Do you give them the tools they need to solve problems? Which is more important to you, people or policy? If it's people, that does not mean you must throw policy out the window. And if it's policy, have the courage to make this clear to your followers. Don't give them a double message.

I've often wished that the people writing the advertising copy about service were the ones running the stores and institutions with which we do business. Service is more than training people to smile nicely and answer questions. Service means giving satisfaction—solving problems, filling needs, finding answers. Do you, as leader, personify the attitude toward service that you want your people to have? Do you have the courage to really serve?

"He had the passion of a missionary and he really wanted to help people" is the answer Judith Welsh gave when asked if she was bitter about her husband's death. Kevin Welsh was a police officer in Washington, D.C. One day, three weeks before the birth of their third son, Kevin answered a call on his police radio. A woman had tried to commit suicide by jumping from a bridge into the river. Kevin and another officer jumped in to save her, but she drowned. The swift currents pulled both officers away; the other officer was saved—Kevin was not. Was his life wasted? Judith said he died doing what his life was about—serving others.

My grade for serving others:

Willingness _____

Ability _____

16. *The courage to follow.* Harry Cordellos is blind, but not without insight. He believes, "There is a real difference between failing and being a failure. The loser isn't the one who comes in last—it's the one who never entered the race." This may sound like a motivational platitude until you realize that Harry Cordellos is a marathon runner. He travels the country running races with a sighted guide. Harry is a leading member of the United States Association of Blind Athletes. When he is not racing he gives motivational speeches to schools, colleges, and conventions to promote the cause of blind athletes.

Harry has all the leadership qualities, yet he must be a follower when he is actually running. As his guide takes him through the streets or over rough terrain Harry becomes an expert "follower."

Even the most exalted leader must be a follower at some point. A wise and humble leader knows when it's time to step down and follow. When you switch to the role of follower, you become doubly aware of the challenges that followers face every day. How do you separate leaders of substance from those who possess only the *image* of being a leader? One way is to observe their willingness to be a follower when necessary.

When you are called upon to share your power, to let someone else take the lead, are you able to step aside? Do you feel that your position is threatened?

My grade for willingness to follow:

Willingness _____

Ability _____

PLANNING FOR COURAGE

When you have graded yourself on these questions, decide which areas you will work on first to make yourself a more courageous leader. What factors are the most important for your personal growth? Make an action plan and incorporate it into your daily activities.

As with mission building, you should start small. Don't discourage yourself by setting your standards too high at first. It is better to advance slowly than not to start at all!

MUCH IS REQUIRED OF YOU

President John F. Kennedy said, "Of those to whom much is given, much is required." The gift of leadership is a great responsibility, one that requires much courage. Your mettle is truly tested when you ask yourself penetrating questions about your own capacity for courage.

How you describe courage may change with time and place, but the need for courage does not. As a modern leader you must be acutely aware of the new generations who are eagerly seeking ideals to follow. You must have the courage to tolerate and promote new standards, while retaining and even revering the best of the old. It takes courage to let go of outdated "oughts and shoulds." It also takes courage to resist the novelty of each flashy new concept that promises easy solutions to age-old problems.

Followers want to be loyal. They are loyal when they feel that they belong and can make a contribution. They want to be productive in an environment of fairness and mutual respect. The new values and work ethics demand the courage to confront changing times.

Michael Maccoby, author of *The Leader,* discusses the new social characteristics of leaders: "A caring, respectful, and responsible attitude; flexibility about people and organizational structure; and a participative approach to management, the willingness to share power. Furthermore, they are self-aware, concerned with self-development for themselves as well as others."

Be honest about yourself and your life ambitions. Ask, "Why do I want to be a leader?" Socrates and Plato challenged their students to have the courage to examine their life. Plato said, "A life unexamined isn't worth living." Have the courage to look deep into yourself to evaluate your courage. Then have the courage to invest in yourself, to build your leadership skills, and develop a philosophy, so that when all is said and done they will say that your leadership "made a difference."

LEADERSHIP QUALITY TWELVE

A LEADER IS COMMITTED
The Glue To Success

"Nothing resists a human will that stakes its
very existence upon the achievement of its purpose."
—BENJAMIN DISRAELI,
Former Prime Minister of England

Four-year-old Francisca was frightened. She liked the man with
the kind face. But her swollen hand hurt and she did not understand why she had to leave her parents. When her father kissed her
goodby she clung to him tearfully. As Señor Pena held her he
prayed that God would be good to his little daughter. She had been
through so much for one so young.

As Ray Gatchalian gently took Francisca from her father he had
to hold back his own tears. He knew how hard it would be if he
had to turn his daughter over to someone, even if it were to get
her medical attention that would save her life. This was a difficult
moment for everyone. But Ray knew that if the surgery was successful, Francisca would be back soon—a healthy, happy little
girl.

Ray met Francisca and her father on one of his frequent visits
to El Salvador. "I fell in love with her," Ray says. "It was so sad
to see her small hand swollen with cancer. There were no medical
facilities in El Salvador that could help her. I thought of my daughter and how lucky we are to live in America. I had to *do* something!"

Ray made a commitment to bring Francisca to the United States for the highly specialized surgery she needed. As he began his mission of mercy his passion attracted other people who wanted to help.

First, he worked with government officials and social workers to cut through red tape. His energy and dedication inspired them to make the extra effort necessary to get the job done quickly. He found someone who would donate transportation. Another provided a home for Francisca before and after the operation. A doctor and staff of six at Stanford Medical Center in Palo Alto, California, agreed to perform the surgery without charge.

When all the arrangements were made Ray returned to El Salvador to get Francisca. He carried the tearful child on the plane and flew with her to San Francisco. The story has a very happy ending. The surgery was successful. The useless, bloated appendage became a healthy, fully functioning hand. Francisca is back home with her family, laughing and playing, thanks to the deep personal commitment of Ray Gatchalian.

Ray earns his living as a fire fighter in Oakland, California. He is a fourteen-year veteran and captain of a fire station in the downtown area. In his "spare time" Ray works with young people, speaks for civic and business groups, writes and makes award-winning films. His moving short film, *Survival Run,* has won thirty-two national and international awards. It is about two runners, one blind and one sighted. *In No One's Shadow* describes the history of Filipinos in America. His most recent film, *Unheard Voices,* is about the children of El Salvador.

In 1985 the Kellogg Foundation awarded Ray a three-year fellowship in leadership. Recipients of this prestigious grant participate in intensive study groups on world problems and go on fact-collecting expeditions all over the globe. Recently he decided to concentrate his efforts on the problems of Central America.

The first time I met Ray I was immediately struck by his quiet confidence. His deep personal power shows in his walk, his handshake and his voice. With a boyish grin and a sprinkling of gray hair, forty-three-year-old Ray Gatchalian looks like a born leader. If you told him that, he'd laugh; he is a very humble man. Ray believes that few people are born leaders. He says, "People think you have to be anointed in some way, or you have to be born into a particular situation to be a leader. Let's face it—most of us *learn* to be leaders, we *learn* to make a difference.

"I have found that a large percentage of the population operates under a dangerous illusion," he told me, "—the illusion that the world's problems are too big and too complex for one individual to make a difference. But I believe one person *can* make a difference. My dad always told me, 'We're here to inspire each other, to bring out the best in each other, and the only way we can do that is to care about each other.' "

Can the commitment of just one person really make a difference? Can it inspire others? Ray says, "You have to act on what you believe. When you do that, then people respond. Sometimes I wonder, 'What am I doing this for? Shouldn't I just be making money, getting a big house and a better car?' But the more I get involved with Francisca and the other children we've brought from Central America, the more I know that I have riches beyond anything I could buy. I hope other people will lend a hand and become involved, too."

Ray's commitment has touched many hands: the hands that applaud and wipe away tears at showings of his films; the hands of teen-aged audiences eagerly raised to ask hard and searching questions; the hands that reach out to his, seeking rescue from war and from the desperation of an existence without purpose or hope.

In his own strong hands Ray Gatchalian holds a small photo. It shows a beautiful little girl from El Salvador, a healthy child with two hands of her own—two hands that prove what just one leader's commitment can do.

YOUR COMMITMENT IS IMPORTANT

Commitment is the glue to your success as a leader. It is the binding force that holds the other eleven leadership qualities together and gives them power.

- Commitment to making a difference is the foundation of your mission that matters.
- Commitment to being a big thinker attracts others to you.
- Commitment to high ethics builds trust in your followers.

- Commitment to being a change master opens the door to your future.
- Commitment to being a sensitive leader inspires loyalty.
- Commitment in team building maximizes people potential.
- Commitment to be an effective communicator forges productive relationships.
- Commitment to being a decision maker unleashes your followers' talents.
- Commitment to using power wisely means mastering influence.
- Commitment to risk taking is expanding the possible.
- Commitment to being courageous strengthens everyone's resolve.

Commitment is important at every stage of your leadership development. It is that intangible ingredient you reach for, deep inside, to help you through the tough times. It is the inner strength that keeps you going when everyone else gives up. And total commitment can create miracles.

WHERE DOES THE FAST TRACK LEAD?

All across the country people tell me that even though they have all the "goodies" the fast track has to offer, they feel something is missing. They have nice homes and good jobs with large salaries and important titles. But they want their life to have more meaning. They want to make a difference, not just make a living. Quality of life is important to people.

Men and women from every state and every walk of life have told me that they want more time for their families and more time for their personal lives. The fast track has become a track to stress and loss of intimacy. People aren't saying they want less money or that they want to leave it all and run off to contemplate the meaning of life. But they want a change.

To make a contribution, to feel that one can make a difference, to have some control over one's life, and to look in the mirror and see someone likable—these are the feelings people value. In big cities and small towns people are becoming more involved in issues and problems that have been ignored for too long. They are finding a reward in giving, not just receiving. This giving is at the heart of grass-roots leadership.

You know what that reward is if you have received a smile and a thank you from an elderly person in a convalescent home,

- or served Thanksgiving or Christmas dinner to the homeless,
- or helped a drug user kick the habit,
- or given comfort to a person dying of AIDS,
- or worked to protect our fragile environment,
- or taught someone to read,
- or protected children from abuse,
- or stood up for the civil rights of your fellow citizens.

THE AGE OF VALUES IS COMING

In the last twenty years people haven't always valued this kind of reward. The seventies was the me decade. The eighties was the materialistic decade. But already we can see that in the nineties our values are changing.

We are helping our fellow human beings more. The eternal values—faith, trust, hope, love, justice, mercy, honesty, service, sacrifice, humility, and charity—are in style again. Already, there are people leading the way. They are showing us that we can make a difference, that each of us does matter in the bigger scheme of life. They are reminding us that grass-roots leadership is important.

———*Grass-roots Leadership Among the Young*———

In 1986 Olivia Milonas was a sophomore at Fieldstone School in New York City. Every time she walked to school she passed homeless people along the way. It bothered her. When she heard about the volunteer program "Midnight Run" that delivered late-night meals to the homeless, she knew that this was a way she could make a difference.

Olivia went to the director of students at her school and found that Adams Jolles, a junior, was also interested in helping the homeless. Olivia says, "Suddenly Adam and I were in charge. We were the school program for the homeless." Soon other kids expressed interest, and in a short time Olivia and Adam were head of a school assembly line that put together thousands of sandwiches to be distributed each night.

Olivia and Adam have handed out their sandwiches in person several times. Adam said, "Each time knocked me out for a couple of days. You hand people sandwiches, they talk to you—maybe get a load off their shoulders—and you feel pretty good. But when you see some of them again, they may be in even worse shape—may not even remember you. You've given them their one meal of the day. Some people were always waiting for us. I'll never look at the homeless in the same way. They're just like me, only homeless."

CONTRIBUTION OR COMMITMENT?

There is an old story about a chicken and a pig who were walking along a country road early one morning. It was time for breakfast and as they approached an old-fashioned eatery they saw a sign in the window that read: Bacon and eggs $1.79. The chicken said, "Well, well—will you look at that! What would breakfast be without my contribution." The pig looked at the chicken in shock and replied, "It's OK for you! For you it's a contribution, for me it's total commitment!"

Admiral James B. Stockdale, leadership expert, wrote, "A leader must aspire to a strength, a compassion and a conviction several octaves above that required by society in general. Glib, detached people can get by in positions of authority until the pressure is on. But when the crunch develops, people cling to those who they can trust—those who are not detached, but involved—and those who have consciences."

Civilian leadership and military leadership differ only in the aspect of battle. Otherwise they are the same. As General John Long and I concluded our conversation on the twelve leadership qualities, he said: "If you are truly committed—that's not a trite phrase in my view—that means you believe in what you are doing, in what your organization is doing. I am talking about the leader's commitment now. You believe in what you are trying to achieve for the organization, believe that its mission is noble. And you are committed to the mission, the people, and the organization. That commitment has got to be genuine, through and through, twenty-four hours a day. You have to love your organization and the people in it."

If you do, people will respond to the commitment. They will give you the benefit of the doubt when there is a close call. They will say, "At least his heart is in the right place. He's been right in the past. Let's go with him." That commitment will pay tremendous dividends as you try to guide an organization."

THE WISDOM TO LEAD

To have wisdom is to have perspective on how and why human beings function and progress. Wisdom will help you lead others to make a life, not just make a living. Your wisdom can help them differentiate between the authentic and the false, between things worthwhile and things pretentious, between lasting and fleeting, between personal power and position power.

Your understanding of human character, coupled with technological and business skills, will help you create an organizational culture that supports human growth. In this kind of culture people feel fulfilled; they have a direct influence on their standard of living and the quality of their lives.

KNOWLEDGE AND WISDOM

Mark Twain said, "Learning you get from school. Education you get from life." It is never too late to become better educated. At ninety-two years of age Justice Oliver Wendell Holmes was ill and in the hospital. His friend President Roosevelt came to visit him. When Roosevelt entered he saw Justice Holmes reading a Greek primer. "What are you doing, Mr. Justice?" asked the President. "Reading," answered Holmes. "I can see that," said the president, "but why a Greek primer?" Holmes answered, "Why, Mr. President, to improve my mind."

Knowledge for the sake of knowledge is not important. It is important that you have the wisdom to apply what you learn. The pursuit of wisdom builds character; it gives you the inner tools to lead others.

Michael Maccoby, author of *The Leader,* wrote, "The study of the Bible, comparative religion, ethical philosophy and psychology, and great literature leads one to explore the inner life,

particularly the struggle to develop the human heart against ignorance, convention, injustice, disappointment, betrayal, and irrational passion. Such an education prepares one to grapple with
his fear, envy, pride, and self-deception. It raises questions about
the nature of human destructiveness and the legitimate use
of force. Without it, a would-be leader tends to confuse his
or her own character with human nature, guts with courage,
worldly success with integrity, the thrill of winning with happiness.

"Without a commitment to culture that supports the practice of
life described in the great humanistic religious traditions, people
find meanings in idols of self, possessions, technology, or organizations. They put their faith in bureaucracies rather than the divine spirit in each other, and the self remains childish and
undeveloped."

DEVELOPING THE NEW WORK ETHIC

What we refer to as the good old-fashioned "work ethic" has
changed dramatically. The old work ethic meant showing up on
time, caring about your efforts, working toward good results. When
jobs were hard to find and people were less educated, the wage
was king. The work ethic led to financial reward. Today "work"
means more than money. There are more people with a good education than ever before and just having a job does not mean what
it did to people in the 1930s, '40s and even '50s.

If you are to be a successful leader today, you must build a
work ethic that corresponds to current standards and values. You
must develop a work ethic with rewards that surpass a mere pay-
check.

First of all, the work ethic does not only apply to a job
or occupation. A work ethic is an attitude about how we pre-
form any task. We can "work" at an occupation, we can "work"
as a volunteer, we can "work" at home. "Work" is a way
to contribute to society, to be a valuable part of a bigger picture.

It is a leader's responsibility to instill the work ethic in the follower. Today, a leader is responsible for creating an environment
where people can find fulfillment. A leader must make people feel
that they are part of a team whose mission inspires them, whose

long-term goals include growing room for their personal ambitions, and whose values speak to their need to make a contribution. If the leader cannot or will not reward people in this way, they will have a negative, self-interested "work ethic." They will have no commitment.

Tom Peters tells us that leaders who develop a clear philosophy of motivating and recognizing excellence are those who improve the work ethic of their followers. These same leaders support education and believe in autonomy for people in leadership positions. They are committed to their followers.

GOOD IS THE ENEMY OF GREAT!

If there has ever been a time when we need great leaders with commitment to great ideas, it is now. We need them in your town and mine. We need them in business, in government, and in community groups.

I can hear someone saying "great," that's a tall order. Don't be put off by the word "great." People need examples of greatness to show them the power of commitment.

————Small Acts of Corporate Greatness————

There are twenty-seven comprehensive cancer centers in the United States. Pat Blum had been the recipient of the care and expertise at one of them, the Sloan-Kettering center. She and fellow cancer survivor Jay Weinberg founded CAN—Corporate Angel Network. The network solicits the use of corporate airplanes to fly cancer victims to these vital centers. Every month at least fifty patients are flown to hospitals without charge and without having to negotiate the difficulties of commercial airports. Since 1981, 400 companies have flown over 1,200 patients and families over 2 million miles at no cost.

How did Pat's commitment to helping cancer patients spark a great idea? Pat is a board member of the Connecticut Division of the American Cancer Society. One night at a meeting they were discussing how to get a patient to the proper place for treatment Pat is a pilot and had often seen company planes taking off and landing. She said, "All of a sudden I saw all those corporate planes as an untapped resource."

You don't have to form a corporation to be great. Single acts of greatness can make a difference, just as each plane that carries a cancer victim does.

Greatness can come in many shapes, sizes, and forms. You can have a great attitude. You can be a great boss. Whether you are a scout leader, a business leader, or a community leader, you can commit to great deeds. A single project can be great. A committee can achieve a great goal. A career can be great. You can be a great friend or a great parent. Life can be filled with many great efforts, tasks, and relationships.

GOOD ENOUGH

Most people go through life saying, "Well, that's good enough." The question is, good enough for whom, for what? For the difficult and challenging time we live in? For a future that needs deeply committed leaders?

Winston Churchill said, "We make a living by what we get, but we make a life by what we give." There are people and projects in this world that are worth the struggle for greatness.

But greatness is not the goal; it is the pursuit of greatness that will set you apart from people who are willing to settle for good enough. It's your commitment to giving that will make you a leader who can make a difference. Good is the enemy of great.

—Two Lifetimes Of Greatness and Commitment—

Bob Hope is a living example of a lifetime of commitment. For more than forty-eight years he has led the entertainment world in giving its talents for the benefit of others.

He did his first radio show for servicemen in March 1941, and continued to broadcast to servicemen and women for eight years. Throughout World War II and the Korean conflict, he traveled more than a million miles entertaining more than ten million troops— appearing at almost every military base in the world. He became an annual visitor at many of them.

In 1948, Hope began what was to become a Christmas custom, when he went to Berlin to put on several shows for the GIs involved in the airlift. The following year Hope and a troupe of Hollywood performers entertained GIs in Alaska. In successive years he took

troupes to the Pacific in 1950; to England and Iceland in 1955; back to Alaska in 1956; the Orient in 1957; Europe in 1958; Alaska again in 1959; the Caribbean (including Guantanamo Base, Cuba) in 1960; Newfoundland and Greenland in 1961; the Far East again in 1962; Europe and North Africa in 1963. For the next five years he and his USO troupe performed in war-torn South Vietnam.

In 1969 his Christmas show became the "Around The World Christmas Tour." On completion of his twenty-third holiday overseas show in 1972, Hope informed the world that this would be his last Christmas Show. But Christmas 1973 found him packed and on the go with a "mini-troupe" of entertainers to veteran hospitals in San Diego, Long Beach, and San Francisco, and to the Naval Center in Bethesda, Maryland, and the Walter Reed Hospital in Washington, D.C. In 1983 the Department of Defense called, and Bob was off again to a trouble-spot in the world— Beirut.

It has been said of Hope that "if he could live his life over again—he wouldn't have time." Today, at age eighty-six, Bob Hope is still on the go, giving benefit shows, founding and directing charitable organizations, and donating his personal time and wealth. In 1988 Bob made the Guinness Book of Records as the world's most decorated and honored man in entertainment. He is hailed as an individual whose credo is the lifting of the human spirit. If anyone doubts it—ask any G.I.! It is said that the strength of his commitment is in his staying power, his "sheer physical stamina which comes purely from his attitude."

Asked about his commitment to the G.I.s, Hope said, "There was so much gratification connected with the shows. You got to thinking of what you were doing and how damn lucky you were to have the chance to do it. You were there, you were the recipient of their marvelous love."

While the herculean contributions of Bob Hope inspire us, there are thousands of men and women all across the country who have also committed to a lifetime of giving.

Ruby Forsythe is eighty-two years old. She lives in an apartment above the school house in Pawley's Island, South Carolina. Ruby has been teaching at Holy Cross Faith Memorial School for forty-nine years. She says she teaches "all the basics, plus the little things that count—honestly, dependability, responsibility." Pawley's Island is a poor community consisting mostly of black Americans. Ruby has always been deeply concerned that the fifty-three children in her class each year get a fair start in life. Many of her pupils have grown up and sent their children to learn about the things that count from her.

Ruby Forsythe and Bob Hope are both jewels of commitment shining brightly, giving us inspiration. Everyone knows Bob Hope; Ruby Forsythe is known to those in her community. But both have touched the hearts of those they have taught and entertained. Famous leader, unknown leader. They are the hope of today and tomorrow. They are the ones that make a difference. "They" are you!

―――――――――――――*Giving In Return*―――――――――――――

Setting an example of sacrifice is a very powerful human motivation. It can bring out the best in others, and help them to see how they, too, can make a difference.

When you look at Mother Teresa's small size and bent body, you'll be unimpressed. You may even doubt her power, her leadership, her unbelievable ability to make a difference. You'll be unimpressed until you look into her eyes and see the depth of her compassion, until you hear her voice and hear the sound of pure love expressed in few well-chosen words, until you are in her presence and feel what omnipotent personal power can do to your soul.

As a young nun Mother Teresa wanted to work with the homeless and hopeless but her superiors felt that she was too frail, young, and inexperienced. She pleaded her case, but they refused and assigned her to teach at a convent in India.

The years passed and Mother Teresa's mission burned deep in her heart. She grew in experience and determination. She never gave up her dream. Finally, at age thirty-nine, she was granted permission to embark on her calling. With nothing more than the clothes on her back and the fire of her mission burning deep in her heart, she left the school and walked into the streets of Calcutta to begin her work. If you have been to Calcutta you know that the poverty is staggering—it is beyond description. Into that destitute privation went this small, gentle giant.

It is said that on that very first day Mother Teresa saw a man lying in the gutter, so covered with disease and vermin that no one would go near him. She kneeled down next to him, held his frail body in her arms and began cleaning him. He was so astonished he asked her, "Why are you doing this?" Her simple reply was, "Because I love you."

Mother Teresa's mission is love. Her Sisters of Charity are now active worldwide. They do no advertising, make no fund-raising efforts, but their holy charge continues. When asked why she doesn't ask for funds, Mother Teresa answers, "God will provide."

One quiet little woman, operating in the worst poverty imaginable, is carrying out her mission with a zeal, setting the example of sacrifice that reaches around the world.

YOUR SACRIFICE

You don't have to go to India to set an example of sacrifice that will motivate and inspire others. You can make a sacrifice right where you are, in any area of your life.

What can you sacrifice? There are many things to sacrifice: some of your time, some of your energy, perhaps even some money, a little ego, some position power, maybe a few of the trappings of success.

What do you get in return? When you make a sacrifice you receive a commodity that can never be purchased. It cannot be bargained for or demanded. It can't be inherited or given. It can only be earned. It comes from service to others and sacrifice of self. It is the profound personal satisfaction of knowing that you have made a difference in someone's life. This calm, quiet feeling in your heart and your soul is where humility is born. And with humility comes the *real* long-lasting ability to lead others.

YOU DON'T CLAIM LEADERSHIP, YOU EARN IT!

You earn leadership when you:

• treat people as if today is the only day you have to help them reach their full potential,

- teach the benefit of setting a good example to the lowest level of people in your organization,
- know that if you take very good care of today, tomorrow will take care of itself,
- accept full responsibility and accountability for your thoughts and actions,
- live each day as if your life were being judged by that one day,
- take time each day to be alone, to communicate with God, to think about your mission and how you are going to make a difference.

Then you *earn* your position of leadership.

No matter where your commitment takes you, no matter what your leadership accomplishes, it is exciting to know that you are in the process of "becoming." You are an ever-changing composite of the things you say, the books you read, the thoughts you think, the company you keep, and the dreams you dream.

Your self-worth is not your net worth. Your self-worth is determined by what you can contribute. It is based on intangible, eternal values. When you have the courage to stand and be counted, and when you understand the awesome power of serving others and the wisdom of self-sacrifice, then your self-worth is greater than your net worth could ever be.

Your potential is endless. Your ability to make a difference has no boundaries. It is said that one person with belief is equal to ninety-nine with only interest. New York Governor Mario Cuomo said, "You can make a difference, if you are different." You will surely be different when you have the courage to be a leader with a strong commitment to serving others. You will be "giving in return."

REMEMBER THE ORIGINAL IDEA

Robert L. McCraken wrote, "We on this continent should never forget that men first crossed the Atlantic not to find soil for their plows, but to secure liberty for their souls."

I am a first-generation American. I believe in the American dream. I have received a great gift from those who have gone before me. My mother was an immigrant from Yugoslavia and came through Ellis Island like millions of others early in this century. When I ride the Staten Island Ferry and watch Lady Liberty coming closer and closer as my mother did from the deck of a ship, when I stand where she stood as a young girl, gripping her most precious possessions, I want to shout at the top of my lungs, "Don't let this incredible experiment in democracy falter! Have the courage that these immigrants had to build a life and to make a better world for your children. Have faith in the golden opportunity within our shores! Be willing to be a leader in your job, your town, the nation! Try to make a difference so that our children and grandchildren can have the same opportunity my mother and I had."

Albert Einstein said, "Many times a day I realize how much my own outer and inner life is built upon the labors of my fellow men, both living and dead, and how earnestly I must exert myself in order to give in return as much as I have received."

When actor Hugh O'Brian founded the HOBY youth program, he wrote a message that is the credo of the organization:

"The Freedom to Choose"
I do not believe we are all created equal. Physical and emotional differences, parental guidance, varying environments, being in the right place at the right time all play a role in enhancing or limiting development. But I do believe every man and woman, if given the opportunity and encouragement to recognize their potential, regardless of background, has the freedom to choose in our world. Will an individual be a taker or a giver in life? Will he be satisfied merely to exist, or will he seek a meaningful purpose? Will he dare to dream the impossible dream?

I believe every person is created as the steward of his or her destiny with great power for a specific purpose to share with others, through service, a reverence for life in a spirit of love.

No matter what your age, your experience, or your position, you can dream a dream that will make a difference, you can have a mission that matters.

In 1965, lyricist Joe Darion put impassioned words to the music of the award–winning Broadway play *Man of La Mancha.* In his song, "The Quest" (more popularly called "The Impossible Dream"), we have the making of a mission that matters:

"To dream the impossible dream,
To fight the unbeatable foe,
To bear with unbearable sorrow,
To run where the brave dare not go,

To right the unrightable wrong,
To love, pure and chaste, from afar,
To try when your arms are too weary,
To reach the unreachable star,

This is my quest, to follow that star,
No matter how hopeless, no matter how far,
To fight for the right without question or pause,
To be willing to march into hell for a heavenly cause."*

*1965 Helena Music Company and Andrew Scott, Inc. Words, Joe Darion, Music, Mitch Leigh.

Your commitment could be inspired by a heavenly cause or it could be inspired by one of those rare moments that changes your life:

- If you have held your brand-new baby in your arms; you understand commitment.
- If you have stood looking up at Lady Liberty; you understand commitment.
- If you have heard your dying parent say, "I loved you more than life itself. I did the best I could"; you understand commitment.
- If you have solemnly repeated a marriage vow that says until death do us part;
- If you have proudly stood in cap and gown at your graduation;
- If you have felt the excitement of putting the key in the door of your first home;
- If you have nervously raised your hand and taken the oath of citizenship with other new Americans; you understand commitment.
- If you and your fellow workers finally reach a long-term goal;
- If you cheer when your protégé wins an award or gets promoted;

- If your company produces a product that helps others;
- If you took the risk to start your own business, you understand commitment.

Faithfulness and persistence are the first two ingredients of commitment. Action is the third ingredient that gives the first two life.

You have the ability and talents to change your world. Don't be afraid to start small, then go for greatness. If you have a purpose, a compelling vision, and a commitment to give of yourself, *you* can be a leader and *you* can make a difference!

ABOUT THE AUTHOR

Sheila Murray Bethel is internationally acclaimed as one of America's leading professional speakers. Her client list includes Fortune 500 companies, the U.S. government, national and state associations, youth groups and professional organizations. She has given over 1,500 speeches and seminars in the United States, Canada, Mexico, Argentina, Australia, New Zealand, and Europe.

Listed in *Who's Who In America,* Sheila is owner and president of Getting Control, Inc., a San Francisco–based marketing and training corporation. She has served on the adjunct faculty of Indiana-Purdue University and San Francisco State University. She is a former instructor for the American Management Association. Sheila is the recipient of the CPAE Award for Excellence in Speaking, given by the National Speakers' Association, and has served on their board of directors for three years.

For information on Sheila Murray Bethel's speeches, seminars and Leadership training materials, please contact her at:

Getting Control, Inc.
1376 Vancouver Avenue
Burlingame, CA 94010
(415) 344-1747

INDEX